Murder Will Out

Irish Murder Cases

'See how love and murder will out'
William Congreve (1620–1729), *The Double Dealer*

'You cannot get there quick enough. You cannot stay there
long enough, and you cannot go back often enough'
Detective Chief Superintendent Dan Murphy,
speaking about a murder scene

Murder Will Out

Irish Murder Cases

Tom Reddy

Gill & Macmillan

Published in Ireland by
Gill & Macmillan Ltd
Hume Avenue, Park West, Dublin 12
with associated companies throughout the world
© Tom Reddy 1990, 2005
First published 1990
0 7171 3823 2
Print origination by Seton Music Graphics Ltd, Bantry
Printed in Malaysia

*The paper used in this book comes from the wood pulp of
managed forests. For every tree felled, at least one tree is planted,
thereby renewing natural resources.*

A CIP catalogue record for this book is available
from the British Library.

1 3 5 4 2

For Maria

Contents

Acknowledgments

IN writing this book I was accorded the good offices of a number of people and institutions, all of whom I wish to thank sincerely for their efforts and patience.

In particular I would like to thank the Garda Commissioner Eugene Crowley; the head of the Garda Press Office, Superintendent Denis Mullins; the Director of the Forensic Science Laboratory, Department of Justice, Phoenix Park, Dr James Donovan; the state pathologist, Dr John Harbison.

I would also like to thank the editor of *The Irish Times*, Conor Brady; RTE's Security Correspondent, Tom McCaughren; the chief librarians of *The Irish Times* and *The Irish Independent*, John Gibson and Michael Daly respectively; the editor of the *Garda Review*, Stephen Rae; the public relations officer of the Association of Garda Sergeants and Inspectors, Austin Kenny; the head of the Defence Forces press office, Commandant Dave Ashe and the librarians and staff of Dublin Corporation's libraries in the ILAC Centre and Pearse Street.

I wish to also acknowledge the help and expertise volunteered for this book by active and retired members of the Garda Siochana — my thanks.

1.

Introduction

IT was snowing when a man forced his way into Todd Burns' wholesale and retail shop in the Curragh military camp on the eve of St Patrick's Day in 1947. The thief forced in a rear door and left the same way, implanting a clear impression of his hobnailed boots in the freshly-fallen snow. He escaped with five wrist watches worth over £24 and £1.50 in cash.

The first Garda on the scene was Sergeant William Lunney who was stationed nearby in Newbridge. As he examined the scene he saw the clear footprints. But he also noted with dismay that a thaw was setting in and that they would soon vanish into a puddle. He needed to make a cast of the prints, the only clue left by the thief, but was equipped with neither plaster of Paris nor wax. The latter would have melted the powdery snow anyway.

Quick thinking saved the day. He rushed to the Curragh General Military Hospital and requested their stocks of bandages used for dressing broken limbs. These bandages would be soaked and wrapped around a broken arm or leg, and as they dried the plaster of Paris with which they were impregnated would harden to form a cast. He brushed the dry plaster of Paris from the bandages, collected up the white dust, rushed back to Burns' shop and sprinkled it on the impression. There was barely enough to make a wafer-thin cast, and unless it was immediately strengthened it would break and crumble into dust. In his second flash of inspiration that evening he remembered passing a building site on his way to the scene of the crime. He returned there and obtained a small quantity of hard wall plaster to strengthen the cast.

Armed with the impression, he went to the camp's military police. The snow had melted but the mark of the thief remained. The MPs examined over 3,000 pairs of boots before they could match the impression, with its specific wear marks, to a pair of boots belonging to a soldier. The thief was confronted, and he returned the watches which he had hidden in a water cistern in the barracks toilets.

The quick-witted Garda was commended by the Garda Commissioner for his work and subsequently went on to become a superintendent.

In another case, a man battered an old woman and her cat to death with a huge and heavy skillet pot. A suspect was later traced and was found to have a piece of bone in a hole in his boot. The piece of bone was the size of the nail on the fifth finger of a child. Detective Superintendent Paddy McLoughlin was in charge of the Technical Bureau and directed that the pieces of bone from the scene should be collected up. Detective Garda Eamonn O'Fiachain brought the pieces to the state pathologist and requested him to rebuild the dead woman's skull. He said it was a job for the ballistics section, as they had experience rebuilding numerous objects, including smashed headlamps from car accidents involving hit-and-run drivers. He gave O'Fiachain two skulls to help him. One had been the skull of an RIC man shot in Cork during the war of independence. A neat round hole was centred in the forehead where a .445 bullet had penetrated. The Bureau men had a half day on Saturday at that time, and as O'Fiachain browsed in the second-hand book barrows on the quays, he came across a book on anatomy. The inscription showed that it had once belonged to a Dr Ball. He had separated from his wife, and his son Edward was convicted of matricide in 1936 although the body was never discovered. With the skulls and anatomy books as a guide, Detective Sergeant O'Fiachain set about his task.

First, all the tissues had to be separated from the bone by boiling. Then the bones had to be identified as either human or animal. There were approximately fifty pieces of human bone and the only clues were the natural cracks and fissure marks found in a human skull. Despite being a jig-saw enthusiast, it was to take a month of consistent work to mesh together the top piece of the skull, which when glued together took on the yellowed shape of a bishop's skull cap. The final piece which was never glued into place was kept as a separate exhibit for the court. Under rules concerning how fit an accused was to plead, the case never came to court, but the ballistics man had satisfied himself that the bone found in the shoe fitted the skull.

These cases are unique not only because of their circumstances, but because they emphasise two important points. First, the ability of the Garda Siochana to use science in crime detection, and second the application of that information to catch criminals.

Today the scientific skills used in crime detection are combined in three departments, the Technical Bureau based in the Depot in the Phoenix Park, the state forensic laboratory, and the state pathologist's office.

Probably the most dramatic illustration of their skills is demonstrated in the investigation of murders. All three services combine their unique talents to play a vital and significant role. That expertise is continually honed and improved and in the case of the Technical Bureau the development of those skills springs from the earliest days of the force when many Garda stations were little more than out-houses and the only technical equipment was a baton or a whistle.

On 21 February 1922 the first recruit to the Garda Siochana was registered. A total of 2,000 were to enrol that year and a further 3,000 the following year. All Gardai at that time were uniformed and no provision was made for a detectives' department. Also in existence at the time was the Dublin Metropolitan Police (DMP) which did contain a detective unit, called the Criminal Investigation Department (CID) or 'G' division. Incidentally it was these men based at Oriel House in Dublin, all armed and plain clothesed, who gave Americans their nickname for undercover agents, the G-men of the FBI. Their primary duty was to guard cash convoys and end the spate of armed robberies in the capital in the early 1920s. In 1922 the number of armed robberies exceeded 100 each month; the following year that had dropped to thirty-three; in 1924 it was only fourteen; and in 1925 it dropped to five a month. Also in 1925 the DMP and the Garda Siochana were amalgamated. Two hundred men were selected as the force's first detectives and were sent on a basic training course for detectives. The course lasted over six months. Classes were held at Kevin Street station and the Phoenix Park depot and the training covered both ballistic and forensic evidence, criminal law, police methods and firearms training.

They were posted to the headquarters of twenty Garda divisions outside Dublin, with the primary aim of restoring law and order in areas where gunmen held sway. The need for specialised skills was soon recognised, and in 1926 the photographic section was established under Garda Myles P. Saul who had been trained in Scotland Yard.

The following years saw the growth of the Garda Siochana as well as an increase in the meagre government allocation to the force. Training, however, was limited and the greatest source of instruction for all ranks was contained in the pages of *Iris an Gharda*, the forerunner of *Garda Review*, the rank and file's in-house magazine. It detailed FBI cases, covered legal problems and technical skills such as the notable essays on photography and its benefit in recording a crime scene written by Detective Officer Saul.

In 1929 the collection and classification of fingerprints was transferred from the general prison section of the civil service under the General Prisons Board. Fingerprints had been introduced to Ireland in 1900 and over the next decade a substantial library of prints of convicted criminals was assembled.

The Garda Siochana's fingerprint system was set up by William Henry, who also received his training in Scotland Yard. He had worked in the criminal records section of the prison service, and when that was transferred to the Gardai he joined the Bureau.

It was in 1931 that the Garda authorities sought 'constructive ideas' from members of the force on any area of police work. The request was welcomed by the Garda Representative Body who pointed out the lack of specialists in the force whose testimony would be accepted as expert evidence. 'Sending a man out armed with a revolver and a detective's identification card to investigate a big forgery case is as incongruous as giving an ambulance man a medical degree and scalpel and directing him to operate on a patient. The chances of success are about the same in both cases,' said the *Garda Review* at the time.

Forty-year-old Detective Sergeant George Lawlor sat down and wrote a 3,000-word essay outlining the problems detectives and uniformed members of the force faced, and offered some solutions. His essay became a blueprint for the establishment and development of the Technical Bureau. The lack of training in seeking clues, and the need for scientific equipment and the case for establishing a specialised detective unit were all tackled in the essay.

Experts in fingerprinting had been appointed to the force, but what use were they if prints were destroyed by an inexpert Garda arriving at the scene of a crime, asked Lawlor? 'It must be admitted that lack of a little practical experience has resulted in cases being messed, or at least the subsequent investigation hampered, with resultant heavy expenses to the state. Indeed I might add in no small way it has reflected on the force at times,' he wrote.

'A detective is held to know more about the investigation of crime than an ordinary Garda,' he added. 'But does he? It must be admitted that in a great many cases he does not. Why? Because he did not get proper training. Certainly a detective must carry a revolver but until lately very little effort was made to have him proficient in its use. After undergoing a course he must have practice at least once a quarter.

'He is required to investigate murders and all serious crime or assist therein. How is he to be successful without proper training? I hold that all members of the detective unit who are fitted for their positions by their aptitude for such work and their present and past ability should undergo a special course of instruction at the Depot. If this course is deemed too expensive then that a Special Branch be formed, attached to the Depot, members to be despatched to any Division where a serious crime occurs, assist therein or take charge of investigation as necessity arises.'

In 1932 the third specialist unit of the Garda was established, the firearms section. It was originally charged with the study and examination and testing of firearms, and was subsequently renamed the ballistics section.

In March of the following year the *Garda Review* editorial under the headline 'Science and the police officer' bemoaned the failure to introduce the latest scientific techniques in crime fighting.

'If the truth be told we are probably the most antiquated police force of them all, and that is a sorry confession. The radio car, the teletype, and those other highly efficient scientific systems that play such an important part in the detection of crime are things that we have read about and that is all.'

Two years later, in October 1934, the Garda Siochana took its most dramatic and innovative step when it provided the expert back-up that the force needed by establishing the Technical Bureau. The Bureau was based in a complex of buildings in St John's Road, Dublin near the Royal Hospital, Kilmainham. Under its director, Chief Superintendent G. Brennan it took control of the existing specialised sections, and went on to develop a number of departments.

It was staffed with Gardai who had an aptitude for technical or scientific matters and they were given training in fingerprints, footprints, forensic ballistics, photography, sketching, model making, forensic chemistry, microscopy and the use of the violet ray. The HQ unit was intended to serve two purposes — to provide both instructors for the school of criminal investigation and a team of investigators ready to be despatched to the scene of serious crimes in any division in the country.

In conjunction with this the Gardai also established an exhaustive system of criminal records. This was intended to give all available information about people wanted for a crime, property stolen, property recovered and suspects. The cross referenced files in the system also classified criminals by their *modus operandi* and other characteristic peculiarities. Work also commenced on producing a manual of criminal investigation.

There was no formal training for detectives until the 1950s when the Bureau organised training courses which were to continue into the sixties.

At this time the Crime branch, known as 'C' branch, one of eight sections within the force, was facing an increasing workload. Headed by an Assistant Commissioner, it was further subdivided into five branches. C1, records and statistics; C2, summary offences, legal matters, licensing laws, missing persons; C3, subversives; C4, Technical Bureau; and C5, weights and measures. The Technical Bureau was itself headed by a Detective Chief Superintendent. The upsurge of violence in Northern Ireland in the early 1970s spilled into the south, bringing an increase in armed crime as guns became more available and banks and other financial institutions became targets for subversives anxious to bankroll their activities.

During the late 1970s and the early 1980s the Bureau was at its largest ever strength; by 1986 there was a staff of over 120, including Interpol, the sub aqua unit, and staff in the Fogra Tora, documents, records and administration sections. The investigation section in particular was increased in size during this period. This section effectively comprised the detectives who met the public — the ones who use the scientific and technical evidence gathered by their colleagues to confront a suspect. They are versed in questioning techniques and are in the vanguard of any investigation. It was these men who were popularly known as the murder squad.

In 1978 the Commissioner appointed a Detective Inspector to head up a training programme and subsequently short-term in-service training schools were opened in Dublin, Cork, Sligo, Kilkenny, Monaghan and Limerick. These courses were open to detectives. The first in-service training school aimed specifically at detectives was run for six weeks in 1979 at Fitzgibbon Street Station in Dublin and had twenty-four participants.

Twelve months later a new four-storey building was opened in the Depot, and the Technical Bureau transferred there.

Military policemen also received training in the Technical Bureau. Although their main function is the preservation of discipline, it was considered important that, if a crime was suspected or discovered on a defence forces installation, MPs would be able to give a professional response. Consequently, although Gardai are always called in to investigate crimes, MPs are trained for the initial stages of an investigation and have taken courses in ballistics, fingerprints, and both criminal and civil law.

The Bureau has made its name internationally in the world of forensic science with two major breakthroughs in forensic investigation. Detective Superintendent Dan Stapleton discovered that broken glass contained a specific fracture pattern. Examined in section under a microscope, the break pattern can identify pieces of glass from the same original sheet or section. This was used to particularly good effect in burglaries and hit-and-runs where some glass particles were left at the scene and others later recovered on a suspect.

During the Emergency there was a thriving black market for stolen bicycles. That was until a member of the Bureau discovered a method of identifying bicycles by their original number punched into the frame even though it had been filed off. When the number was punched on to the frame in the factory it left a faint impression in the molecules in the metal frame. With the frame rigged to an examination bench under a microscope and camera, the filed down number was treated with acid and the number raised briefly — but long enough to be photographed.

However in the history of the Bureau, two particular cases marred an otherwise excellent reputation. In July 1976 the British Ambassador was assassinated. A workman's helmet was found at the scene of the crime. Detective Sergeant William Diggin examined the helmet but found no fingerprint. Later it was examined by the head of the fingerprint section, Detective Inspector William Byrne, who found a mark and subsequently identified it as belonging to a Co. Tyrone man. However Diggin checked the identification charts and claimed they were wrong, and told his superior, Detective Sergeant Pat Corless, who agreed.

Eventually the print identification was discovered to be incorrect. On a hunch, Diggin checked whether he had left the print on the helmet during his examination and found that he had, and the authorities had to withdraw the 'identification' document from the murder file. The fingerprint affair was aired in the media and Dail questions were followed by an internal Garda inquiry. The two officers who made the incorrect identification were moved respectively to senior posts in the Special Branch and the Central Detective Unit. The men who had spotted the error were moved to two inner city Garda stations — a move seen as a technical demotion. Detective Gardai from the investigation section of the Bureau were transferred to outside stations.

A second event that damaged Garda morale were allegations of a 'Heavy Gang' operating within the force and the Bureau in the mid 1970s. The allegations were that confessions were being systematically extracted, sometimes using brutality and intimidation. However these allegations, made by subversives and 'ordinary' criminals sometimes intent on putting up a defence at any cost, were never substantiated, but over a decade later they return occasionally like shadows from the past.

Against these two items is the Bureau's record of excellence in crime investigation. One of the proudest records they maintain is a murder case solution rate of over 95 per cent — one of the highest in the world.

In the late 1980s a group of detectives representing all ranks pointed up their special role within the force when they moved to establish their own representative body.

They wanted better representation, demanding a change in the promotion procedure where plain clothes members were required to revert to uniform duties for at least one year on promotion. They argued that they were a separate rank because their duties and operational methods differed from other members of the Gardai. They estimated over 90 per cent support among the country's 1,500 detectives. However despite their determined effort, the Supreme Court ruled against their appeal action, saying they were not entitled to negotiate on the vital issues of pay, working conditions and pensions.

Forensic laboratories were being established throughout the world's police forces since the 1920s. But it wasn't until 1975 that the Department of Justice opened a forensic laboratory and appointed Dr James Donovan as its director.

By the end of the 1980s the State Laboratory was dealing with an average of twenty-five murders a year, thirty-five suspicious deaths and ten to twelve suicides, in addition to 3,200 drug cases, hit-and-runs, fires, and an ever-increasing number of sex offences.

The state forensic laboratory was originally sited in the Institute of Industrial Research and Standards in Glasnevin but is now situated on top of the Technical Bureau's offices for security reasons. Because of its effectiveness in the war against crime it was seen as a target. The Belfast equivalent of the state forensic laboratory has been both bombed and burned. In Dublin there have been two attacks on Dr Donovan, including a bomb attack in January 1982 which seriously injured him.

In the late 1980s, members of the investigation section were moved to stations around the country as part of a series of measures by Garda managers of a force that was under pressure to produce results and reduce costs. Senior Gardai believed these men could apply their talents more effectively in this way and were still available for major criminal investigations. These arrangements ensured 'more efficient and effective use of personnel resources'.

The problem, as past members of the squad saw it, was that while the team could be put back together, what was to happen when serving members retired and to whom was their expertise to be passed on?

In May 1990 the Garda Representative Association heard calls at their annual delegate conference for the re-establishment of the investigation section. The mid-ranking Association of Garda Scrgcants and Inspectors took up the cudgels on the issue too, emphasising the need for experienced officers on serious crime investigations.

The Garda Technical Bureau has been in a continual state of flux since its inception. It remains to be seen where its future lies, as exciting scientific developments such as DNA identification techniques outpace even the lively imaginations of science fiction writers.

2.

Every Contact Leaves a Trace

'YOU look very smart,' George Robinson told his nineteen-year-old daughter Deborah as she straightened a bowler hat on her fair, collar-length hair.

She wore a dark school blazer-type jacket and jeans and was dressed for a day-trip to Dublin. 'Bobby', his pet name for his daughter, had made them both breakfast at approximately 7.00 am. One hour later she closed the door in the exclusive Upper Malone Road area of Belfast and with a purse full of punts which her father had just changed for her she set out for the secret date.

At 9.00 am on Saturday 6 September 1980 Deborah Robinson boarded one of the three Ulsterbus day trip coaches labelled A, B and C. That evening she had not returned as scheduled, but knowing she was a sensible girl George Robinson presumed she had missed the bus and would be in contact with him. But by 10.30 pm the following evening, George was frantic with worry.

He phoned Ulsterbus to be told there were no other buses due from Dublin. He rang the Northern Ireland Railways' office, hoping she had taken a train if she had missed the bus, but couldn't get an answer. The phone just rang out. As his anxiety increased he decided to go to the railway station and check for himself. He drove the family car to Botanic Station to check train times but he couldn't get in. It was locked up for the night.

He returned home and telephoned the Lisburn Road police station. The officer on duty tried to soothe his fears advising him that if she was not home by the following day he should report her missing to Dunmurry RUC station.

Deborah had not returned or telephoned him by Monday, so he reported her missing. Not content that he had done enough, he called to the Ulsterbus head office and left a photo and description of his daughter, asking the staff to keep a watchful eye on buses from the south.

Deborah had enjoyed sports and the outdoor life and had been a member of the Irish Youth Hostel Association. Grasping at any straws he telephoned two youth hostels in Dublin, but no, they told him, his daughter had not checked in with them.

On Tuesday he rang his wife Lorna, a medical doctor who was on holiday in Majorca. Anxiously she began packing immediately and left for the airport to get an early flight home.

It was 4.00 pm that afternoon when an RUC Chief Inspector accompanied by a sergeant and a woman constable from Dunmurry RUC called to the Robinson home in Fairway Gardens. The Gardai had reported finding a girl's body in Co. Kildare, south of Dublin. It might be Deborah they said. George Robinson called some friends, and one of them offered to go south with him. They left at 5.30 pm. That night Mr Robinson identified his daughter's body in Naas mortuary.

'The irony of the whole situation is that although she had been all over Europe by herself she was never harmed. She was killed on a day trip to Dublin,' said her father.

In the summer of 1979 Edmund Law, aged twenty-five, graduated with an honours degree in social anthropology from Cambridge University. He was offered and took up a social science research scholarship at the famed University. In July 1980 he arrived in Dun Laoghaire on the car ferry with his battered Vauxhall Viva to carry out his research into marriage in the greater Dublin area with specific reference to the constitutional ban on divorce. Both Trinity College and the Economic and Social Research Institute offered him facilities. He was independently wealthy, but was given a grant of £2,225 a year and field allowance of £902 from the Social Research Council in England.

While at Cambridge Edmund Law joined Dateline, the London-based computer dating agency. When he moved to Ireland he wrote to them telling them of his change of address, and requested a geographically relevant printout of Dateline members.

Deborah had joined Dateline in December 1979. She had paid a small fee and by return post received a questionnaire asking for details of her personality, interests and description of the type of person she would like to meet. She later received a list of twenty-seven names, five of whom lived in Scotland, twenty in Northern Ireland and two in the Republic.

On Saturday 30 August the well-spoken Edmund Law rang Deborah's home. Her mother answered the phone and passed it on to Deborah. Yes, she would love to meet, but when and where?

11

After a brief chat the two computer daters agreed to meet the following Saturday in Swords, Co. Dublin, where Law had a flat. She would travel down by bus and ring him when she arrived. She jotted down his phone number before replacing the receiver.

Deborah had received nine 'O' levels at Methodist College, and rather than go to university as her parents had, she opted instead for a course at the Belfast College for Business Studies. There she took a bi-lingual secretarial course. She excelled and was due to travel to London to collect first prize in a French shorthand examination at the end of the month. She worked as a private secretary in the Ulster Weaving Company in Belfast. Her parents were extremely proud of their daughter whom they described as 'serious minded, responsible and a good mixer'.

Deborah had no serious boyfriend at the time she agreed to meet Edmund Law.

Deborah boarded her bus, lettered 'B', as it pulled out of the bus depot. Elizabeth Reid, a secretary from Newtownbreda Road in the city, saw her get on the bus. Later that morning all three day trip buses halted in Dundalk. There was time for a coffee break and Deborah approached her and asked if she could join her group. They chatted briefly and Deborah told them she was going to Dublin to meet a boy.

There were forty-eight passengers on board Deborah's bus. At about 12.30 pm six miles from Dublin, Deborah walked up the aisle of the moving bus and asked the driver Gerard Rogan if he would let her off in Swords village, as she was meeting a friend there. As she got off the bus at Main Street he told her he wouldn't be able to pick her up there on the return leg. He told her that she would have to meet the bus at the scheduled pick-up point in Parnell Square in the city centre.

At 6.30 pm that evening all three Ulsterbuses were scheduled to start the return leg of the journey. At 6.40 pm there was still no sign of the attractive blonde girl with the bowler hat. At 6.50 pm George Rogan turned on the ignition, put the bus into gear and returned to Belfast without Deborah Robinson.

When she got off the Ulsterbus in Swords' Main Street, Deborah walked to the nearest coin box. She rang Law and he immediately left his flat to meet her. He spotted her without any difficulty opposite the 'Quality Shop' as she had accurately described her clothes and her hat.

It was their first meeting. Law invited her back to his flat. It was a two-level, one bedroom apartment in the converted old vicarage.

12

Law had one of the three apartments in the house. He offered to show her around, on the ground floor was a hall and kitchen, upstairs a toilet, study and bedroom. They sat on two chairs downstairs talking about their families and interests. Law then brought her to his bedroom to show her his photo albums. They included family photos. He was the second of three boys; his younger brother was in university, the elder an officer in the Coldstream Guards. His father was the rich and titled Lord Ellenborough, and they lived in Springhill House in Sussex.

As they sat on the end of the bed they kissed briefly and moved into the sunny garden where they sat on a bench. They stayed there for about twenty minutes before going for a walk around Swords, seeing the ruins of the old castle and passed the Amdahl factory with its ornamental pond. Then they returned to the flat where Law made tea and toast.

A detective was later to pace out the route they took, timing and measuring it, and then hunting for witnesses to their afternoon stroll.

It was after 2.00 pm when Deborah said she had to leave. She had shopping to do, and she had to catch her bus. Law volunteered to bring her into town and show her around, but she turned this offer down. However, he did walk her to the bus stop and left her standing waiting for a bus.

Law estimated it was sometime between 3.00 pm and 3.45 pm when he returned from the bus stop. He stayed in his flat until about 6.15 pm when he telephoned another girl he had contacted through a small advert. A woman's voice at the end of the line told him that she wasn't in.

At 7.00 pm a friend of the landlord called and gave him some butter in return for some he had previously borrowed. At about 7.30 pm his phone rang and he took a call from a car dealer, a Mr Sean Bree about a car he subsequently bought, a Mini automatic. His own car had been parked in the Smithfield area one night only a few weeks after his arrival when it was vandalised. He sold the wreck for scrap, and had been looking for a car ever since.

Francis Marrin, the landlord, who also kept a flat in the building, called him at about 9.00 pm to remind him he was having a party that night and that he was to come along. Law again tried to contact the girl he telephoned earlier in the evening, but this time he was told she was on holiday. At about 10.00 pm that evening he went to Marrin's party. There were eight male guests, drinking wine and eating fruit and cheese. Law only knew Marrin, but he chatted with a few people before leaving at about 11.00 pm to go to bed. Guests said he appeared calm and affable. Sunday was another fine day, and after having breakfast Law went to the local Church of Ireland Divine Service at 11.45 am.

Although he had joined the computer dating service, Law had also advertised for female friends on his arrival in Ireland. Shortly after his arrival he placed an advert in *In Dublin* magazine which read, 'English male, working in Dublin for nearly one and a half years, own car, slim, tall, wishes to meet girl friend leading towards possible marriage. Reserved. Makes friends with difficulty.' The advert cost him approximately £1 and he received six replies. He met all the women who replied. Four of them were met in the city centre, and he made arrangements to meet two others at his flat at the old vicarage on the Sunday and Tuesday after his planned date with Deborah Robinson.

On Sunday afternoon he was telephoned by Eilish Lynch, one of the six girls who had replied to his magazine advert. He left his flat and walked down to the ESB office in Swords where she was waiting to meet him. It was about 3.30 pm that afternoon when they returned to his flat. They watched the live broadcast of the All-Ireland hurling final.

Law then brought her upstairs and showed her his photo album. She left him at approximately 11.00 pm that evening, agreeing to meet again the following Wednesday. The following day he had another rendez-vous with another girl who replied to his advert. They met at St Stephen's Green, but they only stayed together for about thirty minutes. Law spent the remainder of the afternoon in the ESRI offices in Burlington Road before returning to his flat.

That evening RTE broadcasted a short news item, about the body of a young girl found murdered in Co. Kildare.

Christopher Walsh was a farmer and lock-keeper at Barretstown, Sallins, Co. Kildare. He had been herding his sheep along the road between Digby Bridge and Millicent Road on Monday afternoon with his wife Alice and married daughter Mary.

It was about 4.15 pm, he estimated, when one of the sheep fell into a deep ditch near the entrance to a field owned by a local farmer, Jim Gibbons. The dog couldn't force the animal out, so Walsh lay on his stomach in an effort to haul the sheep out. As he lay down he saw something else lying at the bottom of the ditch. He pulled out the sheep, and stood brushing his clothes. 'I got a fright there for a minute, I thought there was a body there in the drain, but it's not, it's a doll,' he said to his daughter. Mary Christian, a mother of three, bent down and peered into the drain. 'Come away, Daddy, it's a body,' she said.

As she said this, a self-employed window cleaner, Myles McGrath, drove up towards them in his van. Walsh flagged him down. McGrath noticed his shocked and pale face and got out of the van to see for himself. The ditch was eight feet deep, the sides were steep and covered with overgrown bushes. At the bottom was the body of a girl in blue jeans lying on her back. McGrath got back into his van and drove to Jackson's Mill, one of three houses on the mile long stretch of road, where he telephoned the Gardai.

Sergeant James Corcoran took the emergency call, and Garda Noel O'Donoghue was despatched to the scene. He arrived at approximately 4.30 pm, and immediately ordered that no one go near the body or ditch. This was part of the standard procedure to preserve the scene of a crime.

'Preservation of the scene of the crime is one of the most important things in any murder investigation. It can tell the experts so much, and can give the Gardai the breakthrough in an investigation of vital clues,' says John Courtney, one of the country's most experienced investigators and head of the murder squad.

He regards the Robinson case as one of the most important in his career, as it showed the dogged determination of a team of murder squad detectives who were given a breakthrough clue by a forensic scientist.

Dr John Harbison, the bearded state pathologist, arrived at the scene at 9.20 pm that night. The light was still good, and he was able to see the body without the aid of lamps. Within the next two hours petrol driven floodlamps were erected around the ditch, and Gardai using slashers cut back the briars and bushes growing in the ditch.

At 11.50 pm Dr Harbison crawled into the ditch and carried out his initial examination of the body, and measured both the temperature of the corpse and the air to determine time of death.

The girl's body was lying on its back, the right leg straight, the left bent at the knee. There was an absence of *rigor mortis*, but this was probably because it had already passed. Once *rigor mortis* sets in and passes no further rigidity sets into the body.

He noted that there was a bruise on the left side of the neck, and he initially thought that strangulation may have been the cause of death. It was almost 1.30 am by the time the body was moved to the county hospital in Naas where a post mortem took place later that day.

He estimated that the girl was dead between thirty-six and forty-eight hours at the time he first saw her, which would put her time of death sometime on Saturday night or in the early hours of Sunday the 7th.

There were a number of pressure marks on the face, and a sharp cut on the side of her head. There were some scratches on her face which may have occurred when the body was hurled into the ditch. The post mortem also showed that there were a number of spots beneath the skin which, in addition to haemmorrhages in the whites of the eyes, showed the girl had died from asphyxia. There was gross internal bruising on the neck and death was due to asphyxia in turn caused by manual strangulation. Although there was extensive injury to her neck there was no fracture which may have been because of her natural teenage flexibility. The nature of the bruises suggested she had been attacked from the front. No ligature had been used in the attack, but considerable pressure had been applied to the girl's neck.

After death blood flows to and settles in areas of the body touching and supporting the body's weight. This staining is called lividity and begins approximately one hour after death. Because of this staining of the body, which is easily distinguishable from bruising, Dr Harbison said he believed the body had been moved after death. Simply, the staining that should occur in this natural process showed that the girl had not been killed in the ditch. He believed the body had lain on its left side and not its back as it had been found.

The post mortem also showed that Deborah Robinson had been a virgin before she had been subjected to violent and painful sexual intercourse shortly before her death.

Dr Harbison later estimated that she would probably have taken between thirty seconds and four minutes to die. Volunteers had undergone tests which showed that as they were manually strangled unconsciousness had followed within thirty seconds.

Naas Garda Station, the divisional headquarters for the Carlow-Kildare area with its thirty stations and two sub-stations, became the immediate headquarters for the murder squad. It is less than four miles from the spot where the girl's body was found. Twenty Gardai were assigned the task of combing the area around the ditch where the body was found, on their hands and knees. A wider search area of the ditches surrounding Gibbons' field and the roadway was also mounted using slashers and sticks.

No identification papers or cards were found on or near the body. There was no locket, purse or charms. In a Garda telex to all stations the girl was described as 5'4", blue eyes, fair collar–length hair, plump build. It also described a skin graft scar on the calf of her left leg. The description did not tally with any Garda records of missing people, and it was the RUC who were to link it to the missing Belfast girl Deborah Robinson.

As the body was identified the large Garda search of the area was concluding. The girl's clothing was bagged and sent to the state forensic laboratory which had only just moved to the top floor of the new beige stone fronted office complex at the back of the Garda Depot in the Phoenix Park.

It was there that the small and highly trained staff recently transferred from St John's Road, Kilmainham were to provide the murder hunt's most revealing clues.

The clothes were given to Dr Timothy Creedon who took charge of the forensic investigation. Meanwhile Gardai and the RUC began the difficult task of trying to trace the last movements of the murdered teenager who had been seen getting off a bus in Swords, and whose body was discovered two days later more than twenty miles from her destination in a part of the country she had never visited before.

The investigation initially centred on the area surrounding the place where the body had been discovered. Detective Superintendent John Courtney was put in charge of the case. A native of the Dingle peninsula, the fifty-eight-year-old Kerryman had already won a considerable reputation by solving most of the major murder cases in the sixties and seventies.

At fourteen stone he was the same weight as when he entered the Gardai. He had an impressive record and was partly responsible for the Garda's 99 per cent success rate in solving murder cases, one of the highest in Europe. Courtney plays his cards close to his chest and is known to his colleagues as a great believer in hard work, existing on cat naps and adrenalin. Often that involved twenty-hour days, through Christmas if necessary. Young detectives have been impressed by his staying power, often waking them in the middle of the night to begin a new line of investigation into a case. Outside of his passion for his family of five, the GAA and his job, he has few interests. A shrewd individual, he maintains a close and loyal small circle of friends.

Sunday 7 September was the day of the All-Ireland hurling final in Dublin between Limerick and Galway; the tens of thousands of fans from Limerick who travelled up for the game used the main road — the N7 — which was less than two miles from the ditch

17

where Deborah Robinson's body had been found. Also less than two miles away was Mondello race track where there was a motor racing meeting that day which drew thousands of overnight campers to the area. Also in the vicinity were hundreds of spectators watching the annual Liffey descent boat race.

All these extra people in the area added to the Gardai's mammoth task in trying to identify strangers. It was to become one of the biggest and most extensive murder investigations the country had seen, and one that was to tax the resources of John Courtney.

The Garda investigation now set itself the task of trying to establish exactly who was in the area at the time the body was found and in the forty-eight hours prior to her death.

A total of 4,000 questionnaires were completed by Garda investigators as they visited homes of people living in the area, and tracked down sports enthusiasts who had also been attending events there that weekend. The event organisers provided helpful lists and programmes of people involved in the sports.

As the weeks passed Gardai were to check out inconsistencies in statements included in the questionnaires. One senior Garda makes the point that a lot of time can be wasted with questionnaires by people who cannot correctly remember their whereabouts, or who lie deliberately. For instance, men who are having an extramarital affair consistently hamper investigations by lying about their whereabouts, wasting valuable detection time.

The questionnaire system demands a massive manpower input from the Gardai. Not only do they have to talk to the people they are questioning, they then have to follow up in a huge cross referencing and checking operation. Detectives checking the questionnaires hope they will unearth a mistake, a false alibi or provide clues to vital times not accounted for by a killer living in the area.

Intense investigation showed that between 4.00 pm on Saturday 6 September and 4.00 pm on Monday 8 September a total of 841 cars, trucks and lorries had travelled within a one-mile radius of the spot where the body had been found. Of this number, 122 could not be identified, while forty-two were sighted on the road where the body was found or in its immediate vicinity. If the search radius for vehicles had been extended to two miles, the numbers would have been impossible as that would have included the N7 dual carriageway at Johnstown — the main road to the south.

On Thursday evening Edmund Law was taking a break from his research work in the Common Room in Trinity College. He picked up a morning newspaper that was lying on one of the occasional tables and read of the death of Deborah Robinson. He sat shocked, going over their meeting in his mind again and again, wondering what to do.

He met his Thursday date outside the Hibernian Hotel in Dawson Street at 8.45pm. He seemed nervous and distracted and told the girl he had been with Deborah Robinson the previous Saturday, and that he had to call the police. Law left her before long. He took a bus to Swords, and once in his flat at approximately 9.55 pm he called 999. 'I was with Deborah Robinson,' he said. He also knew her by a pet name 'Bobby,' he said.

Law agreed to go to the Garda station where he was questioned about his movements on the Saturday and subsequently. He told the Gardai that Deborah was dressed in a yellow vest-type top, Lois jeans and a dark blazer. She wore white wedge heel sandals and had glass-type earrings. She also wore a distinctive bowler hat. Law provided blood and saliva samples for comparison testing. He also volunteered hair samples both cut and pulled from his head.

Dr Timothy Creedon had also been given swab samples taken from the dead girl's body during the post mortem. These were of semen and under tests showed that the owner was a secretor, that is someone whose bodily fluids including semen and saliva contain blood antigens which can be grouped and identified. Fortunately for crime investigators, 86 per cent of the world's population are secretors.

Using an isoelectric focusing technique which involves dripping a sample onto a treated plate and passing electric current through electrodes attached to the sample, the secretion will move across the paper to a particular position. This can then be compared to a pH (acidity/alkaline) chart which clearly identifies the sample. This test showed that the deceased's blood group was PGM 1+1-. Because of the rarity of this group, it was possible to exclude 80 per cent of the male Irish population. While this evidence wasn't enough to pinpoint the murderer it was useful in narrowing the field. But it was the second set of tests that Dr Creedon carried out in the biology department of the State Laboratory that were to prove vital to the investigation.

As he took the dead girl's clothing out of the paper sacks in which they had been delivered, Dr Creedon noticed a large number of cloth fragments on the back and seat of the dead girl's jeans. In one corner of the laboratory stands a three foot diameter stainless steel funnel almost four feet high. At its base is a highly polished steel dish, and over this funnel Dr Creedon shook the

19

clothing. The fibres fell into the dish, and the tiny fragments measuring between two and five millimetres in length were ready for examination.

The fibres were examined under powerful Leitz microscopes capable of magnifying up to one hundred times. They clearly didn't belong to any of the other items of clothing brought to the laboratory. It was common enough to find single fibres on articles of clothing, but unusual to find so many yarn fragments on the same item of clothing. Further tests showed that the fibres detached themselves easily from the jeans, so they couldn't have been there long before the girl's death or after it. No other materials were found near the body in the ditch so they had to come from wherever the girl had been before the body was discovered.

A total of forty-five fibres were collected from the pair of blue jeans. These were made from a range of materials including cotton, cotton/polyester, and polyester. They were all of a lightweight material and were red, blue, white and pale green in colouring, and contained some twist.

Under the microscope one of the examined shreds showed blotches of colour which suggested they might have been part of a fabric with a printed design. Again under the microscope, indistinguishable to the naked eye, it was clear that the ends of the fibres had been cut in two different ways. One end of the fibre was cut transversely, and was slightly squashed, in the same way a pair of scissors squeezes and cuts. The opposite end had been cleanly sliced across at an angle as if they had been cut with a slicing action using a sharp blade.

Dr Creedon concluded that the fibres originated from a woven fabric used for manufacturing clothing. Inquiries in the clothing trade confirmed the suspicion, and showed that the squeezed cut would have been made as a pattern was cut out, and the other sliced cut in the overlocking process as the finished garment seams were trimmed. The fibres were the few millimetres of post-overlocking waste.

The wide range of colours found on the jeans tended to rule out any large companies, as they would tend to produce bulk orders and garments of the one type and colour material. However because there were a large variety of threads and colours this pointed to a smaller factory manufacturing a variety of garments in a variety of materials and colours.

Detective Superintendent Courtney organised teams of Gardai to visit clothing factories in the area around Sallins. The net then stretched to the whole of Co. Kildare and neighbouring border county towns. At this stage Edmund Law had contacted the Gardai and his story about meeting Deborah, bringing her for a walk around Swords and leaving her at the bus stop was being checked out. The hunt for the fibres was now extended to a large area with Swords at its centre.

Over the following months Dr Creedon and Detective Superintendent Courtney were to travel hundreds of miles visiting clothing factories. Supervisors in these factories were able to confirm that the fibres were similar to trimming waste, but neither their records or samples ever fully matched the fibres found on Deborah Robinson's jeans.

In December Gardai issued a public appeal in a bid to help them track down the killer. There was now evidence to link Deborah's killer with the clothing trade. The killer may have taken her life in a clothing factory or moved her body in a vehicle normally used in the clothing trade. He may also have been involved in the clothing trade.

As forensic comparisons between the 'Deborah fibres' and supplied samples from the trade continued, Gardai were checking out Edmund Law's story. There were a number of problems. Although she had been spotted in Swords in the afternoon and later on a bus into town, Law had mistaken the day his neighbour's friend returned butter to him, and the car dealer was unable to verify his telephone conversation with Law. The Garda sub aqua team were called in to examine the well in the grounds of the old vicarage where Law lived. The highly skilled group of divers are a regular feature of any Garda search team but on this occasion they failed to turn up anything of significance.

Although the investigation continued in Kildare, its focus now switched to Swords. In a similar operation to that already carried out in the Sallins area, thousands of questionnaires were filled in by Gardai as they knocked on front doors, stopped motorists and interviewed people on the street.

It was Deborah's distinctive hat that gave Gardai another lead as they began to fill in the missing hours.

Mrs Dympna O'Flynn was walking to a bus stop in Swords waiting to go into town at about 4.30 pm when she noticed Deborah. The girl was already standing at the bus stop when she arrived there with her husband. 'I thought she was about twenty-three or twenty-four but she seemed to be dressed like a sixteen-year-old with her jeans turned up at the ends.'

21

The most valuable witness was Sr Mary McGuirk, a post-primary teacher at the Margaret Aylward School in Whitehall, Dublin and a member of the Holy Faith Order. She had been teaching since 1957 and was an observant woman with a lively interest in what went on around her. On Saturday 6th she was playing the organ at a wedding ceremony in Whitehall with the parish folk music group. The ceremony started at 4.00 pm, and was finished at 5.10 pm. This allowed her time to return the missals to the school behind the church and catch her bus into town at 5.30 pm. At approximately that time she boarded a number 41 bus bound for the city opposite the Viscount pub on the Swords road.

She sat on the long seats that run along the front side of the bus, opposite a girl she had never seen before. The girl wore a light anorak type jacket, jeans and a distinctive hat with a wide band on it. The girl looked sad, and the jacket was quite dull for a teenager, the nun thought.

The girl was still on the bus when she got off at Mountjoy Street. She noted her time of arrival at 5.55 pm, breathing a sigh of satisfaction that she was back punctually for prayers which were said in the community at 6.00 pm every evening.

That weekend a Bangharda of a similar build to Deborah and wearing similar clothes retraced what was known of the dead girl's last movements with a televised appeal for help. The film sparked off numerous calls to the Gardai.

It wasn't until Monday that a busy Sr McGuirk managed to catch a few minutes to sit down and read the previous day's papers. In both the *Sunday Independent* and the *Sunday Press* there were photographs of Deborah and of the clothes she wore. Sr McGuirk hurried to ring the Gardai.

As Edmund Law was eliminated from the investigation, Gardai threw their net wider. Now it was clear Deborah had travelled to the city centre, and for some reason had missed her bus home. Detective Superintendent Courtney ordered that the factory checks should now extend to all clothing factories in the city. Meanwhile Dr Creedon had been given 'lifts' — effectively, fibres lifted by applying a piece of special sticky tape on a surface — from Deborah's clothes and home. They did not match the fibres he had in his possession from the dead girl's clothes. Similarly fibres from the factory where she worked as a private secretary did not match.

Dozens of factories had drawn a blank when Detective Superintendent John Courtney and Dr Creedon went into Janet Ltd, a clothing plant in East Arran Street near the Four Courts. The company was small and made numerous small batch orders. Their records were also very comprehensive.

Staff checked back through their records and were able to provide samples of materials used in manufacturing prior to Deborah's death. Forensic testing back in the State Laboratory was able to match the fibres found on the dead girl's jeans with those used by the factory.

Detectives sensed the net closing as they checked the company's employment records to discover that a presser, Richard O'Hara, left the company shortly after Deborah Robinson's death.

O'Hara was born in May 1953 in Belfast. He served as a soldier in England before returning to Belfast and then moved south. He had previous convictions in Northern Ireland and England for assault and theft. He was living in a flat in Parnell Street, off O'Connell Street with his wife Geraldine and four children. He had an argument with his wife on the morning of Deborah Robinson's murder and he left the house in anger. He went to a pub on the quays where he bought himself a 'fix'. He wandered around for a while and eventually went into the Film House cinema which was showing an afternoon film about a robbery.

He later left the cinema hoping he might bump into his wife as she went shopping in Roches Stores across the Liffey in Henry Street. She wasn't to be seen in the busy street, but he bumped into two girls coming out of the shop. He knew one of them from nearby Sheriff Street who worked in the factory and he asked them to join him for a drink in a nearby pub. They agreed and they had one or two drinks together, he told Gardai.

After the couple of drinks he got up and followed them out of the pub and started to walk them home. Near the Rotunda Hospital in Parnell Street he saw and spoke to Deborah Robinson. They fell into conversation and began walking along the street in the direction of Capel Street. O'Hara said that she told him her name was Deb, or Debbie.

As they walked further westwards they came to the market area of the city and passed near the factory where O'Hara worked. He had a set of keys for the factory and opened it, bringing the teenager into the canteen. They sat and he rolled two marijuana joints. She refused to smoke the one he handed her. Then he brought her around the factory into the cutting room.

He claimed they then had sex with her consent. However the post mortem clearly showed that this could not be the case. He claimed then that Deborah began shouting she wanted to go home, and he put his hand over her mouth to stop her. She wouldn't stop, so he put his hands around her neck and squeezed until she died. He dumped her body onto a pile of polythene sacks which were coated with fibres from the cutting process. In doing so O'Hara unwittingly proved the basic forensic principle of scientific crime detection formulated by the criminologist Edmond Locard, that 'Every contact leaves a trace'.

O'Hara then left the body and the factory. It was about this time that he saw the car of Paddy Flood, one of the factory bosses, parked outside a nearby pub. He went inside, took up Flood's offer of a drink and told him that he had been in the factory as the Gardai had contacted him about an open window. Flood thought this odd as he knew O'Hara was not a keyholder who was registered with the Gardai. O'Hara then went home.

On the following afternoon O'Hara returned with a van he had hired from a rent-a-car company based in O'Connell Street. He threw Deborah's shoes, hat and other belongings into the back of the van along with the body. Then he drove down the Naas dual carriageway looking for a place to dump it.

It was still light when he threw the body into the ditch and returned to Dublin. As he was about to return the van, he realised he had overlooked disposing of the hat, shoes and other items. He wrapped them up in a piece of newspaper and threw them onto waste ground at the back of a house of flats in Summerhill.

O'Hara vanished from work for a number of days after the murder. On 12 September he left a note at the factory for another one of the employees he knew, saying he was going to commit suicide. He told Gardai that he went to confession in the Pro–Cathedral at the back of O'Connell Street within days of killing Deborah, as his guilt became too great to bear.

The priest told him to give himself up. He claimed that he walked up to the steps of Fitzgibbon Street Garda Station the following day and was standing in the public office behind a man who was presenting documents to the Gardai for certification. But his nerve broke and he left.

'I don't know what happened to me, but I just turned around and walked out,' he said.

O'Hara returned to work, but left within a fortnight. He went to live in Co. Kerry for a little while with his wife and family. But he left them to live with another woman in Salthill, Co. Galway. He was now wanted for questioning for issuing dud cheques and in relation to a number of burglaries. He was arrested in April 1981.

He was remanded in custody to Limerick prison where he was found to be mentally unstable and was brought to the Central Mental Hospital, Dundrum, Dublin.

He stayed there for a number of months, and was released on 2 December to appear in court on charges of theft. The charges were dropped, and as he walked out of the court he was approached by two experienced members of the investigation unit of the Technical Bureau, Tom Dunne and Pat Lynagh. He was arrested and brought to Castlebar Garda Station. He made the first of three statements there, and was duly brought before Crossmolina Court.

On his way from the court to Dublin he slept most of the way. After he woke and spoke to accompanying detectives he agreed to point out where he had hired the van and where he had thrown the clothing. He also pointed out Fitzgibbon Street Garda Station as they passed it, saying he had been in the public office to give himself up at one stage.

On 29 March 1982 Richard O'Hara stood in a crowded courtroom on the sixth and final day of his trial waiting for the decision of the jury. He had pleaded not guilty. The jury found him guilty and trial Judge Tom Finlay handed down the mandatory sentence of penal servitude for life.

After the trial George Robinson, who had sat through the trial with his wife said, 'Since Debbie's death there has been a gap in our lives. She had been a breath of fresh air to us both. It is very hard to come to terms with the fact that we will have to live the rest of our lives without her.'

3.

The Captain Nairac Mystery

A PHONE call that day had tipped him off, and now he was ready. He checked his appearance in the mirror in his quarters in Bessbrook Mill barracks, Portadown. He was casually dressed in a white shirt with red stripes and a pair of light trousers. He patted down his jacket, smoothing it over the holster and the Browning 9mm pistol. Captain Robert Nairac of the Grenadier Guards was going undercover into South Armagh, IRA bandit country, the area of Northern Ireland most feared by British soldiers.

Dressed in civilian clothes, he was armed with his favourite weapon. He carried the pistol in a shoulder holster, and had earlier been issued with fifty rounds of ammunition. He had modified the grip of the gun to suit his own hand, and had customised its safety catch, extending it and making it easily distinguishable among the other regulation issue weapons of his colleagues.

Robert Nairac was a dedicated officer. He had been born in August 1948 in Mauritius, but was still a child when his family moved to Stonehouse, Gloucestershire. His father Maurice was a retired ophthalmic surgeon. He was educated at Ampleforth College in Yorkshire, before going up to Oxford at nineteen to read history. He excelled at his favourite sport, boxing, and won a 'blue', as well as playing first XV rugby. He joined the Grenadier Guards in his last year at Oxford.

He served in Northern Ireland for four months as a first lieutenant and then returned to England and was stationed in Chelsea barracks, London. He took a survival course at one stage over the next few years in Kenya and volunteered to return to Northern Ireland at the end of April 1976, holding the rank of captain.

He had visited his parents about six weeks previously. He never spoke about his work in Northern Ireland but they suspected he had some involvement with the élite and secret Special Air Services.

At 9.20 pm on Saturday 14 May 1977 Nairac informed Captain David Collett in Bessbrook that he was going on duty. Collett, of the Worcester and Foresters Regiment, was the Operations Officer and was responsible for logging people in and out of the compound gates. Nairac did not tell him the reason for his visit to South Armagh: he never gave reasons for his journeys to officers on the gate. As they made arrangements for his trip, Collett noticed that Nairac was wearing his Browning pistol partly hidden under his jacket. Nairac made arrangements with him to make a series of check-in radio telephone calls using his call sign '48 Oscar'. He was issued with a red Triumph Dolomite car, registration number CIB 4253. His exit from the compound was noted in the log-book. At 9.48 pm he made his first radio telephone call check-in. The second call was logged at 9.52 pm and the third at 9.56 pm when Nairac said he had arrived at the Three Steps public house at Drumintree, near Forkhill, Co. Armagh and that he would remain there until 11.30 pm.

Joseph McCreesh, the owner of the Three Steps bar, was sitting in the front seat of his white Mercedes 200 since shortly after 8 pm that evening. The moon was hidden by clouds, but it was a dry night. He sat in his car every Saturday night watching the car park at the front of the single-storey pub. The pub was near the Roman Catholic church, less than three miles from Dromad village and a couple of miles from the border.

It was about 10 pm when Robert Nairac arrived, locked the car and went into the pub. A band was already playing ballads and popular tunes of the day. He could hear them belting out the music over a crackly public address system as he edged past their minibus which was parked up against the front door.

Nairac went up to the crowded bar and ordered a pint of Guinness and a pack of twenty Carroll's cigarettes. He was served by a teenager, Joseph McCreesh, the owner's son, who later recognised him from a photo. The bar was up against the long back wall of the pub; there was a pool room at one end and the toilets were beside the stage where the band sang through a rising haze of smoke. It was a lively Saturday night crowd, about two hundred strong.

Nairac stayed leaning against the bar smoking for about half an hour. He watched the television over the bar for a while and ordered another pint. Then, drink in hand, he went up towards the stage and as the band broke between songs he beckoned Sean Murphy, one of the musicians, to the edge. He shouted at him over the noise of the pub, 'Could a man from Belfast sing a song?'

He was asked to write down his name and what he wanted to sing, but wouldn't, and just said his name was Danny McClean. He spoke with a soft Belfast accent, and as he climbed up onto the stage the band struck up behind him as he sang two rebel songs. There was a short round of applause, and a few nods and smiles at him as he made his way back down the bar. One man in the bar sat quietly and unobtrusively watching the newcomer. He had noticed the man from Belfast was 'carrying'.

At 11.30 pm Nairac left the pub. As he got to the door two men came up behind him and one leaned forward to say something to him. The two men had been in the pub before Nairac entered and they left with him walking closely in front. No one remarked on the departing trio. Around midnight people still in the now quiet bar heard some shouting and sounds of a fight outside. There were maybe four or five people involved, it was estimated later. It was difficult to tell.

Nairac was due to call in again that evening on the radio telephone, but failed to do so. By 1 am, as he had neither checked in by radio nor returned to base, Captain Collett contacted his commanding officer who called out troops from the barracks for a search. At 5.40 am that morning the British army informed the RUC that an officer was now officially missing. The police were given a description and told that Nairac was armed with a pistol bearing the serial number IT 7774 and two magazines of 9 mm ammunition.

As the early morning light broke over Co. Armagh a few hours later, the car park outside the Three Steps Inn was empty, except for Nairac's car.

Detective Sergeant Henry McCann of the RUC's Criminal Investigation Division telephoned the Gardai in Dundalk at 8 am to request their help in the search, fearing that Nairac had been abducted over the border. Garda Superintendent P.J. Farrelly in Dundalk informed the district border stations and Garda Headquarters in Dublin. A search was mounted immediately south of the border. Now troops and police officers on both sides were hunting for the man, or his body. But it wasn't until the following Monday at 1.30 pm that the British army publicly admitted that a captain had been kidnapped from the Three Steps Inn on the previous Saturday night. The 'South Armagh battalion' of the Provisional IRA claimed responsibility for the kidnapping.

The search on both sides of the border involved tracker dogs, troops, RUC, Gardai, police with specialist sub aqua units and British army helicopters. But they failed to find the missing man's body.

The state later prosecuted a man for Nairac's murder, but without ever producing the body. Forensic evidence was to link a man to Nairac's death but in the absence of a corpse the prosecution's case was to hinge on vital statements made by the accused man.

The first ever conviction for murder in the absence of a body since the establishment of the state was made in March 1935. Rose and Elizabeth Edwards of Castlegrange, Athleague, Co. Roscommon were sentenced to death for the murder of an infant, Teresa Mary Edwards.

Their story began on 2 October 1934 when Elizabeth Edwards of Fuerty, Co. Roscommon was admitted to Roscommon County Home by her local doctor. She was a single girl and had managed to conceal her pregnancy from all her family except her sister Rose by continually lying about her health, saying she suffered from swollen feet, appendicitis and other ailments. She arrived at the County Home at 11 pm, registered under a false name, and gave birth to a healthy female infant thirty minutes later. The following day she admitted her real identity. Her only visitor over the next fourteen days was her sister Rose. During her stay she was warned twice, by a nurse and the medical officer in charge, a doctor, about the necessity of having to feed the child. As she left the hospital another nurse, Sally O'Gorman, also warned her to be careful with the child and not to abandon or ill-treat it, or else she would get into trouble with the Gardai.

On 29 October the matron of the hospital rang the Gardai in Roscommon asking them to check on baby Teresa Mary Edwards. They contacted Athleague Station and Sergeant Patrick Tobin and Garda John Salmon called to the house at approximately 9.30 pm. Lizzie Edwards told the uniformed Gardai that the child had died in her bed on the night she had come home from the County Home. Her sister Rose had taken the child out and buried it the following day. Rose Edwards gave the same story and brought both men to a field and pointed out a spot about 150 yards from the house. Sergeant Tobin searched the field in the chill night air, burning his fingers on a steady stream of matches as he examined the ground. He could find no sign of a fresh grave and gave up the search when he ran out of matches. Lizzie was hysterical at this stage as she did not want her parents to know she had given birth.

The following day Inspector O'Sullivan and three Gardai returned to the house, and asked Rose to show them where she had buried the child. As they approached the spot she had pointed out the previous evening, Rose said, 'Jesus, there was something at it.'

Sergeant Tobin saw a piece of white material sticking out of the ground near the fence. There was a partly severed sod in the ground and the piece of cloth had been inserted into it. Rose Edwards said this was the child's grave.

The Gardai dug at the spot, and found two pieces of cloth. The sods had merely been turned and replaced so perfectly that nothing other than the rags could have ever fitted under the sods. Asked to explain this Rose Edwards's simply said of the infant, 'I put it there anyway, find it if you are able.'

One of the rags in the 'grave' looked bloodstained, and Superintendent Twomey tested it for evidence of blood. He used the Guaicum test, now obsolete. This involved taking a tiny sample of Guaicum resin and adding it to a few cubic centimetres of methylated spirits. Old turpentine is then added to this and the mixture poured on a section of the item for testing. The appearance of an immediate blue-green stain would establish the presence of human blood. The more accurate Precipitin test is now used and is commonly employed to identify badly decomposed remains to ascertain whether they are human or animal.

The Guaicum test proved negative and the rags were retained for further examination by the state pathologist.

The Gardai then began checking back over the movements of the two girls since Rose had hired a taxi to pick Lizzie up at the County Home to bring her home. The driver told the Gardai that instead of driving them home directly via Fuerty, one of the pair told him to drive via Athleague, thus adding a further three and a half miles onto the journey. Rose went into a general grocer's in the village and bought two loaves of bread and the journey resumed. The driver let them out of the car at White's Orchard, about one mile from their home. Gardai began to question neighbours in the hope they might have been seen making the journey from White's Orchard to their home.

One man, James Keegan, recalled meeting the girls and asking how Lizzie was now that she was out of the County Home. Lizzie replied that she felt well again and kept her hands in her pockets as they chatted. Rose Edwards was carrying a parcel under her arm that corresponded to the size of two loaves of bread. Lizzie Edwards had no child with her, he was certain.

The girls said that Keegan had been mistaken. They had brought the child to the house when their mother was absent and then left it in their bed. One sister went to Fuerty to get a bucket of water at the pump, the other to Ausboro's shop nearby to buy bread. Gardai checked and neither bought bread in the shop. They also checked and found that the Edwards had a spring water well on their own land, and had no need to go to the pump for water. Lizzie visited the child in the room regularly, but said it appeared to be ill. She went to bed at 10 pm and Rose joined her an hour later. Rose brought her breakfast in bed the following morning and discovered that the child was dead. She buried it at 2 pm.

In November the details of the case were reported to the Attorney General for a decision. In December, Sergeant Tobin and Garda Connolly were on duty on the farm when they overheard a conversation between the two sisters, as Lizzie said, 'What do you care about them, sure they can't find it now anyway.'

The Edwards sisters were arrested in January 1935, and tried in the Central Criminal Court two months later. They were convicted and sentenced to death but this sentence was later commuted. The Court of Criminal Appeal held that the jury's verdict could not be set aside. The body of the infant was never discovered, although there was much speculation that it could have been dumped into the flooding waters of the river Suck.

Just over a year later, in February 1936, another murder case got under way when the car of a missing woman, Mrs Vera Ball, was discovered by the sea at Shankill, Co. Dublin. Although her body was never found, her son Edward was eventually convicted of her murder.

Now, forty years after the Edwards and Ball cases, another murder hunt was under way although the corpse of the victim had not been found. In the course of the Captain Nairac trial, the prosecution made reference to both previous cases.

An armed guard was put over the red Dolomite outside the Three Steps pub by the RUC in anticipation of the technical examination. Fears of booby traps had led the RUC to be careful when examining the scene of any crime or suspicious object. They called in the army's experts. An ammunitions technical officer was despatched to the scene. He blasted in the front side windows of the car, using a shotgun. No bomb exploded, and after a careful visual examination for any wires or devices, he left the way clear for the first technical examination at the scene.

The Newry RUC's scenes of crimes officer Constable William Poots then began his examination. The area around the car showed signs of a scuffle; there was soil scattered in front of the car, and its wing mirror was broken off and lying on the ground. There were some bloodstains on the gravel in front of the car, and a cigarette packet and a few cigarettes lay scattered on the ground beside some loose change. Constable Poots also took four fingerprints from the near passenger window, three on the interior driving mirror, and three more on the passenger side window.

All the items including some hairs found on a stone in the fight area were bagged, labelled and sent to the Department of Industrial and Forensic Sciences laboratory in Belfast for testing. Meanwhile the search went on. The Provisional IRA admitted responsibility for killing Captain Nairac, but said nothing about where the body could be found. His family were extremely distressed: not only had they lost their son but they had no body to bury and mourn. Archbishop Hume made a television and radio appeal to the Provisionals to give up the body, but his words fell on deaf ears.

The river Fleury runs through the 1,600 acre Ravensdale Park, near Dundalk, Co. Louth, on the south of the border. On Wednesday the 18th two men entered the park intending to go trout fishing on it. It was a fine afternoon and they parked their car on the Dundalk to Newry road which runs parallel to the river, and hauled their fishing gear out of the boot of the car. As they crossed the West Lodge bridge at about 3.30 pm they noticed a number of coins lying on the ground. They looked around the grassy bank and saw two bullets, a piece of wire and bloodmarks on the ground. Alarmed, they went back to their car, and drove to Dromad to report their find. But on the way there they met a Garda squad car on the road and flagged it down. The squad car radioed to Dundalk Garda station. Captain Nairac's disappearance was at the forefront of Superintendent P.J. Farrelly's mind when he visited the scene later. He ordered the area to be cordoned off and sent for the Technical Bureau to examine it. He realised that if there was a link between the scene in Ravensdale Park and Captain Nairac, the case took on a whole new significance: that of a cross-border abduction.

The first Technical Bureau members, including Detective Inspector John Courtney, visited the bridge scene that afternoon. It took four painstaking days of examination before the Gardai were satisfied they had gathered every scrap of evidence. There was a graze on the wall of the bridge, and this yielded a small piece of lead which appeared to be the base portion of the lead core of a 7.54 mm jacketed bullet. Two bullets were discovered at the scene and sent to the Technical Bureau's Detective Garda Mick Niland for examination. One was a 9 mm calibre manufacture made at the Royal Ordnance, Railway Green in England. The other was a 7.65 mm calibre manufactured by Hitenberger Patronen-Zundhutchen in Austria. It bore firing pin marks on its primer. On the ground near the wall of the bridge a portion of a bullet's copper jacket and a number of pieces of lead were also discovered. A single round of 9 mm Parabellum ammunition also manufactured by the Royal Ordnance was discovered as well.

A large number of other items were also discovered at the side of the bridge or in the grassy field on its southern side. These included a white shirt button, two pieces of wire and some hair, a black button on a piece of wood which may have been a post, a rock and a trunk of a tree which were bloodstained. A black button was also discovered in a nearby ditch.

About two feet away from the wall of the bridge Detective Garda Niland took a sample of moss at the land supports of the bridge, and a sample of the bloodstained earth and grass two feet away from the bridge. He took four blood samples from the scene, including splashes on the bridge and on the grass. In total he took eight samples of grass and four of soil. On 25 May he took a sample of the stone work on the bridge with a steel scalpel. He sent both the sample and blade to the state laboratory for examination by Dr James Donovan. On 29 May he went to the bridge again and took samples of soil, a small stone and a piece of grass in the area and sent these with a sample of the blood discovered at the scene to Dr Richard McClean at the state forensic laboratory in Belfast.

Meanwhile on 20 May the military police at Bessbrook were requested to provide samples of hair from Captain Nairac. This seemingly impossible task was achieved quite simply by taking a sample from the hairbrush in his quarters. Nairac also kept a dog, and hair samples from the animal were also sent to the Northern Ireland laboratory for comparison purposes on the same day as the request.

Dr McClean said that hair found on a stone at the Three Steps showed some microscopic similarities to hairs taken from the brush belonging to Captain Nairac. The hair taken from the car park was consistent with having been pulled from the head rather than cut. Stones taken from the same scene were covered with blood and hair, and when this hair was examined it too was similar to the hair on Nairac's brush. Most of the hairs had broken ends and one of the samples was crushed. Later he was to examine hair taken from the scene at Ravensdale Park, and these too were found to be similar to that on Nairac's brush. Blood from the stones at the Three Steps Inn was similar to human blood taken from the bridge in the South.

Dr James Donovan received a steady flow of items for testing as the investigation continued into the disappearance of Captain Nairac. Gardai had painstakingly combed out every inch around the bridge area, and every item that might have been of forensic evidence use was bagged and sent to the Bureau. Not surprisingly, many of these had no evidential value at all. The items submitted included hairs taken from the wall of the bridge. These proved to be human hairs with human blood attached.

Scrapings taken from a mark on the wall were suspected of being made by a bullet, a belief the forensic report confirmed. 'I compared the human hair found in the various parts of the scene with that from the hairbrush of Captain Nairac and I found this hair to be very similar. In other words, the hair from the scene is consistent with the hair of Captain Nairac,' concluded Dr Donovan's report.

As the scientists worked at analysing the dozens of samples they had been given from the two scenes, police intelligence on both sides of the border was at work, increasing surveillance, questioning touts and checking the movements of suspects. In the North the RUC made five arrests.

On 28 May, Liam Townson, a twenty-four-year-old unemployed joiner, was spotted by two detectives in the back seat of a Ford Cortina travelling northwards. They followed the car, and as it pulled up at a security check at Marshes North, outside Dundalk, they arrested him under Section Two of the Emergency Powers Act. Townson was brought to the Garda station shortly before 9 pm. Townson came from a respected family in the community of Meigh, Co. Armagh. His mother was a community nurse, his father a health inspector. Liam was single and one of a family of five boys and four girls. He had moved south of the border because he claimed he had been beaten up by the British army, and was currently unemployed. Townson, thin framed with long straggly hair, was brought to an interview room in the town centre Garda station.

The events surrounding the death of Captain Robert Nairac and Townson's detention in the Garda station in the following hours were to spark lengthy debates, claim and counter claim in the Special Criminal Court five months later, when Townson pleaded not guilty to the murder of Captain Nairac. He also pleaded not guilty to having a .32 revolver, a 9 mm pistol and eighty-three rounds of ammunition with intent to endanger life.

The first interview began with Townson at 9.20 pm that evening, when Detective Sergeant Owen Corrigan and Detective Garda

Terence Hynes from Dundalk Garda Station told him they were investigating the disappearance of Captain Nairac in Ravensdale Park. Townson was to be interviewed until after 4 am that morning as relays of questioning teams asked him about the SAS man's death.

Asked to account for his movements on the night of the 14th, Townson said that he had been in Leonard's pub, Church Street, Dundalk with a man called Peter Fagan. They moved on to another bar in Bridge Street where they stayed until around closing time, and left around midnight. He tried to arrange a lift home because he was drunk. Eventually he got to Fagan's in Proleek where he stayed and he went to bed.

'I was not involved in the disappearance of Captain Nairac and know nothing about him. Oh Jesus lads, I wasn't there,' Gardai were to say he told them later.

The trial continued for twenty-two days. Townson spent two of those days in the witness box, giving his version of events and the court adjourned at one stage after Townson was examined by two doctors and found to be 'mentally unfit' to continue the trial.

Townson was represented by the one of the top legal brains in the business, Paddy McEntee SC. McEntee, the son of a dentist, was born in Monaghan and educated by the Christian Brothers. He went on to University College Dublin where he was a leading light and contemporary in the Dramatic Society of successful entertainers Des Keogh and Rosaleen Linehan. He was called to the Bar in 1960 and practised on the Northern circuit. He had campaigned as an election agent for Fine Gael's Billy Fox, and ironically years later was to accept a brief to defend one of the men accused of the murder of the Senator, the only member of the Oireachtas murdered since the end of the civil war. A superb defence lawyer, his career was to be marked by important legal victories won on behalf of his clients.

Liam Townson told the court that when he was was being questioned after his arrest, his questioners said he 'would be put across the border for this'. He thought this meant he would be extradited to Northern Ireland. Asked what effect this had on him he said, 'I did not think I would ever see the inside of a barracks again. I saw the body of Peter Cleary and he did not have much of a chance as far as I know. I used to meet him at dances sometimes. He was shot dead when he was supposed to be running away from the SAS British soldiers. I thought I was going to be shot too. They said there were five statements in the North all saying [that] I did know something about Captain Nairac and that I was involved in his disappearance and killing.'

Those statements included allegations that Townson had hit Nairac across the head with a gun as he was held by his captors, sitting on the ground with his back to the bridge in Ravensdale Park. Townson was laughing and ignored the man's pleas for a priest. Then he put his gun up to Nairac's head and fired the first shot when the muzzle was only two feet from his head. The gun clicked, and then clicked three more times. Townson swore about the 'blanks', then pulled the trigger again and the gun went off.

In the courtroom, in reply to Mr McEntee, Townson denied telling the detectives that he was involved in the murder.

He alleged that the Gardai had information that he had been met in a pub in Dundalk where he had been drinking McArdle's beer and that he had gone to pick up a gun for a job. Then he had travelled with some men to Ravensdale. He had let off a test shot through the open window of the car as it travelled northwards. Then he had gone into a field at Ravensdale Park where a number of men were holding Nairac and he had shot him, left the body and went back to the town to continue drinking. Mr McEntee put it to his client that several Garda witnesses had sworn that Townson had given this version of events himself, but Townson denied this and also denied drawing a sketch map of the area shown in court.

Townson in response to his Counsel also said that he had at no stage ever confessed to the murder either verbally or in writing.

He also claimed in court that he had been abused by five Gardai. He had been called a 'callous, brutal and murdering bastard', one had kicked him on the shin, and one had slapped him across the back of his head. Townson said that when they went to Ravensdale Park with the Gardai 'the life had been scared out of me because I thought I was going to be given over to the SAS'.

The Gardai denied that they had slapped or abused Townson while he was in custody and said that there had been no threat made to put him back across the border. The court also heard how on the Monday evening Townson had become excited. 'The accused became hysterical. He stretched out his arms with his fists clenched and said, "I will swing for nobody. They will never put a rope around my neck. They can shoot me if they like. I will kill myself tonight. I will tear my heart out,"' one member of the investigation team said. Townson's brother entered the room as they tried to calm the accused, and when asked what they were doing, Liam Townson said, 'It's OK they didn't do anything to me.' Townson was also medically examined while held in custody, and was given a clean bill of health.

Detective Garda Frank Clune supervised a visit by Townson's mother, brother Rory and sister Sheila on the Monday evening. The court was told that during that visit Townson told his mother, 'I am being well treated, I have not been abused at all,' and then turned to the Garda and said, 'Guard, I want you to hear what I have said to my mother. I am being treated very well.'

Solicitor Donal Carroll from Dublin said he had been engaged to act for Townson at 11 pm on the Sunday night 29 May. He rang Dundalk Garda Station and asked the sergeant in charge if he could see his client.

'He told me that some of the Gardai dealing with the case would have to grant the visit, but none of them was there at that time. I complained that this was highly unusual and that I had never met such an attitude before. I told the sergeant that I would be at home all night and could be called as soon as some of the Gardai returned,' said Mr Carroll.

However, he did not receive a call that night. He phoned the station three times the next day and received the same response. Exasperated, he then drove to Dundalk, called to the station at 3.50 pm, and despite promises that he would be allowed to see his client at 5 pm, it wasn't until 7 pm that he saw him.

When he finally met Townson on that Monday evening, he found him sitting crying with his head in his hands, saying, 'I don't want to die, I don't want to die. Please don't give me back to the SAS.' He had no difficulty seeing his client the following day and on the third day, Wednesday, Townson was back to his normal self.

Earlier on that Monday, handcuffed to Detective Garda Lane, Townson was seated into the back of a patrol car between Detective Inspector John Courtney and Detective Garda Lane. Garda Harrington was the driver and Detective Sergeant Canavan sat in the front passenger seat. They drove out the Newry road from the station in the direction of Dromad. As they approached Thistle Cross, Townson gave directions to the driver until they stopped and he retrieved a white plastic bag covered with stones from a ditch. This contained some of his own articles of clothing and shoes.

On the way back to Dundalk, Townson said the guns were hidden near Proleek, and offered to show them the spot. Off the main road they turned right, stopped at a gate and walked across some fields to where Townson pointed out another small pile of stones. Underneath it Gardai found two guns, a holster and several rounds of ammunition.

The guns were examined by the Technical Bureau's ballistics section. One gun was a .32 revolver, capable of firing 7.65 mm ammunition. There appeared to be blood on the barrel and there was hair on the frame. There were two faults in the gun. It could only be fired by the double-action method, applying pressure on the trigger to cock the hammer automatically and discharge a shot. Two consecutive shots could be discharged only if the trigger was released quickly after the first shot had been discharged. But if the gunman didn't do this, the trigger would have to be pushed fully forward before a second bullet could be fired. The reason for this fault was wear on the trigger's pivot pin. The second fault was that it was likely to misfire due to wear on the barrel catch point. This meant that it was impossible to know if a cartridge was in position under the hammer.

The ballistics report written by Detective Garda Niland also showed that the firing pin markings on the two spent cartridge cases found at the scene were made by this revolver. The firing pin markings on one round of 7.65 mm calibre ammunition found at the scene in Ravensdale had similar characteristics to the markings on the test bullet cases fired from the retrieved gun, and this suggested they would appear to be made by the same gun. However, there were a number of 'intermingled and superimposed marks' which obliterated vital characteristics. So while the markings on the jackets of the test bullets and those on the jackets from Ravensdale were similar, they could not be 'positively identified'. The second gun was a Browning number two mark one semi-automatic pistol. The bore of the barrel was clean and did not show any signs of a shot having been discharged from it. The lanyard swivel ring was missing, and the left-hand side of the stock had three finger-shaped grooves filed into it. The right-hand side had been smoothed down, and the safety lever had been built up by brazing.

The gun was identified prior to the hearing as Captain Nairac's by his colleague Captain Collett. He knew the gun because of its peculiar modifications which Nairac had made himself, and because he had seen Nairac leave the barracks with the gun in its holster beneath his jacket. The modified gun was the only one he had ever seen adapted this way in Northern Ireland although he had seen it done elsewhere, he told the court in Dublin. The Captain also identified the holster which was retrieved with the guns as belonging to Captain Nairac.

On 3 June Dr James Donovan of the State Laboratory received samples of swabs taken from the two guns. These contained lead, antimony, barium and copper traces, which meant that both guns had been fired. One of the swabs was from a pistol and there were fewer traces of the four metals on that swab than on the other which came from a revolver. Either the pistol had not been fired for some time or considerably more shots had been discharged from the revolver, he concluded.

On the previous day the white plastic supermarket bag containing a polo neck sweater and black trousers were delivered to the State Laboratory for forensic testing with a variety of other items retrieved from the ditch by Gardai with Liam Townson. These included a fawn-coloured sweater which was missing a portion of the left cuff. Both cuffs had bloodstains. There were also a number of samples of a mossy plant material on the front and on the sleeves. Under the right armpit there was a bunch of human hairs which were consistent with being taken from the head of Captain Robert Nairac, said the forensic report.

The black trousers were mud stained and the mud was similar to a sample from the scene. Threads had been pulled from the trousers at the lower leg and left pocket level as if it had been caught in barbed wire. The trousers were bloodstained in a total of six areas. All the bloodstains were on the outside.

Shoes in another bag belonging to Liam Townson were extensively mud stained. Analysis proved that the mud was the same as samples from the scene. A control sample of moss taken from the scene was found to be exactly the same as that found on Townson's sweater.

After Townson had pointed out the guns and clothing they returned to the patrol car. Garda Larry Crowe was waiting there and Crowe, who knew Townson, asked him if he'd make a statement. Townson said he would if he could sign it with his solicitor. That was OK, said Garda Crowe, and he cautioned Townson as he sat in the patrol car with Detective Garda Lane. Garda Lane wrote the statement as Townson dictated it.

The statement was challenged in court, and a documents expert from London, Dr Julius Grant, a Fellow of the Royal Institute of Chemistry, was given facilities to examine the original statement at the forensic laboratory in Dublin. In direct evidence he could not say for certain whether the document had been written by someone holding it on their knees or alternatively written at a desk. The court had heard that it had been written by Garda Crowe in a patrol car with the paper resting on his knees.

Under cross examination Dr Grant said that he was fairly sure the document was not written on someone's knees. The writing was very regular and uniform. He had the impression it was written at a desk or on a piece of board.

In total Townson was to make seven alleged statements, five outside Dundalk Garda Station and two inside, the Circuit Criminal Court was told.

Earlier that Monday in Dundalk Garda Station Townson had asked Detective Sergeant Michael Canavan how long he would get for the killing, and both Canavan and Detective Inspector Courtney said they did not know. Townson then said he would tell the truth. He was cautioned and admitted he had shot Captain Nairac with a revolver. 'I honestly don't know where the body is. I'm not the OC. I should never have done it. I walked into it like a lamb. He never told us anything, he was a good soldier,' he added.

The court's three judges spent two days considering the admissibility of the seven statements allegedly made by Townson to the Gardai. Mr Justice D'Arcy, presiding, said that the court was satisfied that Townson had been lawfully arrested, and that there was nothing fictional or fraudulent relating to the arrest. They accepted a submission from Patrick McEntee SC, for Townson, that an admitted right of a person to have reasonable access to a legal advisor was also a constitutional right. The court was satisfied that between 4 pm and 7.15 pm on 30 May there had been a deliberate and conscious denial of the accused person's right to have access to his solicitor, and this was also a breach of his constitutional rights.

The court went on to reject five of seven statements allegedly made by Townson, including one taken in the patrol car which was not signed by Townson. The only two statements not tainted with constitutional irregularities was one made to Detectives Courtney and Canavan in Dundalk Garda Station at about 3.40 pm on Monday the 30th, and the second one made in the presence of a number of Gardai at Dundalk after Townson had seen his solicitor.

The judges rejected allegations that there were threats to put the accused across the border. There was evidence that Townson was calm and relaxed and the court further rejected allegations that he had been held down and shouted at. Later in the trial there had been evidence that Townson had been hysterical and distressed, and the court was satisfied that this was not due to any act or defect of the Gardai, and the statement made at this time was also admissible.

The court agreed that there was a breach of the Judges' Rules in regard to the first statement, to the effect that such a statement should be written down and then signed by the accused. The evidence in this instance was that the statement was not written down until an hour and a half later. However the court said it was satisfied that this was because the accused had said he was willing to make a written statement to Gardai King or Crowe whom he knew. This was an acceptable reason for not writing down the statement at the time and justified the breach of the Judges' Rules. The statement had in fact been made and was voluntary and therefore admissible.

In the confession admitted, Townson said that he had been approached in a pub in Dundalk where he was drinking and was asked to get a gun to carry out a job. He had a lot of drink taken at the time, but agreed, got the gun and went to Ravensdale Park. Captain Nairac told Townson he was a 'stickie', a member of the Official IRA, and he named a man from Dromintree. But Townson said he did not believe him, and said he was a British soldier and he had to kill him. He hit him with his fist and struck him on the head with the butt of his gun. Nairac said to him, 'You are going to kill me, can I have a priest?' The Captain was in a bad state at that stage. 'I aimed at his head and only put one into him,' he said. Then he walked back across the fields leaving the body there.

In summing up, the judges said that when Sergeant Canavan said the voluntary statement began at 3.50 pm, and Detective Inspector Courtney said it had been completed at 3.50 pm, the court was reasonably satisfied that despite the discrepancy the voluntary statement was made by 4 pm. The court was satisfied that when Sergeant Canavan had made the alteration of times in his notebook he had no ulterior motive and they were satisfied with his perfectly innocent explanation in this matter.

The court was satisfied beyond any doubt that Liam Patrick Townson had shot and killed Captain Nairac and that this was murder, and the mandatory penalty was penal servitude for life. Townson was also sentenced to five years for having ammunition and firearms with intent to endanger life.

The body of Captain Nairac has never been found. Detectives investigating the case say that because of the geography of the area with its numerous lakes there was always the possibility the body would not be recovered.

Five men were also convicted in Northern Ireland in connection with the death of Captain Robert Nairac. In December 1989, Liam Townson was released from Portlaoise prison on Christmas parole. At the time of writing Townson still has no release date, although the men convicted in the North have all since been released, the latest in 1987. In a letter to the *Sunday Tribune* Townson promised he would seek out his former colleagues, if paroled, and ask them to hand over the body of the British army Captain.

4.

The Shooting of Bob Browne

THURSDAY 2 June 1983 was the feast of Corpus Christi, and a holy day of obligation. All over Ireland people got up earlier than usual and went to mass before going to work; others took time off work for a morning mass, joining young mothers with toddlers, the unemployed and the retired. Others just waited for an evening mass.

The population of Co. Kerry was no different. In the Browne household in Killacrim a few miles outside Listowel, thirty-nine-year-old Anne was chivvying her children to hurry up or they'd be late for 12.15 mass. She was a brunette, pleasant and cheerful, a lively dancer and still considered an attractive woman; the mother of six, the eldest of whom was seventeen and the youngest thirteen months. She eventually got three children seated in the family's beige-coloured Ford Cortina. One of the teenagers remained at home with the family's newest addition, eighteen-months-old baby Rachel. John, her husband, better known as Bob, drove the car. He was seven years older than she and no longer worked after a large insurance company payout following a hand injury sustained six years previously when he worked as a labourer at the ESB power station in Tarbert. He had been steadily drinking the £63,000 compensation payout ever since.

Bob drove into Listowel and parked the car beside the post office. Anne, Richard, Paul and Michelle Browne walked to the nearby church.

Bob Browne turned and walked towards his nearest favourite pub, Sheehan's in William Street, to start another long day's drinking. He was well known in the town and surrounding country-side, for he was a native of the area and had been raised in Dysart, Lixnaw. He went to the local school until he was fifteen and then, like most of his classmates, left to go to work. He worked as a farm labourer for the next four years, until he became a water keeper with the Limerick Fisheries Board. In October that year he married

Anne Stack, who was only a year out of the Presentation Convent school in Listowel. Her family was originally from Abbeyfeale in Co. Limerick but had moved to Glenderry, Listowel, in the early 1950s. In 1956 the family had again moved, this time to Irremore, Listowel. Anne had not excelled at school, and had been working as a domestic servant when she married.

Newly wedded, John and Anne Browne decided their future lay in England where the construction business and the economy were booming in the mid 1960s. They stayed there for four years, then returned, and John was re-employed by the board in his old post. He continued to work there for the next three years before taking up a more lucrative job as a labourer with APC construction at the ESB power station site until the accident. Along with his compensation payment he received disability benefit of just over £100 a week.

He had made an attempt to buy a house in Tralee but the deal fell through, and subsequently Kerry County Council built him a house on his own site. Over the past few years, as time hung on his hands, his drinking had become heavier and heavier and had hardened into a routine. He was not a sociable drinker, preferring to drink alone at the bar, brooding over a pint of Guinness, reading the day's paper, or watching the television. He caused no trouble in the town's bars despite his sometimes prodigious drinking feats and had never been barred. On one occasion he had stayed away from a bar in the town for a few months after he had swapped angry words with another customer and the barman had to intervene.

Bob had a pint or two in Sheehan's that day, and then went to Kennelly's further down the road. He finished his pint and walked to Mulvihill's in Market Street where he had arranged to meet his wife and family at 1 pm. They arrived as he stood at the bar and he bought them all a drink. Approximately one hour later they left and walked back to the parked car. Sixteen-year-old Michelle sat into the driver's seat, and as they drove home Bob asked to be let out. He walked off in the direction of the town while the family continued on.

Bob Browne began to walk out the Ballybunion road, thumbing a lift. He was picked up by farmer Timothy Hartnett who also ran a caravan park at Gortnaskely, Ballybunion. He dropped Browne off in the seaside town and drove on. Browne was ordering a pint of stout in Brosnan's bar in the Main Street a few minutes later. He stayed there until after 4 pm, when he left to thumb his way back to Listowel.

At 5 pm Catherine Relihan, the barmaid in Walsh's pub in Limerick Street, Listowel, served him. Two hours later he was still there. He moved on to Mulvihill's bar where he had again arranged to meet his wife and had a drink with her before leaving at about 9 pm. He returned then to his starting point, Sheehan's, where he had another drink. By 9.45 pm he was in O'Connor's bar in Upper William Street where he stayed lowering pints until after 11.30 pm.

Bob left the pub by the front door and turned for home. It was a dry breezy night and it wasn't the first time he had ever walked home after a day's drinking. At 12.20 am he was seen thumbing a lift outside the Listowel hospital. He stepped into the road to flag down a passing car but the car continued, and he kept walking. Five minutes later he passed Cahill's house at Greenville, and fifteen minutes later Val Connors' gate at Gurtcreen. He kept walking towards his home, past Scartleigh cross.

Earlier that evening a neighbour, P.J. Hayes, a farmer at Gort-namincha, had been to 7.30 pm mass in Listowel. He had driven home in his red Opel Manta and around about 10.30 pm he had gone to Wolf's bar for a couple of drinks. He had delayed talking to people as he left and it was almost 1.15 am when he got into his car to drive home. He was nearly there when he saw something lying near the middle of the road. As he slowed he realised it was a body. Recognition dawned on him: it was the body of a man to whom he occasionally gave a lift home. It was the body of Bob Browne.

He hit the brakes and reversed the car. As it backed along the road the headlights swept over the huddled body a second time. He parked the car with the two left-hand-side wheels up on the pavement, turned off his headlights and switched on his hazard warning lights. Bob Browne was lying on his front, parallel to the centre of the road. His head was turned towards the fence on the left-hand-side of the road and there was blood on his trousers. P.J. Hayes stooped down and felt his forehead. He was cold to his touch. Browne was either dead or very bad, he guessed, as he ran to his own home. He burst into the house, and his sister Alice who was reading in bed, dressed hurriedly and ran to their father's car clutching a couple of blankets to put over Browne's body. P.J. went back to the scene with Alice.

No other car had pulled up beside either the body or the still flashing lights of the Manta in his absence.

The Hayes family shared a communal telephone line so he decided to drive to Listowel, which was just over two and a half miles away. Although Finuge village lay one mile in the opposite

44

direction, they had had trouble getting a line out when they needed it in the past and he thought that calling personally to the station would be the fastest way of raising help.

About one mile away as the crow flies, near the Listowel to Lixnaw road, Mrs Julie Lyons had spent the evening watching television in the family caravan as her two toddler children slept. She watched the end of 'Falcon Crest', the last programme on RTE for the evening, and, unable to sleep like her children and husband Pat, she stayed up reading for almost an hour. Suddenly the silence of the countryside was shattered by two loud bangs. She looked out her window and saw nothing she could associate with the noise. The incident stuck in her mind. It was an odd occurrence, she thought, as she settled into bed that night.

At 1.40 am the Gardai arrived in a marked blue and white patrol car. Garda Daniel Lynch knew Browne and was able to identify him. Lynch was accompanied by recruit Garda John Barry. They began an initial investigation, noting down details of the fifteen feet wide stretch of roadway which served the old Scartleigh creamery. There was a large bloody wound to Browne's right leg above his kneee and flesh was visible through his torn trousers. It looked like a hit and run accident. Bob Browne was pronounced dead by a local doctor called to the scene.

An ambulance was at the scene ten minutes after the Gardai, but the body was not moved until they had completed their initial inquiries. It was 2.35 am before it was brought into the mortuary in St Catherine's Hospital, Tralee and porter Joseph McCarthy locked the door and returned the keys to the hospital reception.

At midnight Anne Browne was at home. Her son John was watching television. She made tea and then, tired out, told him to wait up for his father as she went to bed. At 1.30 am she woke with a start, reached out and missed Bob from the double bed. She pulled on her dressing-gown and went to the sitting room. John had fallen asleep on the couch as he watched television. She shook him gently, woke him and sent him off to bed; then she went back to bed herself. At about 1.45 am her daughter Michelle came into her parents' bedroom and woke her mother. She had been out on a date. Was her dad home, Michelle asked in a worried voice. Alarmed, Anne said 'No, what's wrong?,' Michelle said she had seen blue lights flashing down the road. It looked like there might have been an accident with the Gardai and ambulances called out in the middle of the night. Anne Browne jumped out of bed, put on her dressing-gown and they both went out onto the road outside the house. As they stood outside the porch they could see the blue lights in the distance.

Meanwhile Garda Lynch had contacted Listowel curate Fr Patrick Moore. Once dressed he went with him in the patrol car to Bob Browne's house which was almost a mile from the scene of his death. It was about 2.30 am when they pulled up outside the house. Both mother and daughter were in their dressing-gowns when they answered the knock at the door. They asked what was wrong, already beginning to dread the worst as they looked at the concerned faces of the Garda and priest. 'Where's Dad?' Michelle asked.

Garda Lynch said there had been an accident and broke the news as gently as he could that Bob Browne was dead. Both women burst into tears. They were shepherded back into the kitchen where Anne sat on a chair and told Michelle to calm down in case she'd wake the baby. 'How will I manage now? He looked after everything,' said Anne through sobs.

The phone hung on the kitchen wall and Anne tried to ring her brother-in-law, Billy. Numbers were scrawled in a list on a pad hanging beside the phone. Anne ran her finger down the list, found Billy's number and dialled, still shaking from the shocking news. She couldn't get through and rang the exchange; the operator then tried, but Billy's number still rang out. Anne mentioned another name to Michelle but her daughter insisted that someone should go and wake Billy. P.J. Hayes had joined them in the kitchen and he volunteered to go to Billy Browne's house in Tannavalla with Garda Lynch. Fr Moore stayed talking to the two women as they left. Anne stayed up, unable to sleep.

At 4 am the Tralee hospital porter Joseph McCarthy opened the door of the morgue. Three nurses stripped the body and placed the clothes into a bag which they then sealed. They locked the door behind them again and handed the bag to Billy Browne, who had gone to the hospital.

Later that day Gardai examined the scene in daylight. Sergeant Michael O'Donohue from Lixnaw Station was one of the Gardai examining the roadway which was bounded by ditches and open fields. There was a long streak of blood on the roadway and blood spots were noted on the post of a gateway entrance to one of the roadside fields. He also discovered a piece of flesh two inches long on the grass verge at the side of the road. He pointed it out and gave it to the Listowel district scenes of crime officer Garda George Gaine.

On Friday Browne's front door was open all night as a steady stream of relatives and neighbours called to offer their sympathies.

46

At about 9.30 pm Jeremiah Sullivan, a forty-two-year-old father of five, called. He was of medium build with grey hair and a ruddy complexion. He and Anne were friends and regular dancing partners and often visited the music pubs in the area together. He had rung the house earlier in the day and Michelle had told him her father had been killed in a hit and run accident.

Gardai investigating the incident had called to Sullivan's house as part of their routine investigation and asked him had he seen anyone in the area that night. He told them that he had met Anne Browne in the square in Listowel at 9 pm on the Thursday evening. She got into his car and they went to the Western Inn in Abbeyfeale a few miles from Listowel. They stayed there until closing time, and returned home via Finuge. He dropped her off at the grotto, and she walked the rest of the way home, while he went back into Listowel for a bag of chips. He then drove home alone, passing the scene of the incident, and arrived at about 12.30. He hadn't seen Bob Browne that day at all. The only person he met on the way home was a cyclist on Markey's bridge, he told the Gardai.

Soberly dressed in a dark blue suit, it was the first time Jeremiah Sullivan had ever been in the Browne home. He spoke only briefly with Anne in the kitchen before leaving.

The following day, Saturday the 4th, Gardai in Listowel got two anonymous phone calls. The first was from a male caller with a Kerry accent who said he was from Ballybunion and ringing from there. He said he was coming from Tralee via Finuge shortly after midnight on Friday morning with his girlfriend when they saw a car outside Scartleigh creamery. The second call, again male and anonymous, began by asking, 'Well, what about the murder?' Garda O'Neill asked, 'What murder?' and the caller said, 'Well, the hit and run so'. The caller then said he had seen a white Ford Capri parked at Scartleigh creamery near Gortnamincha.

P.J. Prendergast, the consultant pathologist to St Catherine's Hospital in Tralee, began the post mortem shortly before midday. He found that there was a large soft injury to the right side of Bob Browne's leg, and what clearly looked like the peppered markings caused by shotgun pellets. Dr Prendergast informed the Gardai and it was decided this was now a matter for the state pathologist. Superintendent Liam Leonard opted to call in the murder squad. The post mortem was adjourned to allow Dr Kieran Cuddihy of Ardkeen Hospital in Waterford, the assistant state pathologist, to continue the examination.

It was on Saturday that Anne Browne was told that her husband had been shot, and had not been the victim of a hit and run incident.

On Sunday morning the doors to the mortuary were unlocked, and Dr Cuddihy began his post mortem examination. It showed that there were two major shotgun wounds to the body. The largest was on the back of the left shoulder with a pellet spread of almost nine inches. There were no exit wounds at the front of the body from this shotgun blast. Pellets had penetrated into the left lung and the fourth left rib had been completly shattered. There the blast had ripped a hole four inches wide and another two inches by three inches. The second shotgun wound was to the inside thigh of the right leg. A total of sixteen pellets were removed from the chest of the corpse, and a further five from the leg. Microscopic examination showed they were size four shot. Dr Cuddihy concluded that the cause of death was due to a loss of blood and inhalation of blood into the left lung due to shotgun wounds.

Detective Garda William Brennan from the ballistics section of the Technical Bureau attended the post mortem in Tralee. He had been with the Bureau for over five years and formally identified the injuries as caused by shotgun blasts. That afternoon he drove to Gortnamincha and organised a search party made up of local Gardai. A sketch and a map showing the long bloodstain on the roadway had already been made by Gardai. The bloodstain ran in a line for approximately 262 feet.

Training for scenes of crimes examination is explicit and concentrates on minute detail. In early training sessions for the Technical Bureau at the St John's Road complex in Dublin an overgrown section of land at the back of the main building was used for training purposes. Every square inch of the land was searched on hands and knees and Detective Gardai had to be able to account for even a match head at the cordoned-off area after the search was completed.

At Gortnamincha, Gardai were strung out on their hands and knees across the fifteen-feet wide stretch of road, gradually inching forward from the spot where the body had been found to where the blood streak commenced and beyond. Garda Thomas Wright discovered the first cartridge case almost hidden in the long grass on the side of the road near the first bloodstain. He didn't touch it and it was photographed by Detective Garda Peter O'Connor, one of the official photographers attached to the Bureau who take, develop and print their own photographs. Once the cartridge was photographed as it lay on the grass it was picked up, put into a self-sealing plastic bag and labelled.

Later that afternoon, as the search continued, another shotgun cartridge case was discovered on the roadside, approximately 110 feet from the first shell case. It too was photographed, bagged and labelled. Both cartridge cases were similar — twelve gauge Eley Grand Prix.

Meanwhile Dr Maureeen Smyth, a scientist with the State Laboratory, was in contact with the detective team from the investigation section of the Bureau led by Detective Superintendent John Courtney, who was leading the inquiry in his home county. A practised analyst, she had tested the strip of flesh found at Gortnamincha. It had been tested for a number of different blood groups, and proved to be O PGM 1+1+, a combination present in approximately 22 per cent of the Irish population. It was also the combination of groups present in Bob Browne's blood. To the experienced murder squad team it looked like the strip of flesh had been torn from Bob Browne by the force of the shotgun blast.

After the result of the post mortem was known, Detective Superintendent John Courtney requested that Superintendent Liam Leonard, the highest ranking Garda in the Listowel area, issue revocation orders under the Firearms Act 1975 which would allow Gardai to take possession of shotguns from owners who had licensed them in that Garda district.

A total of fourteen shotguns were gathered by detectives visiting farms in the area that day. One of the last farms visited was Jeremiah Sullivan's. It was approximately 9 pm when three detectives called to his house at Ballingerah, Lixnaw. They were there to collect a Pedretti/Rustler single-barrel breech-loading shotgun owned by John Sullivan, Jeremiah's nineteen-year-old son, for which he held an unlimited firearms licence.

Neither John nor his father were in, but another son, fifteen-year-old Noel, brought them to his brother's bedroom where the gun was kept in a wardrobe. They also took a box containing twenty-five cartridges which lay on the floor of the wardrobe beside the gun. As the Gardai were about to leave Jeremiah Sullivan arrived home. He told them that he never used the shotgun, that it was his son's. He had bought the cartridges they were holding for John at Crowley's firearms dealers in Listowel the previous Thursday when he had been in the town.

Dozens of Gardai, uniformed and plainclothes, had been issued with questionnaires aimed at detailing the movements of the population in the area on the night of the shooting. Gardai were given instructions that the questions were to be put to everyone in the vicinity over ten years of age. That Sunday afternoon the Gardai called to Anne Browne as they sought more details about where Bob had been that day. Anne said that Jeremiah Sullivan rang her on Thursday afternoon at about 4.30 pm to arrange to meet her that evening at about 9 pm. At about 7 pm Bob rang her from a coin box and asked her to meet him in Mulvihill's in about an hour's time. She met him at 8 pm in Mulvihill's in Listowel and had a few drinks and left him at 9 pm to walk to the square for her prearranged meeting with Jeremiah Sullivan. She said that she told her husband about the meeting. They drove to Abbeyfeale, stayed in the pub there until about 11.15 pm, and he then drove her to the grotto which is about a six-minute walk from her home. She had known Jeremiah for the past five, going on six years, and their relationship was strictly one of friendship. Bob had been fully aware of it, she told the two detectives.

That Sunday night, 5 June, Jeremiah Sullivan and Anne Browne went for a drink to the Western Inn at Fealesbridge, Abbeyfeale. The following day at about 10.15 am Tim O'Connor looked out the window of his sitting room which overlooked the car park of the Western Inn. A man got out of a blue Ford Cortina, walked to the closed door and knocked loudly. But Tim O'Connor made no move. People had called before opening hours previously looking for drink and he found his best strategy was not to answer the door at all, to avoid arguing with them. It was easier to leave them knock. But when the man persisted for ten minutes, O'Connor relented. When he opened the door he didn't know the man, who wanted to go inside and talk. O'Connor closed the door behind him as they walked into the bar. The man said it was a nice pub; he often called, it was a convenient pub. He said he lived in Lixnaw and that his name was Jerry Sullivan. He said that he had been in the bar with a woman friend the previous Thursday evening for the night and he had lost a ring. Had anybody found it, he wondered? They had been sitting at the top of the bar near the window. The ring had been wrapped in his handkerchief and it must have got lost when he used his handkerchief to blow his nose. No one had found a ring or any other piece of jewellery, said Tim O'Connor. He had been with a woman friend, said Jeremiah Sullivan. She had fair hair, perhaps he remembered? At no point did Sullivan refer to the fact that he had been in the pub only the previous evening, the Sunday. It was only later that Tim O'Connor remembered him from the previous evening. He had been looking out the window of his living room again as his wife Maureen was running the bar. He remembered Jeremiah Sullivan getting into the same car with a woman, a brunette.

When the Gardai subsequently called, Tim O'Connor told them that he hadn't been in the bar the previous Thursday evening, that his wife Maureen had been behind the counter serving. But he came down at around 11.30 pm to close up as he usually did and there were eight people in the pub. He knew six of them as regulars, although one of the regulars he knew only by sight as coming from Abbeyfeale and not by name. The other two were strangers to him. None of the eight people he saw in the bar that night was the man who had identified himself as Jerry Sullivan.

Jeremiah Sullivan had been raised in Lixnaw. He went to the local school until he was fourteen years of age and then left to work as a farm labourer locally. Occasionally he went to England on the boat like hundreds more as a seasonal worker for the sugar-beet campaigns. In 1963 he left Ireland for Britain with Maureen, his wife. They returned a year later and lived with his parents as he looked around to buy a farm. In a couple of months he had bought his first holding, a ten-acre farm at Ballinageragh, Lixnaw, for £900. Seventeen years later he bought a further twenty acres from the Land Commission to supplement his small holding and his work as a farm labourer contractor. He was a non-drinker and was known as a hard worker who earned a good living for his family with his two tractors and small amount of agricultural machinery. His wife Maureen had left him at the end of the 1970s.

Jeremiah had been seeing Anne Browne for the past six years, but it was only in the past twelve months or so that they had been seeing each other more frequently, meeting at least twice a week.

On Tuesday 7 June Garda Liam Moloney in Abbeydorney, a small village near Listowel, was station orderly, signing social welfare forms in the station. When the station phone rang he picked it up and heard a crossed line as two voices spoke to each other, unaware that he could hear them. As he tried to figure out what was happening he looked out the window and saw a local man standing in the phone kiosk across the road. He recognised the voice on the line, and realised that the Garda phone was picking up calls from the coin box. He put the phone down, making a mental note to have it repaired. At just after a quarter to midday the phone rang again and Garda Moloney picked up the receiver. Again it wasn't ringing for him; it was another faulty call. He heard a man's voice and the words 'informer' and a woman's voice answering, 'Is that right? OK.' He looked out the window and there was a man in the phone kiosk again. He ran out of the station as the man got into his car, a blue Ford Cortina with a vinyl roof, and noted down the car's registration number, TZX 500, as it drove off.

Mary Hoare, the receptionist with *The Kerryman* newspaper, was at her desk in the office foyer on the Clash Industrial Estate in Tralee when the phone rang. A male voice, speaking with a Kerry accent, told her that the IRA were claiming responsibility for the death of Bob Browne. 'And there is another man who will be knocked off as an informer,' she was told before the caller put the phone down.

Later that day Garda Jim Sullivan from Lixnaw Station met Jeremiah Sullivan and like everyone else in the parish they chatted about the killing of Bob Browne. There was a lot of talk about himself and Anne Browne, said Jeremiah Sullivan. He had always been a friend of Bob's and had given him occasional lifts in his car. He'd heard the dead man was going out with women in Bally-bunion.

On Thursday 9 June Garda Moloney from Abbeydorney met with Garda Jim Sullivan from Lixnaw and they naturally spoke about the main talking point of north Kerry, the Browne murder. Garda Moloney mentioned the phone call he had overheard, and how he had written down a description of the car and its registration number. He had later checked with the car registration office in Cork to discover it was registered to a Michael Stack of Ballyheigue in Kerry. But the Garda from Lixnaw recognised the description and car number. It had been sold, he said. It was now owned by Jeremiah Sullivan.

Meanwhile the Rustler shotgun taken from John Sullivan's wardrobe was undergoing forensic examination. When the gun was seized there was a faint odour which was common in any gun recently fired. When it was broken it was evident that the barrel had been slightly fouled. Now in the basement of the Technical Bureau the shotgun was test fired by Detective Garda Edwin Handcock. He was to use a system of examination that dated back to the early 1930s in most police laboratories in the world. When a bullet is fired from a rifled weapon, the grooves and the 'lands', the smooth surfaces on the barrel between them, are gouged into the bullet. Similarly the breech block, firing pin and interior marks on a non-rifled weapon such as a shotgun also produce their own 'fingerprint'.

The first conviction achieved through such identification was primitive by modern methods. Professor Alexander Laccasagne, who founded the medico-legal department in Lyons University, identified the pistol used in a murder in 1889 when he extracted the bullet from the body and compared it to bullets fired from other pistols. In 1900, Dr Llewellyn Hall published a book on fire-arms which set out the first accurate method for identifying bullets and cartridges. He test fired bullets into boxes of wadded cotton wool and then extracted them and, using a magnifying glass and micro-scope, compared them. The next great stride in ballistic science came from yet another American, Phillip O. Gravelle, a microphoto-grapher and chemist, who invented the comparison microscope in the early 1920s. Essentially it consisted of one viewing lens with two microscope lenses. This allowed the viewer to place bullets side by side and, now clearly magnified, they could be easily compared. In subsequent years a photograph of the two bullets could be taken through the viewing lens using special equipment. These photos could then be produced as courtroom evidence.

In the Technical Bureau, the cartridge case that was fired by the shotgun seized in Sullivan's bedroom was placed under one set of lenses in a powerful comparison microscope. One of the cartridges retrieved from the scene was placed under the second set of lenses. The markings were identical. Unlike the test shots made with other guns, the marks made by the Sullivan Rustler test cartridge case matched those on the Gortnamincha cartridge case. This was proof positive that the Sullivan shotgun had been used in the slaying of Bob Browne. An attempt had also been made to change the shape of the firing pin which comes into contact with the base of the cartridge, triggering the small explosion that sends the shell rocketing down the gun barrel.

A file had been used on the firing pin and as the person using the file had attacked the pin he had also rubbed against the outer edges of the breech face. 'The purpose was to thwart any subsequent identification of the firearm by means of cartridge examination,' the forensic report concluded.

The evidence had been mounting steadily, but the forensic report on the shotgun was conclusive. There had been an attempt to set up a number of false trails which resulted in Garda man-power being diverted to investigate possible IRA actions and false car sightings. From the beginning, the reasonable assumption from the condition and placement of the body was that Bob Browne had been a hit-and-run victim. All these factors combined to slow the investigation, but now the forensic proof was incontrovertible.

At 8.25 am on Saturday 11 June Detective Sergeant Timothy Callaghan went to Jeremiah Sullivan's house and arrested him. He was brought to Tralee Garda Station. At the same time another group of Gardai went to Anne Browne's house and arrested her and also brought her to Tralee Garda Station.

Jeremiah hadn't been sleeping at nights since the shooting of Bob Browne, he said. He was worried and looked drawn and haggard. His two sons John, the holder of the shotgun, and Noel were also arrested, but like Anne Browne were later released.

Jeremiah appeared happy to get the story off his chest. As two detectives brought him into an interview room in the Garda station, he said, 'I did it.' Asked what did he do, he said, 'I shot Bob Browne.'

The story of Bob Browne's death came tumbling out during the day. On the previous Thursday week, Jeremiah got up at about 7.30 am as was his normal habit and had a cup of tea in the kitchen with his son Noel, who was due to take his Intermediate Certificate exam in a fortnight's time. The pair then went out to milk their six cows, coupling them up in two lots of three to the milking machine. Noel cycled to Lixnaw for 9 am mass and when he returned Jeremiah had prepared breakfast for the family. Jeremiah worked on the farm until around midday when he hitched up the trailer to a tractor and with his son Noel set off for the Presentation Convent in Lixnaw where he had been contracted to ferry some cattle to the market sale ring. They left there at about 2 pm, after Sullivan had been paid his haulage fee.

It was while he was in the town outside the post office that he ran into Bob Browne, who had a 'good few drinks on him'. Bob Browne accused him of taking around his wife, and threatened him, 'If I don't get you tonight I'll get you tomorrow morning, I'll blow your brains out.' Sullivan says he was scared of the threat. Browne was a big man, just six feet tall and, 'He was that kind of a treacherous guy that would do that,' he said.

Jeremiah and Noel returned to the farm where they had a light meal shortly before 3 pm. Jeremiah rang Annie at home and arranged to meet her that evening at 9 pm. In the meantime he tended to their cows and twenty-four head of cattle before going to a neighbour's place to spray potatoes. By 7 pm Jeremiah Sullivan had washed and changed his clothes. He took the single barreled shotgun from his son's wardrobe, wrapped it in an old jacket and placed it in the boot of his car. He put the box of cartridges beside it, then got in behind the wheel and drove to mass in Listowel. When mass ended he walked up to the Listowel Arms Hotel which is tucked into the corner of the town square. He met a few acquaintances in the bar and ordered a pint of lemonade.

Meanwhile Anne Browne had changed her clothes too and was dressed up for a night out. She went into the town to Mulvihill's pub, where she ordered a drink and waited for Bob. He was a few minutes late, and they stayed talking in a corner of the pub until they left. Annie went towards the Listowel Arms Hotel and met Jeremiah in the square at about 9 pm. Jeremiah drove the car out the Abbeyfeale road and parked in the Toer creamery yard where they stayed for about two hours.

Anne's relationship with her husband Bob had been deteriorating over the past few years. There were numerous rows and Anne had turned to Jeremiah as a friend. They first met at a dance in one of the local pubs. She was good company. Anne lied to her husband about where she was going. Michelle, her daughter, would often drive her into town saying they were going to Unislim classes. Other times she said she would be visiting friends. Bob had drunk the compensation money, 'and owed more to the bank. When he'd died he'd drunk the lot,' said Annie subsequently. Jeremiah was 'good to talk to' but there had been no sexual relations, she said. 'There was never such a thing. We just liked to be in one another's company. We shared interests in dancing and music and talking.' They spent the evening sitting in the car in the creamery yard smoking cigarettes and talking about bands that were due to play in the district.

That night Jeremiah dropped Anne back at the grotto as usual and she walked the last few hundred yards home. After she got out he turned the car and went back to Listowel, parking it in the middle of the Market yard. He walked around the town for a while ending up opposite the Garda station outside the chip shop. He entered the crowded shop, bought a carton of chips for forty pence and returned to his car. As he sat in the driver's seat eating the chips Bob Browne walked past him with a roll in his gait. Sullivan watched him, finished the chips, drove out the road he had come in, and parked the car in Scartleigh creamery yard. He got out of the car, opened the boot and took out the gun and two cartridges from the box. He put one in the breech, and the second in his pocket. It was a dry moonlit night. He waited for ten minutes.

As Bob Browne passed the creamery gates on the other side of the road, Sullivan let out a shout. 'Hi Bob, I want you, are you as good a man now as you were today?' he asked. Bob Browne didn't say anything. He knew the voice of the man with the gun and he started to run up the road. Sullivan loosed off a shot at the running man but Browne just kept going. He broke open the gun, fumbled in his pocket for the second cartridge and dropped it into the breech. He was running after him now, gaining, but it was darker as trees threw their shadows across the ditches onto the road. Sullivan took aim and fired again. 'I don't know where I hit him, but I think it was higher than the first shot,' he was to say later.

Sullivan went back to his car and drove home, passing Bob Browne lying on the roadway. One doctor estimated that Browne could have been alive for fifteen minutes after the second shot as he gradually bled to death. Sullivan left the shotgun in the car and went to bed without turning on the light in the room in case he'd wake his son who shared a room with him.

At 6 am he was up and out of bed and down to the shed where the car was parked. He took the gun which had been rewrapped in the jacket out of the boot, picked up a hard metal file off the bench and began filing down the firing pin and the top of the barrel. He replaced the gun in the boot and went back into the house. After his son John went to work he returned the gun to his wardrobe.

That night when he called ostensibly to offer his condolences, he told Anne Browne to say that they had been in the Western Inn at Fealesbridge the previous evening if anyone asked her. He sat on a chair against the kitchen wall and looked shaken, Anne remembered.

That Monday Jeremiah told his nineteen-year-old son John that he had used his shotgun to shoot Bob Browne the previous Thursday night. The teenager asked had his father fired into the air or at Browne. No, he'd shot him in the knee. Browne had tried to duck into the creamery yard said Jeremiah. The Guards will know from the shotgun cartridges who killed him, said John. No they wouldn't, said Jeremiah, he'd fiddled with the gun using a file.

At 7.30 pm on Saturday 11 June Jeremiah Sullivan was brought before a special sitting of Listowel District Court where he was charged with 'feloniously, wilfully and with malice aforethought murdering John Browne'.

When the charges were read over to him, he said he had nothing to say, and he was remanded in custody. Later that month he applied to the High Court for bail and was granted it on entering a bond of £1,000 and two independent sureties of £5,000 each, on condition that he report to Lixnaw Garda Station twice weekly. At his trial Jeremiah Sullivan denied the charge of murder, but admitted manslaughter. Prosecuting for the state, Mr Anthony Kennedy SC said that there was 'some sort of relationship' between Jeremiah and Anne. 'She had been drinking with her husband in a nearby pub and left him to go and meet the accused and they spent the rest of the evening together in his car,' he said. The attempt to set up an alibi for the couple in the Western Inn in Fealesbridge was 'ham fisted', and the anonymous phone calls were also a 'cock and bull story', said Mr Kennedy.

In his statement given to the court Jeremiah Sullivan said, 'There was no such thing as an affair between Mrs Browne and myself. There was only the music and the dancing. My own wife is gone five years.' Mr Patrick McEntee acted for the defence. Michelle Browne told the court that her father had telephoned their house from Listowel on the Thursday afternoon. She picked up the phone and he told her to put a shotgun he had in the boot of his car along with some cartridges. 'He said he was going to shoot Jeremiah and my mother. He had found out Mr Sullivan was going with my mother. I didn't take much notice of him. He was drunk. I told him I wouldn't bring the car into town. I left the house ten minutes later, and took the keys of the car with me in case he came home and took the car and the gun,' she said. She admitted that she had not given the Gardai these details when they were investigating the murder.

Anne Browne said that when Jeremiah had asked her to say they were in the Western Inn she agreed. 'I went along with that. I didn't know what to do,' she said.

At the end of the three-day trial in February 1984 the jury of seven women and five men spent four and a half hours reaching a verdict of guilty. Mr Justice Barron sentenced Jeremiah Sullivan to penal servitude for life.

5.

Fingerprints and Footprints: Three Cases

THE problem of identifying criminals has continued to intrigue criminologists all over the world. One of the earliest methods of identifying a criminal in Ireland was by the scars and burns left by pitchcapping. The barbarous practice of covering the heads of political rebels and law breakers with molten pitch left them marked for life, and served as both a warning to other malcontents and as a badge of guilt. This form of punishment continued until the 1850s.

The first person to invent an international identification system was Alphonse Bertillon, a records clerk with the Paris police. His daily duties included noting down the details of arrested criminals. This set his mind working on a classification and identification system, and in October 1879 the twenty-six-year-old clerk sent off a report outlining his ideas. The identification system he proposed was rejected by the then prefect of police, and it was three more years before his replacement asked Bertillon to put it into practice on a trial basis. It consisted of taking eleven basic measurements of the subject, two photographs and a *portrait parlé* (a 'spoken portrait') that would mention any special facial marks. He claimed that the likelihood of any two people having the same measurements which included the width of the head, the length of the right ear as well as height and trunk measurements, was over four million to one. But even as his system was adopted in France and numerous other countries over the next decade, already work was beginning on an alternative fingerprint identification.

In 1858 a civil servant in India, William Herschel, first asked a man to sign a document using his fingerprint. Two years later as a magistrate he insisted that pensioners should receipt their payments from the government by providing an inked fingerprint. In 1877 he wrote to the inspector-general of Bengal prisons reporting his ideas on fingerprinting. Eleven years later a Sir Francis Galton, a cousin of Charles Darwin, turned his interest to the problem of human identification and recalled reading a letter in the magazine *Nature* about fingerprinting.

The editors sent him to Herschel, and Galton spent years studying fingerprints, assuring himself of their individuality and devising a system of identification. His system was complicated, and it was a Yugoslavian police officer, Juan Vucetich, who worked as head of the statistics bureau in La Plata, Argentina, to devise a practical but basic system of classifying fingerprints. He is also credited with solving the first murder by identifying a killer through her fingerprints.

In 1891 a British civil servant, Edward Henry, was chief of police in Nepal. He had imported the 'bertillonage' system, more properly known as anthropometry. But it was complicated and depended on extremely accurate measurements.

He had read about Galton's work, and on leave in England he contacted Galton. Given free access to the research, Henry had finalised his new classification system by 1896. It was based on the numbers of loops, arches and whorls on a finger around the delta or triangle on the top portion of a finger or thumb. The following year the system was used to solve a murder case in India, and in May 1901 Henry was recalled to London and appointed Assistant Commissioner at Scotland Yard and charged with establishing the fingerprint section. From this beginning, fingerprinting went on to become an essential weapon in the armoury of every police force in the world.

Some time after 3 am on 16 April 1959 Mrs Margaret Anne Finn, a sixty-one-year-old widow, heard a noise outside her house at Knockbeg, Collooney, Co. Sligo. She got out of bed, turned on the light and went to investigate.

At approximately 3.30 am her next door neighbour Mick Noone was wakened by a woman's voice shouting his name. He jumped out of bed, dressed quickly and rushed into the kitchen. There he saw his son Gerard, the only other occupant of the house, standing outside the back door dressed in his shirt and trousers and barefooted. He told his son to arm himself with a poker from the fireplace, and then the two men left the house. They found Mrs Finn leaning across the hedge by her gate pillar. The back of her head was bleeding heavily. 'Will you help me in?' she mumbled as Mick Noone lifted her into her cottage. He sent Gerard to Mrs Christina Harkin, a neighbour, for help. Noone put the injured old woman sitting in a chair, wiped her head with a towel, and when

Mrs Harkin arrived she helped him to lift her onto her bed. When they asked her what had happened she muttered almost incoherently 'the girl'.

The Gardai and the local doctor, Denis Boland, were called to the house. The old woman was now unconcious and she was taken to Sligo County Hospital where she died a few hours later. The subsequent post mortem carried out by Dr Maurice Hickey, the state pathologist, showed that her skull had been extensively fractured: her death had been due to brain injuries resulting from multiple head injuries. He concluded that those injuries could have been caused by blows from a heavy instrument, or alternatively by a fall against an upward slanting stone or a gate pillar. There was also minor bruising to the backs of her hands.

The murder squad, led by the head of the Technical Bureau Detective Superintendent George Lawlor, examined the scene. They believed that someone had tried to break into the cottage through a front window that night. Mrs Finn may have recognised him and when she came out to chase him away he turned and attacked her with a heavy instrument. Her cottage door was discovered open and the electric light on.

The front window was open a number of inches and despite close examination revealed no fingerprints. But under the window in the soft clay there were poor impressions of a bare footprint. Other footprints trailed around the house and a clearer print was identified in her back yard beside the wall dividing her house from Noone's. One particular impression was made by a bare right foot as its owner climbed the dividing wall from Finn's into Noone's.

There was a nice irony in the fact that George Lawlor was in charge of the case. Twenty-eight years earlier, in September 1931, he has been a detective sergeant stationed in Galway when a circular 'routine order' was issued seeking constructive ideas from members of the force in any area of police work. Lawlor wrote an essay which outlined the necessity of establishing a technical office and some of the skills and methods they should employ in modern crime fighting. One of his suggestions was that all recruit Gardai should be taught how to take casts of footprints. Plaster of Paris was not suitable for damp conditions, he wrote, but a good substitute was bees- or candle wax. Now, as head of the Technical Bureau, he was to use his own suggestion to catch a murderer and establish a legal precedent. A beeswax cast of the best of the footprints was made by Detective Sergeant O'Connor. 'It contained much detail particularly the portion at the base of the big toe', Detective

Superintendent Lawlor was to write subsequently in *Iris an Gharda*, the Garda magazine.

A hedge grew at the end of Mrs Finn's back yard, and behind it was her vegetable garden. Detectives searching the vegetable patch discovered a tubular bar, one inch in diameter and eighteen inches in length, which was bloodstained. A second bar, made of brass and measuring thirty inches long, was found lying against the hedge.

Michael Noone and his son Gerard were questioned by the Gardai about how they found Mrs Finn, and suspicion immediately fell on Gerard. The youth claimed that he had got up when he heard the shouting, opened the back door of the kitchen but had not gone outside as he was dressed only in his shirt. He carried his trousers in his hands and was barefoot.

His father remained positive that his son was wearing his trousers and was outside the kitchen door when he came into the kitchen. The younger Noone was taken into custody at Collooney Garda Station and an inked impression was taken of his right foot. Subsequently he was arrested and charged and while on remand wrote a letter to his father in which he said, 'I'm sorry for what happened and I hope you will forgive me; that's all until I see you next week.'

Noone's trial took place at Green Street Courthouse in Dublin in July of that year. The prosecution case was that he had originally set out simply to rob money from the dead woman. It centred on six points: (1) that no fingerprints were found on the window and that a pair of black nylon gloves was found in Gerard Noone's pocket; (2) that he had no money on the evening before the killing yet showed a wallet full of notes to a friend after the murder and told a lie about a former employer owing him money in order to justify his sudden wealth; (3) that he was seen cycling towards his home carrying the brass bar which was found lying against Margaret Finn's hedge; (4) that he wrote a letter of admission of guilt to his father; (5) that his bare footprint was discovered in the clay in Finn's property; and (6) that he was seen in his bare feet outside his kitchen door shortly after the murderous attack took place.

The same equipment was used to take the foot impressions as that of fingerprints of suspects, and it was only necessary to ink the toes and sole extending down to the arch of the foot because it is on this surface that the capillary ridges appear. A total of twenty-one points of similarity between the photograph of the wax impression and the inked footprint were noted by Detective Garda William Byrne of the Technical Bureau in Garda Headquarters who first made the identification. Superintendent Lawlor said that he could have marked as many more characteristics.

Defence Counsel for Noone, Mr Oliver Gogarty SC, objected to the footprint evidence at the beginning of the three-day trial on the grounds that it was a new form of identification. Mr Justice Dixon overruled the objection but agreed that it 'was indeed a new method of identification'.

Cross-examined witnesses included the state pathologist Dr Hickey who said that the head injury could have been caused if the dead woman had been running and had fallen violently, and that a blood smear found on one of the pieces of piping could have been caused by the deceased woman falling on it herself.

In his statement to Gardai, Gerard Noone said that he had cycled to Collooney and arrived home at about 10.30 pm. As he went into his own home he saw a girl's bike outside Mrs Finn's house but he did not know who owned it. His father was in bed, and asked him to check if Mrs Finn had left a cake of bread on their doorstep as she usually did. His father confirmed this detail to the Gardai in a separate statement. Gerard checked, said there was no bread, made tea, and then went to bed and read for a while before he went to sleep, only to be awakened by a 'half shout'. He opened the back door and remained inside as he was dressed only in his shirt and was barefoot. He got dressed, pulling on boots and trousers, after his father had told him it was Mrs Finn shouting and had turned on the light.

Mr J.S. McGivern SC prosecuting said that it was the state's case that Gerard had not deliberately set out to murder Mrs Finn, but had inflicted the beating in an attempt to 'silence' her so that she could not identify him after he robbed her.

Noone pleaded not guilty to the murder of Mrs Finn. However, after a three-hour absence the jury found him guilty of the charge but gave a strong recommendation to mercy. Mr Justice Dixon said that the evidence in the trial was circumstantial but that was just as capable of providing a proof as direct evidence. He ordered that Gerard Noone should be detained at the pleasure of the government.

A very similar case was heard in the Central Criminal Court almost thirty years later. Bachelor Patrick Kearney, aged eighty-two, lived in his two-storey house at Holly Lodge, Marian Avenue, about 400 yards from Ennis town centre. He was considered well off and had numerous business interests. He had sold the family pub for £78,000 shortly before Christmas 1986 and had also sold a farm for several thousand pounds some years previously. Kearney was a shrewd man and owned several sites around the town which were estimated to have potential as valuable building development properties. He had a huge interest in horses and was known as a mild-mannered but strong-willed man. Mr Kearney had lived with his sister May for most of his life in their public house at Lifford, about 1.5 miles from the town centre, but he sold the pub and moved when she died. On Sunday 5 April 1987 his body was discovered in an upstairs bedroom at about 3 pm by a neighbour, Mrs Teresa Naughton, who had a key to the house.

'I was in the habit of visiting him about twice a week and when I saw Pakie last Thursday he was in great form. The next time I saw him, about three o'clock on Sunday, he was thrown on the floor beside his bed with bloodmarks on his face', she said. The house had been ransacked. A highly distressed Mrs Naughton asked a passer-by to call the Gardai.

Sergeant John Norris from Ennis Garda Station was one of the first Gardai called to the scene on the Sunday afternoon. He found the dead man lying entangled in bedding and covered in congealed blood, upstairs by his bed. The body was formally identified by the dead man's solicitor. In the kitchen downstairs the two lower panes of the window were broken. The following day a post mortem was carried out in Ennis General Hospital by the state pathologist Dr John Harbison. The pensioner had suffered a violent assault, and had been badly beaten. There were severe injuries to his head and forehead, and as a result of these he had died from asphyxia after inhaling his own blood from a haemorrhage. Mr Kearney also had five broken ribs.

Reporting on the brutal attack, the *Irish Independent* quoted a Garda saying: 'It is unlikely that his attackers would have got very much for although he was wealthy he was a very shrewd man and was unlikely to have much money in the house. He was a sharp terrier-like person, who would put up a fight if threatened.'

Once the death was reported, the house was sealed off and the scene preserved for technical examination. The murder squad was called in and a painstaking examination of the scene of the crime was undertaken. Detective Garda Brendan McArdle noted the position of blood smears on pillows, wallpaper, doors, windows, and on trousers and biscuit tins at the foot of the dead man's bed. He also collected broken glass from the kitchen windows and brought them for examination to the State Laboratory. Dr Sheila Willis, the head of the chemistry section in the Department of Justice's forensic laboratory, examined the glass taken from the broken kitchen window and discovered that it contained a partial footwear impression.

Two days before the body was discovered an unemployed lorry driver, Edmund Ignatius Kelly, aged twenty-five, of Mountain View, Ennis had been drinking in Murphy's pub in the town, and told a companion: 'I have a good one, I'm going to rob Paddy Kearney.' The Kellys were known as an extremely respectable family in the community, but when the Gardai got to hear of this remark, suspicion immediately fell on Kelly. On Tuesday 7 April, just two days after the killing, Detective Garda McArdle searched Kelly's bedsit flat and took possession of a pair of Doc Marten boots, a leather jacket, a jumper and a towel. He handed these into the Technical Bureau for forensic examination.

Dr Willis examined Kelly's Doc Marten boots. She took impressions of both boots, and found that several irregularities on the heel of the right boot corresponded exactly with the impression on the glass.

'The probability of another shoe picking up one mark with the same shape and identity is unlikely. In this case there were several identical marks. I am satisfied that the impression on the glass was made by the heel of the right boot of Edmund Kelly,' she concluded at Kelly's trial. During the cross-examination of Dr Willis she said that there could be up to 50,000 pairs of similar boots in the country. The indentations she had noted would have arisen through normal wear and tear and by walking on stones and glass.

Kelly was interviewed by the Gardai three days after the body was discovered. Detective Garda McArdle told him that they had the results of tests which showed that his bootprint had been found on a piece of glass taken from the murder scene. Kelly replied, 'There are lots of people wearing Doc Marten boots.' Edmund Ignatius Kelly was then arrested under the Offences Against the State Act. After the maximum detention period of forty-eight hours was over, he was released from custody. But he was rearrested outside the gates of the Garda station, this time on a charge under the Offences Against the Person Act.

The examination of Holly Lodge was so detailed that even the contents of the fire grate had been raked over by the Gardai. Attention to detail paid off again, as detectives discovered a matchbox in the cold grate, and it was extracted and taken away for technical examination. A fingerprint was discovered on its surface. When he was in custody Kelly's fingerprints were taken. Detective Garda Myles Fitzgerald said he examined a fingermark on the match box and a set of fingerprints of the accused. The matchbox print had more than twelve characteristics matching the left forefinger of Kelly. 'I am satisfied beyond any doubt it was made by the middle joint of the accused's left forefinger,' he told the court.

A bloodstain found on Kelly's jacket was of the same blood group as Patrick Kearney's. Kelly was medically examined on his first day in custody in Ennis Garda Station by Dr Richard Feore who said that he showed no signs of any wounds or lacerations on his body.

Kelly was charged with the murder and malicious wounding of Pakie Kearney sometime between 3 and 5 April. Kelly pleaded not guilty to both charges, but later during the trial which took place in February 1988 he pleaded guilty to manslaughter — a plea that was accepted by the state prosecutor Mr Feargus Flood SC. Kelly was also charged with assault with intent to rob, a charge to which he pleaded guilty.

Prior to the trial Kelly was assessed by a consultant psychiatrist over a three-week period after he had been charged. Mr John Fennelly said that he had carried out the psychiatric examination, and told the Central Criminal Court: 'When we spoke about the offence he could remember nothing about it.' His Defence Counsel Mr Martin Kennedy SC said that Kelly had told him that he had previously suffered blackouts due to drink.

Kelly was found guilty of the charges, and Mr Justice Kevin Lynch sentenced him to twelve years imprisonment on each charge, the sentences to run concurrently. 'I have a duty to elderly people living alone to protect them,' he said, adding later: 'You beat him mercilessly. You snuffed out his life in a savage assault.'

Timmons's pub stands on the corner of Watling Street and Victoria Quay near Guinness's brewery in Dublin. The thorough system employed for washing glasses in the two-storey pub was to help the Gardai solve a murder committed on the premises in September 1977. On Thursday nights, all the pint and half-pint glasses were washed in detergent. In addition the glasses were given a daily wash by hand and left to drip dry on the draining board beside the sink. Glasses that were stained and didn't come out sparkling from the hand wash were transferred back to the board at the right-hand side of the sink and were then vigorously rewashed using a hard bristle brush. They were then stacked with the clean glasses on the draining board at the left-hand side of the sink. As the glasses dried out they were moved further along under the counter to the left and nearer the draught tap dispensers. The system of stacking dirty glasses and washing them in a strict rotation routine ensured clean and shiny glasses.

Twenty-five-year old Michael Timmons, the son of the owner, and John Kilcline, an elderly barman, were on duty serving both the bar and lounge on Wednesday 7 September. Michael began work shortly after 10.30 am that morning, and later pulled the first pint of the day, selecting a clean glass from under the counter top. There were about twelve people in the bar area, which is L-shaped. The short leg of the L-shape runs parallel to the quays; the long end along Watling Street. The bar entrance is off the quay. There were a couple of customers in the lounge which ran behind a wooden partition and looked out on Watling Street.

John Lawlor was forty-one years of age. He was born in Tallaght, Dublin and met his Irish-born wife when he was working in England as a bus driver. They moved from Wolverhampton to Australia and lived there for five years before returning to Dublin. John got a job, doing what he did best, as a bus driver for CIE. But he only stayed with them for four years, seeing a good opportunity in the haulage business. He formed his own company, rented a yard in Saggart, Co. Dublin and by 1977 he had a number of lorries working for him and included CIE among his clients. His personal fortune had improved, and his wife and four children had moved from Tallaght to a bungalow in Ballymore Eustace.

By 7 am on the morning of 7 September 1977 Lawlor was up and about the bungalow. He had a cup of tea and got into his car to pick up his brother-in-law, John Carroll, in Tallaght. He left his car outside his brother-in-law's house in Newbawn Drive and the two of them went from there in one of the company trucks to the goods yard at Heuston railway station where they began loading Guinness kegs onto the truck for delivery to the Guinness plant at nearby St James's Gate.

At about 12.30 pm Lawlor told Carroll that he had an appointment with a man at 12.45pm, and after that a meeting with his solicitor. It was lunch–time and they had finished their fourth load of the day. He took the loan of a one pound note to buy a drink before leaving him.

He walked up the quays and entered Timmons's pub. The man he was to meet, John Francis Gavin, was already seated at the bar wearing a long blue trench coat. John Kilcline had served him a pint of stout and he had taken a few sips.

Gavin was a thirty-eight-year old married man recently living in Finglas on Dublin's northside. He was a postman's son from Carrick-on-Shannon, Co. Leitrim. He had been in jail on a number of occasions. He served six months in Mountjoy in 1958 for inde-

cent assault. After his release, and still a teenager, he
and joined the British army. When he left the army he
England to work, but had run foul of the law on several o⌐
and had been sentenced for a range of offences including ⌐
ful wounding and assaults. In 1975 he had been arrested ur.
the Prevention of Terrorism Act, but within a few days had returne
to Dublin before an exclusion order could be enforced against him.

At 12.45 pm John Lawlor joined Gavin, pulling up a stool beside
him. Michael Timmons noted the round-faced and heavy-set Lawlor
entering the bar, bid both men a 'nice day' and took their order.
Lawlor opted for a pint of Smithwicks, and Gavin ordered a second
pint of Guinness. Timmons pulled two-thirds of the pint and left it
to stand on a tray under the tap. Both men chatted quietly together.

Christopher Byrne was another haulier who was working at
Guinness's that day. He had arrived at the brewery at 11 am. By
12.45 pm he had finished loading, and was on his way into Timmons's bar for a drink after a thirsty morning's work with his
helper, nineteen-year-old John Healy. Gavin looked around as the
door swung open and the two men entered the bar. Christy Byrne
bought himself a bottle of Guinness and Healy a Harp lager shandy.
Healy sat at the bar on Lawlor's side. He paid no attention to
Lawlor and Gavin as they talked to each other.

An unemployed kitchen porter from Tallaght, Edward Melia,
was also sitting at the bar having a small whiskey with a friend,
Dinny Dunne. Gavin sat to his right.

Outside the bar on Watling Street a man had pulled his blue
Honda motorbike onto the pavement. He had a helmet slung across
the handlebars and was aged about thirty, needed a shave and had
a quiff in his brown hair.

Michael Timmons topped off the pint of Guinness after it had
settled and lifted it onto the counter, letting the creamy head
dribble down one side of the glass. Gavin paid for the drinks, and
took a packet of twenty Rothmans from his pocket. He took a
drink from his glass and put it back on the counter. It was 1.03 pm.

Suddenly Gavin stood up, his bar stool scraped across the heavy
lino backwards, brushing against Healy he took a step towards
Lawlor. He pulled a silver plated handgun from his jacket and with
his arm outstretched to within inches of Lawlor fired at him. Lawlor
staggered backwards as the shot burst into his chest. Lawlor's glass
flew into the air and broke on the floor with a sharp crack. Gavin
shouted, 'Everyone down, get fucking down,' as he fired another
shot into Lawlor. The wounded and shocked man was still on his
feet, and as he staggered to the centre of the bar Gavin fired again.

The pub was in uproar, men dropped to the floor, and hid behind tables. Darts players ran to the nearest door, the toilet, to get away. Some people were shouting; no one knew what was happening.

'I thought it was a robbery. I got down and crept to the toilet and when I got there it was packed,' said Edward Melia.

Gavin shouted again, 'Get down' and then transferred his revolver from his right hand to his left hand. Then with his right hand he pulled a shotgun from his long coat. The stock of the shotgun was full, but the barrels had been sawn off. He raised the shotgun, and used the pistol in his left to steady his aim as he stepped over to John Lawlor who now lay outstreched on the floor of the bar. He put the barrels of the gun close to Lawlor's head and then discharged both barrels. 'No one move or try to follow me,' he shouted before shoving the shotgun back into a large pocket in his coat and turning to run out the door. The powerful motorbike was now waiting outside the front door, its rider astride the machine, revving its engine. Gavin jumped onto the pillion seat and the bike sped off towards the city centre.

The pub owner, Noel Timmons, was in the living room of the family flat over the bar and lounge when he heard the commotion downstairs. He heard the first shot and went to the top of the stairs, heard more shots and someone shouting that a shooting was happening in the bar and ran to their private phone to dial 999. Michael Timmons was already rushing up the stairs two at a time to phone for help by the time his father had dialled the emergency number.

Jimmy Graham, a painter from Bray who worked in Guinness's brewery, had been playing the 'Burmah Road' in the pub for about thirty minutes on his lunch break with some of his workmates. Their view of the incident was interrupted by the right angle turn in the bar. He heard a loud bang and someone shouting to everyone to get down. He jumped towards one of the corners, and fell to the ground. All around him people were hitting the deck. He kept his head down, and when it was over ran for the phone in the bar to call the Gardai. He saw Lawlor lying on the ground and asked him, 'Are you alright, are you alive?' But he got no reply.

John Mullins from Walkinstown had been in the bar for almost an hour when the shooting happened. He heard the loud pistol reports and dropped to the floor like the seven others with whom he had been playing darts. John Kilcline the barman came around the bar to tell them the gunman had gone. 'Someone's been shot, he's lying out front,' he told the darts players. Kilcline then went to the toilet, opened the door and told the six or seven people inside the shooting was over.

Inspector Donal Donahue from Pearse Street Garda Station was in a patrol car when he heard the radio alert call, and was the first member of the force on the scene. At 1.07 pm, just four minutes after the shooting, Gardai were arriving at the scene and Inspector Donahue began allocating tasks. One Garda was told to close the door and not let anyone enter or leave. Another was assigned the task of taking the names and addresses of everyone present. Another began taking descriptions of the gunman. Meanwhile everyone in the pub was ordered away from where Lawlor and the gunman had been sitting, and told not to touch anything.

One of the customers drew the blinds on the pub.

John Lawlor's body was lying near the centre of the bar floor to the right of the doorway. His head lay six feet from the centre, his legs bent at the knees facing the window overlooking the river Liffey. His blue working shirt and trousers were stained a deep red.

John Kilcline pointed to the pint tumbler still partly filled with Guinness on the counter top where the gunman and Lawlor had been sitting at the bar. 'That's the glass he was using,' he said. It was the only glass with Guinness in it and was positioned between the Guinness and Smithwick's dispensers.

Detective Garda Patrick Grehan from Kilmainham detective unit had also responded to the radio alert. He took the gunman's glass into his possession immediately, carefully putting it into a box and then marking the box. He explained later that that he thought it might be a vital piece of evidence. His foresight and experience were to play a vital role in the investigation. He waited until the arrival of the members of the Technical Bureau and then handed the box to one of them, Detective Garda Fitzpatrick.

At 1.10 pm ambulancemen Christopher Dillon and Alan Naughtan from the Dolphin's Barn station knocked at the closed door and were admitted to the bar. Christopher Dillon checked the body for pulses in the neck and wrist but could find none. They radiotelephoned for a doctor. At 1.55 pm Dr Perceval Patton officially pronounced the man dead. Ten minutes before the doctor had arrived an alert to all train, port and airports had been sent out by Gardai with instructions to stop a man answering to the description provided by eye-witnesses.

The fingerprints of the dead man were taken before the body was moved that evening at 5.45 pm to the mortuary of the Richmond

Hospital in Brunswick Street on the other side of the Liffey. John Carroll, the victim's brother-in-law, and an employee of the haulage company, John Barron, formally identified the body. Dr John Harbison then began the post mortem.

The following day the Provisional IRA issued a statement claiming responsibility for the 'execution' and further claiming that 'after an investigation into the role of John Lawlor in the recent arms and explosives discovery in Dublin it was found that he was "instrumentally involved in the seizure and had gratuitously given important information to the Gardai"'.

The Provos' suspicions arose because Lawlor had allegedly been running guns for them. When an IRA arms dump was discovered on a farm in Ballymore Eustace, Co. Kildare, Lawlor was among those pulled in for questioning. He was questioned for three days but was then released without charge. Further raids and arrests of republican suspects followed shortly after in Dublin city centre. The IRA had apparently formed the view that Lawlor volunteered the information that made these raids possible in return for immunity from prosecution.

The investigation into Lawlor's murder was led by Chief Superintendent John Joy from Dublin Castle and Chief Superintendent Anthony McMahon from the Technical Bureau.

Gavin's fingerprints were on the pint glass which Detective Garda Grehan had so carefully removed from the bar. They were also on file in the large card index boxes of the Technical Bureau's fingerprints section. It was a straightforward matter to extract his prints from the file box and to compare them with the prints on the glass. An ingenious system had been devised to find the file card which most closely matched prints found at the scene of a crime. Every file card had holes denoting print characteristics punched in it. The specimen print card was placed at the front of each row of the file cards and a skewer run through the holes in the file cards until a card was found that matched. This was then lifted out for detailed visual examination. In this way, the prints on the pint glass were confirmed as belonging to John Francis Gavin.

Gavin had a criminal record and his description and record were also on file with the Criminal Records Office in the Phoenix Park; they had a large department of collators whose job was to maintain files on numerous suspects, including subversives who came under regular scrutiny. The system was computerised in the 1980s, giving the Gardai immediate access to a whole range of confidential information about a suspect. This includes name, address, the names of other people who have come under Garda scrutiny at the same house, or on the same road, car registration number, car tax details and details of a person's criminal record. If they are in jail, it notes their release date; if they are on bail, it notes that; it also tells if they are wanted in connection with any crime. It maintains a live register of queries by Gardai over the past six months, and can provide a background briefing note about a subject at the touch of a computer terminal button in the Technical Bureau.

Gavin was obviously an immediate suspect. Although his precise whereabouts were unknown at the time of the shooting, Chief Superintendent Joy's branch men had information from their touts that Gavin was their man, thus reinforcing the fingerprint evidence. Rumours had circulated in the criminal underworld that a 'hit' had been contracted, but no names either about the target or the hitman or other details were available.

The post mortem began with an X-ray to discover whether bullets remained in the body. The largest wound was on the right side of the neck approximately 3 inches by 1½ inches; the second largest was of a jagged shape, of 2¼ inches in diameter at the right side of the neck. The first bullet wound to the head left an entry wound of almost half an inch in diameter in the temple, and a corresponding exit wound at the back of the head. The post mortem also showed that the major wound 'was almost certainly caused by a sawn-off weapon because it was inflicted close enough to contain the wad and yet its diameter of over three inches with early pellet spread would suggest a range of about three yards had it been from a long barrelled choked weapon'. The shotgun had not been loosed off at contact range because of the absence of powder burning. Dr Harbison concluded that Lawlor had died from shock, haemorrhage and lacerations to the brain due to shotgun wounds.

Detective Garda Patrick Ennis was a member of the Technical Bureau's ballistics section, housed in the basement of the Bureau office block and complete with its own firing range. He examined the scene of the shooting. The lino-covered floor around the body was pock-marked with shotgun cartridge pellets, and a number of shotgun wads had become embedded in the floor. There was a hole from a shotgun blast three inches in front of the body which measured 3 inches by 1½ inches. He picked up a number of pellets and a discharged bullet near the foot of the dead man. It was made from lead, with no metal covering jacket and was a .38 special. A bullet embedded in a wooden panel over the bar was taken out and brought for further examination to the Bureau. Detective

Garda Ennis also discovered a bullet hole in the wooden partition separating the lounge from the bar. He traced the path of a bullet through the hole, through the entry porch and noticed marks where it had scratched the black painted stone reveal on the door as it ricocheted; he was able to recover the spent bullet from the street. He also concluded that the shotgun cartridge wads were similar and fired from a 12 gauge shotgun. His investigations into the flight trajectories of the bullets showed that the handgun shots had been fired by someone standing close to the bar. The shotgun injuries had been caused, according to similar investigations, by someone standing close to the main door and facing the bar counter.

The Gardai were convinced they knew who the killer was and among the many houses raided that night and over the following days were the homes of at least three people whom Gavin knew in Carrick-on-Shannon. But the gunman was now on the run, avoiding familiar haunts, friends and acquaintances. Within two days the newspapers had highlighted the major clue in the search, the forgotten packet of cigarettes and the fingerprints left by the gunman on the pint tumbler. 'Gunman runs Garda gauntlet in escape bid,' the *Irish Independent* said on the 9th, claiming the 'Provo assassin' was avoiding border checkpoint patrols by the British and Irish in his bid to cross into the six counties. The man had been sighted on a motorbike on the Donegal-Tyrone border, the paper reported. But Gavin had successfully gone to earth. He did not surface for over three years.

On 25 May 1981 three detectives were in an unmarked car cruising around Galway city when they received a radio call to go to Cedarwood Close where there was a fracas. It was 4 am, and when they arrived two dishevelled men were in the street, their faces bloodied. They had been at a party in a house on the estate when a row had broken out between them and they had spilled out into the street, waking neighbours who called the Gardai.

One of the men rushed up to the detectives as they stopped. 'He's a dead man, arrest me I'm Jimmy Gavin, I'm wanted for murder. I shot that fucking Lawlor below in the pub,' he said.

Detective Sergeant Denis O'Connor said that he looked like he needed a doctor more than anything else, but Gavin persisted, 'No, no arrest me. I want to give myself up. I shot that fucking Lawlor in the pub. Ring Dublin Castle they'll tell you,' he said. 'There will be six men shot in this town in a week. Ye'll find their fucking bodies in the road and that's all ye can do about it,' he added.

The Gardai brought him to hospital, although the other man in the street had reasoned with him not to go. Gavin's nose had stopped bleeding and he was patched up in the Regional Hospital, given an anti-tetanus injection and then the Gardai brought him to Eglinton Street Station. He was given two cups of tea and Gardai began to hunt through back editions of *Fogra Tora*, the force's intelligence magazine.

Fogra Tora carries details of people wanted for interview in connection with firearms offences, serious crimes, stolen property and other offences. One edition showed four photographs of Gavin, including two side photos. There was also a fingerprint, a notice that he was wanted in connection with the Timmons pub murder and a description. The description and photos showed Gavin, with receding curly hair, clean shaven, tight lipped, standing five feet seven inches with stocky build and a sallow complexion. He had a small scar on the left side of his nose, and the tips of his third and fourth finger on his left hand had been amputated. He also wore heavy glasses.

At 5.30 am that morning Gavin was arrested. He subsequently denied he had made any admission to Gardai that he had shot John Lawlor.

Gavin's trial began on 14 October 1981 in the Special Criminal Court in Dublin. The most damning piece of evidence against Gavin was the presence of his fingerprints at the scene of the crime. This evidence was further backed up by descriptions of him by eye-witnesses at the scene and his own admissions of guilt to Gardai in Galway.

Six items were taken from Timmons's pub by Gardai for forensic examination and subsequently these were presented in court as exhibits. They were a half pint glass which had been standing near the dispenser, which had not been served to any customer and one fingerprint identified it as belonging to the barman Michael Timmons; a pint glass from where John Healy had been sitting which showed four prints that matched prints taken from Healy by a member of the Technical Bureau; a half pint glass into which a bottle of Guinness had been poured and left stand had two fingerprints belonging to Michael Timmons. The pieces of a broken pint tumbler picked up from the floor of the bar were also taken by Gardai and these showed two prints from the dead man, John Lawlor.

Detective Sergeant Martin Hogan from the fingerprints section also told the court that the Gardai had taken possession of the box of cigarettes left on the counter and a pint glass of Guinness draught which the killer had been using before taking out his guns. Detective Sergeant Hogan was able to identify a number of finger-marks as belonging to James Gavin. He compared these prints with a set of prints he had taken from Gavin when he was in custody in Galway's Eglinton Street Station, and he had no doubt but that two of the prints on the glass were made by Gavin's right thumb and the middle finger of his right hand. He also told the court that when he had done this he told Gavin of his findings, but Gavin made no reply.

Gavin pleaded not guilty to the charge of murder. Before reaching its verdict the court rejected a call to have his admission in Galway ruled inadmissible and also turned down a claim by the defence that he had been held in unlawful custody and his constitutional rights infringed.

Mr Justice Hamilton said that the court was satisfied that Gavin had shot Lawlor after having a drink with him in Timmons's bar. The judges were also satisfied that Gavin's fingerprints were on the glass left on the counter after the shooting and that the state-ments he made to Gardai were true and admissible in court. 'The court is satisfied beyond all reasonable doubt that the accused is guilty of the murder and it imposes the mandatory sentence of life imprisonment,' said Mr Justice Hamilton. Leave to appeal was refused.

6.

Ordeal by Fire

MARTIN Glynn was a bachelor of eighty-five years of age. He had been released from hospital in February 1981, and now two years later he was crippled with arthritis and had to use a wheelchair to get around. He lived with his spinster sister, Maggie, a sharp-tongued woman two years his senior on their twelve-acre farm at Keaves, Ballinamore Bridge, Ahascragh, Co. Galway, about twelve miles from Ballinasloe.

They lived in poor circumstances. The land was little more than scrub and suited only for rearing sheep. Martin was bedridden most of the time, only using his wheelchair when lifted into it. Maggie also suffered from arthritis and walked with the aid of a walking frame.

It was a miserable existence. Maggie occasionally travelled the twelve miles to Ballinasloe on a shopping trip if she could get a lift there and back from a neighbour. But money was scarce and there were few luxuries. Martin always had a bottle of Guinness by the bedside, but otherwise the extras associated with a comfortable life were few and far between. Maggie was known in the locality as a contrary and cantankerous woman. She had sent the Meals on Wheels people flying from her door in a torrent of abuse, shouting after them not to come back as their meals were 'only trash'. Fiercely independent, she had also told the district nurse to stop calling, telling her tartly that they would manage by themselves.

In early 1977 Maggie had taken the initiative of asking Christopher Kelly to come and live with them. Martin was now unable to walk and Maggie was too frail to lift him into his chair or onto his bed. They were also getting too old to run the small holding. Maggie Glynn knew the Kellys as old family friends from nearby Castleblakeney for well over twenty years. Christopher was one of three children; his younger brother Michael worked as a steel erector; the third child had become a nun.

Christopher stayed with them for nine months, then his brother Michael went to live with them. He shared a bedroom with Marty. Maggie slept in her own room on the other side of the small kitchen. The twenty-five-year-old only stayed a few months. The Glynns weren't paying for his work either on the farm or in the house, and he was still working as a steel erector. They had promised him the farm after their death, but he stuck by his decision to leave them.

Over the next four years he called to see them about twice a year. In December 1980 Maggie wrote to him, asking him to come back. Martin was getting worse and she was finding it more and more difficult to cope. She promised him their farm and money after their death.

Michael went back to live with them, but discovered that they had made no wills. So he telephoned a solicitor from Roscommon and arranged for him to call to the house in the late spring of the following year. The pledge was made and the papers were signed. Under the terms of the wills Michael Kelly was also their executor.

Dr Joseph Daly had been the family doctor for a number of years, and he called once a month, despite the sometimes frosty reception. Both Marty and Maggie were in poor health and they needed constant medical attention, but they refused his requests that they should enter a nursing home. They wanted to die together, and were determined to have their own way despite the hardships. They appeared to be ungrateful old people, and could be extremely difficult at times. 'Any time you would go in there you would hear complaints', he later recalled.

Maggie was only five feet two inches and overweight but she still ruled the house with an iron hand. Michael Kelly continued his daytime work but his evenings were supposed to be dedicated to the Glynns. Maggie often reprimanded Kelly when he stayed out late at night, or when Marty would have to stay in bed the whole day if he hadn't been dressed and put in his wheelchair. Kelly argued back fiercely on one occasion and Maggie threw a cup at him. On other occasions, exasperated at what she saw as his uncaring attitude, she would lock him out, forcing him to sleep in his car.

On Saturday 14 November 1981 Maggie went to bed at about 10 pm. She took her walking aid and the clock with her to bed, Michael Kelly was to later tell Gardai. She also took a candle from under the kitchen table and lit it. She wouldn't turn on the light in her room at night and would get ready for bed by candlelight.

Once in bed she'd lean out and blow out the candle. The light switch was too far from the bed for her to reach without getting up.

Kelly locked up and turned off the light in the kitchen. When he went into his bedroom he called across to Marty asking was he alright, as he pulled the cap off a large bottle of Guinness. He placed the bottle beside the one he'd earlier opened for Marty so he could slake his thirst if he woke during the night. Marty said nothing; he just continued to snore. Kelly hopped into the cold bed wearing his shirt and underpants. A two-bar electric fire was still on in the room.

'I woke up to see flames lepping,' he said afterwards in a statement to the Gardai in Ballinasloe. 'I awakened in the morning and I got a strong smell of smoke. I think it was around 9 am. I was frightened and jumped out of bed and put on my clothes and wellingtons. I could see a lot of smoke coming from Margaret's room, I shouted at Martin, and I can't say if he responded, but I took it for granted he was OK. I shouted Maggie, Maggie, but got no answer.

'I saw her bed was in flames. I was choking with smoke. I caught her feet and tried to pull her, but smoke and flames drove me out of the room. I was nearly suffocating myself and at this stage I decided to go for help.

'The dog was yelping but I'm not sure whether he was in Maggie's room or the kitchen. I went out through the front door and just before leaving I tried to locate the keys of my car but failed to find them in the smoke and ran to Michael Donoghue's home next door for help.'

Michael Donoghue had been up at about 5.40 am that Sunday morning. It was a fine day and the countryside was quiet. At about 9.30 am as he walked back into his own yard Kelly came around the gable end of his house.

'What's wrong with you?' asked Donoghue.

'I don't know. Come out, the whole house is in fumes of black smoke', he said.

The two men ran to Glynn's farmhouse. Thick black smoke was pouring out the front door. Donoghue took a deep breath and rushed into the house, towards Maggie's room. Kelly followed him in. In Maggie's room there was a 'big roll of fire in the centre of her bed,' he recalled. They turned and tried to force their way into Marty's room, but the dense smoke and flames stopped them. The smoke was so thick they couldn't even see the walls or furniture in the room; they shouted in to Marty, but there was no response.

As they gulped in fresh air outside with great heaving breaths, Kelly asked, 'What am I going to do, what will I do?' Donoghue had almost smothered in the joint rescue attempt and he wheezed out that he'd have to telephone for help. Kelly said he had no keys to his car, and as Donoghue's bicycle was punctured, Kelly set off on foot running down the boreen.

He called to seven houses in all. His first call was to McHugh's, then on to Smyth's, Mannion's and Burke's. Then he tried Tom Geraghty's where he was given the loan of a bike, and he then cycled on to Dooley's who telephoned the fire brigade. Another neighbour ran for a priest and a doctor. Meanwhile Kelly turned the bike around and cycled back to the Glynn's farm. It was still ablaze, and both he and Tom Geraghty managed to fight their way into the house briefly before they were driven out. Kelly went in again and pulled out a gas cylinder which was used for cooking, and managed to turn off an electric heater in the bedroom he shared with Marty Glynn.

Firemen were pulling on breathing apparatus as they drove up the last of the 500 yards of the cul-de-sac into Glynn's yard from the main road. They were already at work by the time the local doctor, Joseph Daly, arrived.

Patrick Cahill, the station officer in Ballinasloe, was one of the first firemen into the Glynn's cottage. In one of the rooms he described what he said looked like a 'white turnip or a football', but it was later found to be the body of Margaret Glynn.

The fire was concentrated at one side and the head of the bed. He found the remains of four candles around the bed; a fifth candle was in the bedpan beneath it. They were lying on their sides and none of them were lighting. He had had to use breathing equipment to get into the house.

Dr Daly spoke to Kelly and some of the neighbours as they watched the firemen fight the blaze. Smoke was billowing out of Maggie Glynn's window, and it was to be some time before he was allowed into the house. Kelly told him that he was woken up by the smoke and couldn't find his car keys. Some of the neighbours had gone to mass, and it had been difficult raising the alarm. When he was eventually able to get into the house he discovered that both Marty and Maggie were dead. She was badly burned on the left-hand side of her body.

Garda Brian Courcey was the first Garda to arrive on the scene. He was now assigned to Ballinasloe but had spent more than six years in the local Ahascragh Station, and he knew both Kelly and the Glynns from his time in the area. He too talked to Kelly as they watched the burning house.

'Martin and Maggie are dead in the fire. I did my best to save them. I went to Micky Donoghue but both he and Tom Geraghty have bad chests, they were no help to me at all', he told the Garda. Garda Cleary kept a note of his conversation with Kelly and other people he interviewed at the scene. As the firemen continued their task, he asked him if he had tried to put out the fire himself. 'I was beaten back with the smoke and I lost the keys to my car,' he said. He told him how he had tried to rescue the brother and sister, but neither answered his calls. 'I was beaten back by the smoke and had to run outside. I'm lucky to be alive,' he said.

Fr James Smith, the parish priest of Ahascragh, arrived at about 10.20 am. He annointed the body of Martin in the house, later commenting that his body was still warm, and Maggie as her body was taken by ambulance to Ballinasloe hospital

Sean Cleary was second fire officer in Galway. He began a post-blaze investigation at 12.30 pm that day. He saw no sign of staining which one would associate with smoke or heat distortion, and it was difficult to believe there had been a fire. The fire had been contained in Maggie Glynn's room. The bed had obviously been involved in the fire, the headboard of the bed and the two mattresses, one of foam and one of horsehair, were extensively damaged. There were four candles under the bed, but because there were no holes in the bottom of the mattresses, he concluded the candles had not been the cause of the fire. On the wall beside the bed there was a heavy concentration of heat or smoke staining. This rose up to a peak on the wall. However there was no heating appliance in the room, and no fire in the open grate. He estimated that the fire had burned for approximately two hours.

The state pathologist, Dr John Harbison, was contacted in his home at Howth, near Dublin, and arrangements were made to have the post mortem take place in Portiuncula Hospital, Ballinasloe the following day.

Meanwhile Michael Kelly agreed to go to Ballinasloe Garda Station to make a statement about the fire. It was here that Kelly gave the first inkling that life with the Glynns was difficult. He didn't get paid for his work with Martin and Maggie; sometimes she would give him a pound or two but there was no wage for the work. Maggie would lock him out if he didn't arrive home at a reasonable time, and if he arrived home after 10.30 pm he knew the door would be locked, he said. He'd sleep in the car or return to his family home when that happened. He had been locked out about ten times in the past year, he told Gardai. One month earlier a sheep had died on the farm. Maggie had told him to report it to the Gardai; he hadn't, but she had found out anyway and scolded him. Marty and Maggie rowed frequently, he said, and he would never interfere when they were arguing. Maggie would turn on him, and would throw whatever came to hand at him. They had been pressurising him to give up his day job as they needed him around the farm and the house on a daily basis. They were threatening to change their wills which left him the farm and money unless he agreed, he said.

Their quarrelling had extended beyond the limits of the farm. Maggie Glynn had complained to the Gardai that Kelly had threatened to kill her, grabbing her walking fame and waving it menacingly over her head and shouting. But Kelly dismissed the complaints; Maggie was 'a bit mad', she was an old woman and he paid litle heed to her rambling speeches, he said.

On the previous day he had got up at about 8am, and went to Ballinasloe 'to price a job'. Maggie was up and about the house, but Martin was still in bed as he left the house. He ate a midday meal there, and at about 5 pm met his neighbour Michael Donoghue and talked to him for almost an hour before returning to the Glynns. Maggie, who was seated by the fire — Marty was still in bed — was annoyed with him for being away for the full day. He made tea for both of them. He fried a chop for Martin, and cooked an egg for Maggie who complained of having a headache. He told her he'd call a doctor in the morning if the pain persisted. Marty said he might get up but didn't. He read the paper for a while, then watched about thirty minutes of 'The Late Late Show'. But he switched it off when Maggie complained of a headache and returned to reading the paper again. He went to bed sometime after Maggie which he estimated to have been after 10 pm. He signed the statement and left the station. He returned to Keaves to the fire-damaged house, walked through the yard and up to the uniformed Garda on duty, who was preserving the scene of the fire for technical examination.

Kelly asked the Garda if he could enter as he had to collect something in the house. He walked through the front door and watched by the Garda went straight across the room to a cupboard in the kitchen. He opened the cupboard door, lifted a mirror that was lying on the shelf, and took out a bunch of car keys which were lying hidden beneath the glass. Then he turned and left the house.

The following day Dr John Harbison carried out the post mortem on the two bodies in the mortuary of Portiuncula Hospital. Kelly had already formally identified the bodies to the Gardai. Martin's body had been brought to the mortuary wrapped in a dirty candy striped sheet. He had slept as was his usual habit in his shirt and vest, wearing his underpants and socks against the cold night air. The post mortem showed no evidence of burning by the fire in the house to his body. Neither was there any burning or soot damage to his tongue. A number of samples were taken from the body for scientific examination, including blood, brain, liver and urine specimens. But it was microscopic examination of Martin's lung tissue that was to show up the cause of his death. He had died from pneumonia sometime that Saturday night or Sunday morning. The eighty-seven-year-old bachelor was dead before fire had ever broken out in their single-storey farmhouse.

'The cause of death was pneumonia. He died of natural causes, and his appearance suggested he died before the fire. This was confirmed by absence of carbon monoxide in the blood,' Dr Harbison said later, confirming his own post mortem results. The logic of the blood test was irrefutable. If Martin had been alive at the time of the fire and had breathed in smoke, it would have remained in the blood system and would have been identifiable to scientists as carbon monoxide. However, laboratory tests on the three samples taken from Martin Glynn's body showed that there was no carbon monoxide in his blood. So he had died before the fire.

Maggie Glynn's body had also been brought to the hospital wrapped in a sheet. She had been dressed for sleep in her winter woollies, including a heavy blue jumper. The left side of her body from the top of the head to her calf was badly burnt. The left-hand side of her head was burnt beyond recognition. Her injuries were horrific: the left-hand side of her face had been burnt to the bone. The right-hand side of her head was virtually unmarked in comparison. There was a remarkably clear dividing line between the two sections of the dead woman's head — the burnt and the unburnt sections.

Again the post mortem showed that there was no evidence of scorching of the tongue from smoke inhalation or evidence of soot in the lungs. The evidence clearly showed that Maggie Glynn had also died before the fire broke out.

It was here that the special detection skills of the pathologist come into play. It could have been assumed that Maggie Glynn had died by asphyxiation due to smoke inhalation. Instead, the post mortem revealed the cause of death to be something quite unexpected. Dissection of the head showed that there was a large section of bruising which went downwards over the right cheek bone into the side tissues of the neck and behind the right sterno mastoid muscle. The larynx was also flattened anteriorly, had been displaced and was bruised. The thyroid cartilage opened easily indicating a mid line fracture anteriorly.

The larynx appeared fractured although this could not be verified. 'In view of the injuries around the larynx and bleeding into the lungs, I formed the opinion that she died from asphyxia due to strangulation,' concluded Dr Harbison.

The throat injuries clearly showed that Maggie Glynn had been strangled. The half burning of the face suggested that a burning cloth or rag had been placed over her face in an attempt to disfigure and hide the tell-tale bruising, and effectively cover up the death, Dr Harbison concluded. There were no defensive injuries to Maggie Glynn.

Mrs Mary O'Connor, a forensic scientist in the State Laboratory, had been given blood samples taken from the pelvic area of the two bodies by Dr Harbison at the post mortem. Tests for carbon monoxide showed clearly that there were levels of less than 2 per cent in the samples of carboxyhaemoglobin. Internationally accepted tests carried out under controlled conditions showed that during the progress of a structural fire oxygen is consumed inefficiently and the fire atmosphere contains large quantities of carbon monoxide. Blood has a high carbon monoxide affinity, and as a result of someone breathing in a fire atmosphere their blood carboxyhaemoglobin levels increase quickly. Scientists have established that where those levels are higher than 50 per cent the person breathing that atmosphere would die from carbon monoxide poisoning. Under normal atmospheric conditions blood tests will show that the maximum level of carboxyhaemoglobin would be 3 per cent.

The blood tests further proved that neither Martin nor Maggie Glynn had died in the fire. Martin had died of pneumonia during the night; Maggie had been strangled and then an attempt had been made to disguise the fact by setting fire to her and her bed. Newspapers carried the grim story after the post mortem. 'Two fire deaths: findings spark off a murder probe' read one headline. The report claimed that the initial investigation suggested the deaths were accidental, but that the murder squad had been alerted as the results of the post mortem clearly showed that death was caused by foul play. A Garda spokesman confirmed that the case was now being treated as murder.

The following day Kelly visited the parish priest, Fr James Smith, to make arrangements for the burial of the Glynns. He made a 'very generous donation' and spoke to Fr Smith about the couple's death.

'He was a bit worried but not agitated or distraught. He talked about the tragedy with me and said the Gardai were giving him a hard time. I told him that was to be expected in the circumstances since he was in the house the night before. He told me he woke up to find the house full of smoke,' said Fr Smith. The Gardai had questioned him closely about the death of the Glynns. It didn't take long for their inquiries and knowledge among local members of the force to put Kelly at the top of their suspects' list. He was known to be greedy for the Glynns' land. He was always afraid that Maggie Glynn might sell her brother's land when he died to provide some comforts for her old age or to pay for her hospitalisation. This would have left Kelly without reward for his labours.

Gardai called continually to speak to Kelly, asking him about his relationship with the Glynns, how he got on with Marty, how he coped with Maggie's bad temper. On 22 November, seven days after the fire, Kelly was arrested under Section 30 of the Offences Against the State Act for maliciously damaging the Glynns' house at Keaves, Ballinamore Bridge. Gardai confronted him with the evidence from the post mortem and scientific analysis of the blood samples. Detective Garda Joseph Shelley and Detective Sergeant Pat Lynagh from the investigation section in the Bureau interviewed him.

Kelly admitted it was difficult to live with Maggie, she locked him out, she abused him, and when asked how could he explain the marks on her neck he was silent for a minute and then made the admission. 'I did it, she drove me to it,' he said between tears. By 8.30 pm that evening, three hours after his arrest, he had broken down a number of times and signed a statement detailing his movements of the fateful previous Saturday week.

He had driven in his car from Glynns at about 11 am that Saturday morning to his aunt's flat in Ballinasloe. He went from there to his father's house, but no one was at home. He returned to the Glynns, but couldn't get in. Maggie was fighting with him again. 'Go away to wherever the hell you were all day,' she said. He rattled the door and tried to get in, but it was locked. Maggie was seated by the fire; Marty was still in bed. He knew it was no use and went to visit their neighbours the Donoghues, hoping her bad mood would have passed on his return.

Within the hour he was back, but Maggie was unrelenting. 'Only for Jimmy Dennehy calling we could have starved with the hunger and with a pain in the head,' he said Maggie called out to him, as she refused to open the door.

He turned back to Donoghue's again. He said he tried to return twice again, bringing Michael Donoghue with him the second time. It was now between 2.30 am and 3 am. Maggie came from her bedroom to see what the noise was and when she peered out and saw it was Kelly she told him to leave. He claimed he heard Maggie tell Marty that they'd let him in one more time to bring in the turf for the fire before locking him out again.

Michael Donoghue was watching this with interest. He had accompanied Kelly to Glynn's, and had already told Kelly to go home to his father's house which was four miles away, for the night. His wife Bridget was already annoyed at Kelly who was in and out of their house all night. He said that he saw Kelly knocking at the door, then pushing against it as if there was something blocking against it. Kelly said something to Maggie and then O'Donoghue heard him shout, 'I'll not go you fucking old bitch.' Kelly got in and picked up the three broken pieces of a stick which had been used to jam the door closed on the dresser in the kitchen.

Kelly shared a room with Marty, and he lay on top of the bed-clothes for the remainder of the night. It was a restless sleep and he woke at dawn. As he lay on his bed he noticed that he could no longer hear Marty breathing. He crossed the room to his bedside. Then a sickening realisation dawned on him. Marty was dead. 'Maggie had me driven daft,' he told the detectives as they wrote down his statement.

'I went down to her bedroom. It was bright. A candle was lighting on the bed beside her chair. I picked up a blanket from her bed, and put it over her head, and she started shouting, "Don't do it Michaleen."

'I kept pressing on her neck until she stopped breathing. I then lifted the blanket off her head and held it over the candle until it caught fire. When it was on fire I threw the burning blanket on the inside of the bed near the wall. The top part of the bed went on fire, and the room was soon all smoke,' he said.

'The reason I killed Maggie Glynn was because she had me driven insane giving out to me and saying bad things about me,' he said. The following day, Monday, at a special sitting of Ballinasloe District Court he was charged with the murder of Margaret Glynn and of setting fire to the house knowing that she was in it at the time.

After he was charged, he said, 'I did not know what I was doing.' At the trial in the Central Criminal Court in Dublin sixteen months later, Mrs Bridget Donoghue told how she was 'shocked' by the death of her neighbours. Under cross-examination she denied suppressing any knowledge about the case. 'All that is in my statement is the whole truth and nothing but the truth,' she said. Mrs Donoghue told the court that it was Kelly's place to look after the old couple, but that she knew he had been locked out that evening and had spent most of the night trying to get back into Glynn's.

'I knew he was locked out but I didn't know why. It wasn't unusual for him to be locked out during the day. We didn't like to interfere. She was very active; she would be able to look after Martin and make tea for him.'

Mr Donoghue told the court that he had met Kelly the night of the fire and that Kelly had said to him, 'Anybody who comes now — the Guards or security men — don't let on where I was last night.' Mr Donoghue said that he and his wife were often called in to help the Glynns, when they had fallen asleep at the fire for example as had happened on a number of occasions. Asked if they were bad-tempered, he replied that the years had taken their toll.

Cross-examined during the trial, Dr Harbison said that he could not accept that the bruising on Miss Glynn's neck was caused by her twisting and turning in an effort to get away from the fire. 'If some clothing had become twisted around her neck it would have had to have been caught in something solid,' he said. However he admitted the principle that a person could strangle accidentally.

If Miss Glynn had been alive at the time of the fire she would certainly have died from her injuries caused by the fire, he asserted. There was no asphyxial haemmorrhage above the area of bruising on the neck, but he did find some in the lungs and these would have been indicative of the effort made to breathe. 'I cannot accept that a person would burn without inhaling smoke if she were alive at the outbreak of the fire', he added.

On 24 March 1983 the jury of six men and six women retired for four and a half hours to consider the evidence. Kelly had pleaded not guilty to the murder charge and denied the arson charge. Mr Justice Gannon directed that Kelly be found not guilty on the arson charge, following lengthy submissions by both Defence and Prosecution Counsel on whether Kelly knew that Maggie Glynn was dead when the house was set alight.

The jury returned to find Kelly guilty of murder.

Mr Justice Gannon said, 'The jury have spent a long time on this and have come back with a unanimous verdict. They have found you guilty of intentionally killing this woman. In the circumstances I have to enforce the statutory penalty which is penal servitude for life.'

Kelly broke down and wept as he stood to hear sentence passed on him.

7

The Body in the Street

AT about five past five on the morning of 18 April 1956 a milk roundsman called to the Dublin Skin and Cancer Hospital, Hume Street to make a delivery. He noticed a large bundle of clothes lying on the pavement outside No. 15 across the road from him. After he finished unloading crates of milk bottles he paused for a cigarette, looked around him and noticed the clothes were still on the street. He was the only person in the road at that hour of the morning.

About fifteen minutes after he had left, a van driver for Independent Newspapers, Nicholas Ellis, began delivering city editions of the popular broadsheet. He saw no one in the street, and didn't notice the large bundle of clothes.

John Moran lived at No. 17 Hume Street, on the top floor of the four-storey building. He was an unemployed baker, and left the house shortly before 6 am to report to his trade union office in the hope of work. As he came out of the house, he slammed the door behind him and reached into his pocket for the first cigarette of the day. He paused on the top of the four granite steps that led to his front door and lit up. He looked up and down the street as he did so, and then turned to his right towards St Stephen's Green and continued on to work. He noticed nothing odd about the road.

Milk roundsman Patrick Rigney left the Lucan dairy of Dublin Dairies in the weak, early morning light shortly after 5 am. At approximately 6.30 am he was driving his milk float along Merrion Row. He was travelling at about 20 miles an hour, and slowed further after turning into St Stephen's Green because of the danger of cars zooming out of nearby Hume Street. As he passed the junction he glanced to his left up Hume Street. He saw a woman crouched on the footpath about forty yards away from him. She turned her head towards him as he passed, and as she looked at him he noticed her fair hair puffed up onto her forehead.

The early morning sunlight glinted on her glasses. The woman had a stocky build, wore something white, and he guessed her height was about five feet. It was a brief glimpse, but one he was certain about. He was certain she wore something white, it might have been a scarf, a coat or a blouse. 'I am not sure what it was. I was only passing by,' he explained.

An *Irish Times* van driver, John Harding, entered the street shortly after 6.30 am, but nothing struck him as unusual as he continued on his morning round.

Patrick Rigney made his delivery in St Stephen's Green and then turned back into Hume Street to make a delivery on the other side of the road.

As he drove up the road he noticed a large bundle of rags lying half on the pavement and half on the steps that led to the basement entrance to No. 15. His helper made a delivery to No. 11 and he went to investigate the bundle of clothes. When he got closer he realised there was a pair of legs sticking out from the bundle, and that it was the body of a woman. He took a closer look and saw that her head was covered with a black skirt and that she was naked from the waist down. A black overcoat loosely covered her body. A stocking hung around her neck and the legs had been bound together over the knees with a second stocking and a pair of knickers. One leg was stretched into the basement area, the other onto the pavement. She was barefoot. On the first or second step of the basement staircase was a package. As he was about to turn away to summon help, he thought he heard a noise and looking down into the tiny yard at the foot of the stairs he saw a face looking at him.

'I saw a woman's head looking up at me. The basement door was shut. The woman was standing with her back to the wall which supports the railings facing the basement window. I think she had fair hair, raised up on her forehead, puffed. I only glanced at her and made to get away as quickly as I could,' said Mr Rigney.

He ran back to the van, drove to the top of the road, turned left into Ely Place and around the corner again into Baggot Street, and called a nearby Garda.

This was the second body found dumped in Hume Street. In June 1951 the body of another young woman had been found lying on the pavement in the small street. The post mortem showed that she had died as the result of an abortion. The Garda files on the case remained open.

As Rigney and the Garda rushed back they were joined by a second Garda who was on duty in the St Stephen's Green area. One of the Gardai knocked on the front doors of the hospital in Hume Street for medical assistance. Nurse Catherine Mary Doyle crossed the wide road with the Gardai and carried out the first examination of the body, which lay almost opposite the porticoed front entrance to the hospital. She confirmed that the woman was dead, and realised that rigor mortis had probably set in as the woman's arm was stiff as she tried to lift it during the brief examination.

However the scene had changed slightly, Mr Rigney told the Gardai. The black coat covering the woman had been pulled down further on the body, and a brown paper parcel was now further down the flight of stairs resting on the fifth and sixth steps. The package was later opened and it was found to contain a pair of shoes and a woman's handbag. In the handbag Gardai found a bank book and a list of names and addresses. A new red umbrella lay beside the package.

As the area was cordoned off Gardai noticed a drag mark of dust about three feet long on the pavement. The dark mark started near the head of the dead woman and swept away in the direction of No. 17.

Gardai cordoned off the scene, the state pathologist was alerted and a murder hunt under Detective Superintendent George Lawlor swung into operation. A house surgeon from the Skin and Cancer Hospital, Dr Michael Murphy, also examined the body, and said he believed the woman had been dead three or four hours.

A large number of uniformed Gardai were in Hume Street in the first few hours of the investigation. They noted down anything they thought relevant, including sightings of people living in the street.

One of the occupants of No. 17, two doors away from No. 15, came to the front door of the house shortly after 8.10 am and was noticed by Gardai in the area. Nurse Mary Ann 'Mamie' Cadden, a retired midwife, was wearing a red dressing-gown. She stood watching the Gardai and the gathering crowd for about one minute, and then stooped down to collect the morning milk.

The state pathologist, Dr Maurice D. Hickey, known among Gardai as MD Hickey MD, arrived at the scene with his black bag at 8.20 am. The first thing he did was to take the body temperature which was 29 degrees centigrade, eight degrees below normal for a live human being. He was to make two different computations as to the time of death, each depending on various circumstances. His calculations were based on the observation of rigor mortis in the corpse and body temperature.

If the woman had died in the position she was discovered in on the street, death would have taken place sometime between 2 and 3 am. If however she had died indoors, as was most likely, death would have taken place sometime between 9 pm and midnight. The precise time of death would depend on how warm the room was and whether the body had been covered after death.

When the body was lifted he discovered a small dried bloody puddle about one and a quarter inches in diameter. There were dust and bloodstains on a number of garments worn by the dead woman. One of the stains looked as if it had been rubbed into the material, which would be consistent with the body having been dragged along the ground. There was a strong smell of disinfectant coming from a dishcloth found attached to the woman's underclothes. He noticed the drag mark near the woman's head, and at the request of the Gardai examined it. He could find neither blood nor hair in the three foot long mark.

After the initial examination he ordered the body to be taken to the City Morgue beside Store Street Garda Station, where he began his post mortem examination. On the examination slab, the stripped woman appeared to be about thirty years of age and had been approximately five months pregnant. He examined the skin on the woman's neck after he removed the scarf that had been wrapped around it but there was no evidence of bruising, as might be expected in a case of strangulation.

The right-hand side of the heart was ballooned and contained a quantity of air. Air had been injected into the woman's bloodstream, had travelled to her heart, caused a froth there, and had jammed in her heart stopping her blood circulation. She would have lost consciousness within a few seconds and death would have followed within the next two minutes.

Part of the afterbirth and the caul in which the foetus lay had been separated from the womb wall. This was probably caused by the insertion into the neck of the womb of some type of instrument which had been used to pump in a liquid or a gas which intended to cause an abortion. There were no injuries to the birth passages. There was also a strong smell of disinfectant from the womb.

He was subsequently to examine a common medical syringe and some rubber tubing which was attached to a nozzle and conclude that it had been filled with a disinfectant fluid and used on the dead woman to procure an abortion. The injection would have inserted air bubbles into the afterbirth and this would pass through the blood circulation to the heart, causing death. The use of the syringe and attached tubing and nozzle to cause the abortion would require some medical skill, as instanced by the fact that neither the vagina nor cervix were damaged. Dr Hickey also found blood-stains on the lower part of the body and there were slight scratch and tear marks on the woman's back indicating that she had been dragged over a surface. Her clothes were grimy and torn, and suggested she could have been dragged for some distance as the dirt was ingrained or rubbed in. However the marks were superficial and it was impossible to determine whether they had occurred before or after death, reasoned Dr Hickey.

He wrote that he was satisfied that the woman could not have died in the street unless the operation had taken place there. Death had been caused by an air embolism which had stopped the circulation of the blood. He also took a large number of samples of hairs and fibres which he began examining after the post mortem.

Meanwhile the Technical Bureau was examining the scene. Fingerprint experts, a model maker, map makers and a photographer were busy at work as teams of Gardai began calling to houses in the area. One of the houses they called to was No. 17 which had been divided into flats. Detective Gardai Sullivan and Scally interviewed everyone in the house, including Nurse Cadden, a fifty-seven year old single woman. She lived alone in a 12 foot by 8 foot flat at the back of the house. She said that she had had a very bad attack of arthritis the previous night, had been unable to sleep and had left the wireless on all night to keep her company. As the two detectives were about to leave, the phone in her room rang. She answered it, and they could hear a man's voice at the other end of the line, as she replied, 'Yes, yes,' and 'Oh yes', at intervals.

Asked if she had heard any noise the previous evening, she said 'Sure, I could hear no noise, my room is away at the back.'

Another woman, Mrs Mary Farrelly shared the same landing on the first floor, and rented two rooms. Nurse Cadden went with them to her flat, and listened as Mrs Farrelly said she hadn't heard any noise that night as she was asleep in bed. Garda Scally told them that a woman's body had been found down the street just two doors away. Mrs Farrelly, an elderly woman of seventy-four, was shocked. She blessed herself, making the sign of the cross on her head and shoulders with her right hand, and said, 'God bless us. Is it known who it is?' Nurse Cadden said, 'Isn't it terrible? Sure it must have been a man who did that.' The two detectives closed their notebooks, and walked up the stairs to the next landing to continue their inquiries.

At about 8.30 am that morning, John Moran the young baker who lived on the top floor, returned to No. 17 Hume Street. He saw the crowd of curious on-lookers and the Gardai, and asked a passer-by what was happening. He stayed watching the proceedings for a few minutes, then unlocked the front door and went to his flat. He came downstairs after a few minutes intent on telephoning a friend, Elizabeth Bourke, who had visited his flat the previous evening.

As he passed the first floor landing he noticed Nurse Cadden's door was open. He rapped on the door frame and went into the flat. He asked if he could use the phone in her room, and told her about the body and the Gardai. 'Oh! The poor bitch,' she said.

Moran's mother Lily had been staying with her son in his flat the previous evening and she told Gardai she had heard nothing odd, and hadn't left the flat that night.

Mrs Mary Flanagan lived in the hall flat at the front of No. 17 with her husband and son. Mamie Cadden's flat was over her kitchen and Mrs Farrelly lived over the rest of the flat. She had gone to bed at 11.30 pm and had slept soundly, waking at 7.30 am. She was oblivious to the dramatic events unfolding outside her front window.

James Kirwan lived at No. 15 on the first floor, with his bedroom window fronting onto the street. He had gone to bed about 1.30 am that morning but had been unable to sleep. He stayed awake reading in bed until about 3.30 am when he switched off the light.

Shortly afterwards, as he lay awake, he could hear a noise coming towards him, a sort of rushing noise, growing in intensity as it approached. 'The sound was like someone shoving a brush up the street. It was not a jerking sound but continuous. There were two pauses in the movement,' he remembered. The sound lasted for six or seven minutes and the two pauses for about thirty seconds each. He didn't know exactly what time it was but the early morning light was beginning to flood into the room.

Another tenant in the house, Miss Mary Galvin, was coming home at about 3.30 am and hadn't noticed any body in the street.

Detectives investigating the murder returned to interview Mrs Mary Farrelly who also lived at the front of the house on Hume Street. This time as she spoke to the Gardai alone, she said she hadn't heard anything that night, but early in the morning something had happened. She had fallen asleep, only to be wakened at about 5 am by a noise which sounded like someone moving furniture outside her doorstep onto the stairs. The noise went on until after 6.30 am. Although she often turned her radio on early in the morning, it was switched off and she could clearly hear the noises she described.

As detectives tried to pin down the time the body had been dumped in the street they cast their net further. This meant questioning anyone who passed near the area over the next few nights, in the hope there might be a pattern to their movements, and so turn up anyone who had passed the area when most of the capital's citizens were in their beds. One such man was Dublin Corporation employee Martin Byrne who worked as a lamplighter. He was in Hume Street at about 4.45 am on the morning of 18 April, but he saw nothing suspicious on the footpath outside No. 15.

Gardai were also trying to establish the identity of the dead woman. Her name was not on any of her clothes and the tags had been cut from her black overcoat.

In the woman's bag detectives found a two penny (2d) bus ticket from Nelson Pillar in O'Connell Street for the number 10 bus. That fare would have taken her to a bus stop past the luxurious Shelbourne Hotel on St Stephen's Green which was just a stone's throw from where her body was found. Alternatively, her destination may have been further as there were more bus stops on the south city route before the next fare stage was reached on the route to Donnybrook. The bus conductor, Loughlin McEvoy, was able to identify the ticket as one he had issued on the bus to the dead woman.

The woman's bank book, with the Provincial Bank of Ireland, where she held a deposit account helped to identify her, along with the names and addresses she carried in her handbag. She was a Mrs Helen O'Reilly, aged 33, who had been born in Ballyragget, Co. Kilkenny. She had married eleven years previously, and had lived with her husband John F. O'Reilly in Clifden, Co. Galway before they returned to Dublin and bought a small hotel in Parkgate Street. She was now living in Preston, in Lancashire, with her sister although her six children were in homes in Dublin.

Her husband John, aged forty, had been working in the Channel Islands when they were occupied during the war and had then travelled to Germany. He broadcast from Berlin under the name 'Pat O'Brien', and in 1943 parachuted into Clare from a German plane but was captured. He was interned in Mountjoy jail but escaped shortly after his arrest. He fled to his home town of Kilkee. His father, a former RIC man who took part in the capture of Roger Casement in Co. Kerry in 1916, informed the authorities of his son's return, and John O'Reilly was returned to Mountjoy jail until the end of the war.

He later worked for Bord na Mona before leaving for England and subsequently going to Nigeria as an electrician fourteen months before Helen's body was found in Hume Street.

Detectives interviewed two men whose names and addresses she carried in her bag. They lived in Preston and were able to identify her from photographs. James Wilson Buyers had met her over the previous six days, having first encountered her in the Central Hotel, Preston. He last saw her on 4 April. Another Preston man, Hugh Binning, had also seen her on the same day, had given her a few pounds when she showed him her bank book and wrote his name and address on a slip of paper which he handed to her.

A steward on the ferry mv *Leinster* identified the dead woman, and said he had known her previously. He had last seen her at the entrance to the second-class passenger section of the ferry as it sailed for Ireland on 4 April. A passenger on the ferry, Herbert Doyle, was traced by detectives and he confirmed that he had met her on the ferry and travelled in to Dublin's Abbey Street off O'Connell Street with her where they parted.

Gardai were to track down almost a dozen people who had contact with the dead woman over the following days in the lead up to her death.

She stayed in Thomas Crow's flat at 21 Ely Place for two nights — 4 and 5 April — then moved into a boarding house at No.2 Lower Buckingham Street from 6 April for a week. The owner of the boarding house, Mrs Kathleen Woods, said that she had spoken to Helen who told her she was pregnant. She seemed to be depressed and unhappy. She also slept in private flats around the city, including the flat at No. 21 Ely Place where she had first stayed on her arrival in Dublin. On 13 April two married women, Jane Kelly and Elizabeth Mitchell, met Mrs O'Reilly in O'Donoghue's pub in Merrion Row. They had not known each other previously and all three left the pub together at about 10.15 pm . They accompanied her around the corner into Ely Place, and she went into No. 21. When Thomas Crow arrived home at about 11.30 pm she was waiting for him in the hall. She stayed that night and left the following morning at about 11 am, leaving a raffia bag and a holdall behind her. Mr Crow later gave these to the Gardai when they called to interview him.

The following evening Mrs Mitchell recognised Mrs O'Reilly in Buckley's pub in Lower Baggot Street. A number of witnesses said they met Mrs O'Reilly wearing a perky green beret and a long black overcoat.

Two days before her death she was seen shopping in Moore Street market with a woman and child. On the day before her body was found she was seen drinking in a number of pubs in the city centre including O'Dwyer's pub in Moore Street at 2.30 pm . A teller in the O'Connell Street branch of the Provincial Bank recalled serving the dead woman at one of the hatches in the bank. She was wearing a black overcoat, and had withdrawn £15 from her deposit account. She was last seen alive at 5.15 pm in Mooney's pub in Talbot Street. The bus ticket found in her handbag was issued for the 6.20 pm bus from the Pillar.

Nurse Mamie Cadden had spoken to her neighbour privately about the woman's death. She told Mrs Farrelly that she had been asleep all night and hadn't heard a thing, contrary to what she had told the Gardai.

Nurse Cadden was still a fresh-looking woman for her years and her sharp features reflected her sharp tongue. She cursed and swore freely as she lost her grip on a fiery temper. She had two past brushes with the law and immediately became suspected of some involvement in the death of Helen O'Reilly. On the afternoon of the day the body was found, two detective sergeants, with Detective Inspector Scanlan and Superintendent Moran, went to Nurse Cadden's flat with a search warrant. The superintendent knocked at her door, showed her the warrant and told her why they were there. 'Search away. You will not find anything here,' she said.

The search of the flat didn't take long. The Gardai took away a number of items for further examination, and these included two strong lamps normally used for surgical examinations, some rubber sheets, and a manual of practical anatomy.

Sitting on top of the wardrobe was a blue hat box, which one of the detectives lifted down to search. 'That box has not been down for years,' she said. But as the detective opened the lid he could plainly see fingerprints in the dust marks.

Wrapped in a cloth inside the hat box were two duck-billed specula, which are used for womb examinations, a forceps, two syringes and some rubber tubing. There was a minute bloodstain on the forceps. She showed the Gardai how the two pieces of rubber screwed together and said she used them for enemas as she liked to keep her distance from her patients. She explained the specula away by saying she had them when she was running a nursing home in Rathmines.

Detective Sergeant Martin who took the hat box for examination was to say later that the Gardai had been unable to identify the fingerprints on the box. There was also a fur cape in the hat box which was taken away for forensic examination. As the Gardai searched the flat talking to Mamie Cadden they noticed the pungent odour coming from a bucket of disinfectant standing in a corner of the room. The detectives asked her to give a statement to account for her movements of the previous day and she readily agreed. Detective Sergeant Carey wrote the statement out and she signed it.

In it she said that she went to bed from about 2 pm to 7 pm and slept, then dressed, made her tea and visited her neighbour Mrs Farrelly. She stayed chatting with her for about twenty minutes before returning to her room, where she went to bed again until about 10.30 pm . The doorbell was ringing and she got up, put on her dressing-gown and hurried down the stairs to answer it. She stayed talking to the male caller for about an hour in the hallway. He was a former patient of hers, and she had been treating him for baldness but didn't want to treat him that evening. She thought he was from Kilkenny, but she wasn't sure and didn't know his name. The man left to go to a hotel in town and she went back to her room, taking some tablets for her arthritis before getting into bed at about 11.20 pm . She slept soundly through the night until about 8 am when she was awakened by the postman's knock. He only knocked for the ground floor tenant, as their doorbell wasn't working.

She had slept well and there was no noise or disturbance during the night. The first she heard about the murdered woman was when the Gardai called to the door.

Another item taken by the Gardai for examination was her diary, which was given to the Technical Bureau's photographic department for examination.

Superintendent Moran had examined the hallway outside Mamie Cadden's flat before he had entered it with the search warrant. He noticed two marks running parallel to each other for about four feet along the lino on the hallway floor. The section of lino was marked, taken up and brought to the state pathologist, Dr Hickey, for forensic examination. From Mamie Cadden's flat the Gardai also took samples of hair from two coconut fibre mats. These were also sent to Dr Hickey for examination.

Mamie Cadden ran her own private practice from the single-room flat. She advertised her skills in treating baldness, rheumatism, sciatica and other medical problems in the evening papers. She was born in Scranton, Pennsylvania, but had lived in Ireland since she was a child. She was registered as a qualified midwife on

10 December 1926. She ran a nursing home at 183 Rathmines Road but that had closed in 1939. The nursing home took in all kinds of cases, including maternity cases, and it was this link that was to lead to national notoriety and bring her to the attention of the Gardai. Nurse Cadden and another woman were charged in 1939 of conspiracy to abandon a child and of abandoning it so as to cause unnecessary suffering or injury to its health.

The infant was about six weeks old and was found abandoned on a grassy roadside verge in Dunshaughlin, Co. Meath. A red sports car diven by a woman with bright blonde, flaxen hair was seen near the scene, and Nurse Cadden was implicated. Both women were refused bail and had to apply to the High Court to receive it before being tried in the Central Criminal Court in Dublin. She was photographed continually by the newspapers and as outraged public opinion grew in the case she dyed her hair black. She was convicted on both charges and was sentenced to twelve months imprisonment to run concurrently.

In April 1945 she was convicted again in the same court of unlawfully using an instrument to procure a miscarriage and sentenced to five years penal servitude.

As the Technical Bureau began its examination of items taken from Mamie Cadden's room, and Dr Hickey examined samples he subsequently took from the room and compared them with those found on the body, the investigation continued. Mrs Farrelly was interviewed again, and asked about what she remembered of 17 April, the day before Helen O'Reilly's body was found in the street. At about 3.45 pm that afternoon she heard voices coming from Mamie Cadden's room. They were women's voices, she said. Mrs Farrelly had to leave her flat for a while, and when she returned at 5.40 pm she heard the voices again. She left her flat again, returning at about 8.30 pm . As she pottered around, she heard Mamie Cadden emptying water into the sink outside her door. She heard her spilling the water and saying 'bloody water' loudly.

She swore a lot and used bad language frequently. 'Bloody water' was probably a swear word, she said, and not necessarily a reference to the water being bloodied. Mamie Cadden came into her flat and they chatted for about twenty-five minutes before she left saying she was going to bed. At about 10.40 pm she heard her going downstairs and talking to a man in the hall. As she left the flat she locked the door. This was not her usual practice: normally she left it open.

Elizabeth Bourke, a pretty young woman, had been visiting her friend John Moran the baker and his mother in his top-floor flat at

No. 17 Hume Street on the night before the body was found. She left them at about 10.55 pm and as she walked through the front hallway she saw Mamie Cadden talking to a man at the hall door.

Miss Mary White was also a visitor to the house that night. With a Mr O'Leary and and a Mr O'Neill she called to a friend in one of the flats. She left at about 10.20 pm with Mr O'Neill and saw Mamie Cadden chatting to a man in the hallway. Mary White returned to the house twenty-five minutes later and the couple were still talking in the hallway. She went into her friend's flat, announced she had to leave almost immediately, and within ten minutes had passed Mamie Cadden and the man again in the hallway.

Michael McAuley was a car park attendant in Hume Street and he often called to Nurse Cadden, sometimes bringing her an evening newspaper. He met her that afternoon and she said she had received a letter from her landlord. She asked him would he come to her flat and see whether it was a forgery or not. At about 6.15 pm that evening he called to the bed-sitting-room flat and she showed him the letter. He read it and as it gave her notice to quit he suggested she consult her solicitor.

She was in a temper and often 'went up in flames' in her anger, he said. Although he knew she suffered from arthritis she made no mention of it on this occasion. She said she would 'fix' the landlord and threatened to knife him. He paid little heed to the statement, he said, taking it as a 'comic expression'.

On Saturday 21 April the body of the dead woman was released from the City Morgue and brought to the Pro-Cathedral at the back of O'Connell Street. Mass was celebrated by the Very Reverend Dr McNevin, Administrator. Plain clothes detectives mingled with the small crowd at the mass. On the coffin a wreath of irises was laid, and a card on the wreath was inscribed, 'From her loving husband Jack'. The funeral took place after requiem mass to Glasnevin Cemetery.

Detective Superintendent George Lawlor was the head of the Garda Technical Bureau and ran a tight ship. He had a very disciplined mind and imposed a strict discipline on the men in his charge. But despite that he retained an avuncular interest in the their well-being. Once he led a raid on a house and a large quantity of pornographic material was seized, including a number of films. To prove to a court that these had pornographic content, they had to be viewed and reported on. However, Lawlor ordered that only two senior officers were to view the movies, as he was concerned that they would affect the moral well-being of junior members of the Bureau.

Lawlor was about five feet seven inches and brushed his thinning hair back from his creased brow. He wore heavy round-rimmed glasses and was often photographed at the scenes of crime with his hands in the pockets of his heavy large overcoat, his wide belt pulled tightly across an expanding waistline, pipe stuck into the corner of his mouth. The diary of Mamie Cadden intrigued him. Eighteen entries in particular held his interest. They were for appointments. There were no names beside any of the times, just a word or two to link a person with the appointment. In most cases Mamie's clients were identified by an item of clothing. Each appointment had a fee set beside it, all for less than £1, except for two appointments, one in March for £50 and the other for a woman wearing a blue coat for another £50 on 17 April, the day before Helen O'Reilly's body was found.

The entry for 17 April was almost illegible. It had been heavily overwritten in black ink, to read 'blue coat 2 pm'. Detective Superintendent Lawlor wasn't satisfied with the diary. The large amounts of money on two instances needed explanation. Also they were the only two entries that appeared to have been interfered with by overwriting.

The diary was given to the Bureau's photographic department, which had almost twenty years' experience of dealing with altered documents. Because white light consists of a spectrum of colours, objects appear coloured because of the light which falls on them and what they reflect. Some objects absorb only certain wavelengths: for example red objects absorb green and blue lights, yellow objects absorb blue lights, and green objects absorb blue and red lights. Using a specially adapted camera which was fitted with a choice of colour filters, the Garda photographers took photos of the diary and were able to eliminate the black overwriting. Gardai could now see the original entry for 17 April written in red ink which read 'black coat 8 pm '. It was enough to prompt the Gardai to call again to Nurse Mamie Cadden.

Detective Superintendent Lawlor questioned her in her flat on 26 April. A reporter from the *Irish Times* had already called to the house that day, and spoken to her. She had planned to go to the Canary Islands but had to alter her plans, she told him.

'I was going because I believe they have a cure for rheumatism there. But I have had to cancel my trip because of all this business. I have been receiving anonymous telephone calls at all hours of the night. They are made by a man. I have told the police about it,' she said. She had also been ill in bed with arthritis since January, she added.

The investigation into the death of Helen O'Reilly was led by Detective Superintendent Michael Weymes of the Central Detective Branch from Dublin Castle. Just two years earlier the Garda's Deputy Commissioner Major General W.R.E. Murphy had compiled and edited a manual on orders and instructions which clearly outlined the responsibilities of each Garda and the various specialist units. The investigation of the body in the street began with the uniformed Gardai, and was passed on to the district investigation unit which then worked under the Central Detective Branch, which in turn worked in close liaison with the Technical Bureau.

Detective Superintendent Weymes who led the investigation joined the Gardai in 1928, following in the tradition of his Co. Louth family. He was promoted to sergeant six years later while stationed in Galway; ten years later he became an inspector and in 1954 was promoted to superintendent. In 1967 he was promoted to the rank of Deputy Commissioner and the following year became the eighth Garda Commissioner.

A tall bulky figure, he always pointed to Detective Superintendent Lawlor as a perfect example of a police officer. 'George was the very model of a police officer. He wasn't the first head of the Technical Bureau but he did run the Bureau during some of its most celebrated cases. He was quite outstanding in his dedication to the job in his own professional efficiency and in his ability to adapt to any situation he encountered. Most especially I remember him because he never kept anything to himself during an investigation. Some detectives when they get a clue or a lead won't spread it around and very often that means that other members of the investigation team are missing a vital piece of information which could piece the puzzle together. But George insisted that all information be pooled and it was largely because of that approach that he was so succesful,' he said.

Detective Superintendent Lawlor began what was to be a three-hour interview with Mamie Cadden by cautioning her that she was not obliged to say anything, but she said she would answer and he wrote a full note of her answers.

He questioned her first of all about the curious entries in her diary. On Friday 9 March there was an entry that read 'lady 8 pm black coat'. It was an appointment with a lady whose name she did not know and she could not say whether she ever treated her subsequently. An entry for 23 March which simply read '7 pm ' referred to a gentleman calling to her. Two other entries that day, one for '1 pm Merrion Street' were separate incidents. She could not recall whether these patients attended her flat or not. It was simply a record that someone at some time had made an appointment to call and was no guarantee they had in fact turned up. She would not treat anyone unless they had an appointment, she said.

In addition to her advertised skills, she also treated duodenal and varicose ulcers, she said in her statement.

Despite insisting that all her anonymous clients make appointments, her late-night caller of 17 April had just arrived on her doorstep, she said. This contradicted her earlier statement that the man was calling for treatment of his baldness.

'I spoke to him about his arthritis and also about cortisone. I did not know who he was until I went to my door to let him in. Then I recognised him as one of my patients who I had not seen for a long time. I asked him to come back again some other time, although he had come nearly two hundred miles to see me,' she told Detective Superintendent Lawlor. She refused to name the man, and he had not called back since that night, she added.

'If I knew this dirt was going on I would have let him up to my room, to show him there was no corpse in the room,' she said. Mamie Cadden said that the forceps was normally used for delivering babies and was used as a clamp to stop the flow of blood from the umbilical cord once it was cut. 'I have had that instrument since I was in Rathmines,' she said. It was now used as a tongs for picking things up. 'I never used it since I was in Rathmines for any surgical purpose. If there are hairs or blood on it I cannot account for them,' she said in response to questioning.

The syringe which was taken away for forensic examination was used solely for enemas, while the two sections of rubber were to give her more distance from the patient.

Asked about the other entries in her diary, Mamie Cadden said the fee of £50 for a consultation on 30 March was for her professional services given to two or three members of the one family. The diary entry read '£50 navy blue coat'. The woman who paid her wore a navy blue coat, she said.

The entry for 17 April was overwritten because she had run out of red ink. She had written over it in black ink to make it more legible, she said. But this was clearly not the case said Detective Superintendent Lawlor: if anything the entry was barely decipherable now, and had been changed from blue to black coat. Mamie Cadden insisted that the entry was '2 pm blue coats' and was for two women patients who wore blue coats who were to call for hair treatments. They had not turned up for their appointment, she said.

Lawlor said that the dead woman Helen O'Reilly had worn a black coat and he had information that she was in Mamie Cadden's flat the night before her body was found. Mamie Cadden picked up an evening paper that was lying on her bed and waved it at the detective. There was a picture of the dead woman in it. 'I never saw her face before. I passed a remark when I saw her photograph to a man who was here that she had the mouth of a prostitute,' she replied.

Detective Superintendent Lawlor then left the flat but returned thirty minutes later with a number of other police officers and a Garda photographer. A police car pulled up outside the house, and a crowd of approximately 500 people had to be held back by uniformed officers. Dressed in a fur coat and fur cape, Mamie Cadden was escorted from her flat into the back seat of the police car and brought to the Bridewell Garda Station behind the Four Courts. The following day — 27 May — Nurse Mary Anne Cadden was arrested and charged with murder. 'I'll say nothing, I'll tell it to the Judge or Justice rather,' she told the arresting officer.

She was then brought through the underground tunnel that links the Bridewell with the Inns Quays District Courts, and was held for a while in the recently opened underground holding cells until her case was called, before being brought up the wooden staircase into the well of the court. As she was brought before the bench she said that she was unable to stand up, and would provide medical evidence to that effect. She denied the charge, saying she had never even heard of Helen O'Reilly.

The trial opened in the Central Criminal Court on 22 October 1956. A total of ninety-four witnesses were to give evidence in the case. Eighty-eight were called on behalf of the prosecution and just six for the defence. Mamie Cadden pleaded not guilty and was not called to give evidence in the trial. There were over one hundred exhibits in the trial, the most striking of which was a two-feet high scale model of No. 17 Hume Street and the adjoining houses on either side. The replica model was perfect in every detail, even down to the same wallpaper on the model rooms. It was to be referred to continually throughout the case, and was preserved subsequently in the Technical Bureau for teaching purposes.

Mr Desmond Bell SC who led the prosecution team said that the state would show beyond all reasonable doubt that Miss Cadden had performed an illegal operation on Helen O'Reilly and that she died as a result of that operation. In this case the state had no witness to say that Miss Cadden carried out this operation.

'The state would show by circumstantial evidence that the deceased was in the accused's room, and that her body was dragged from that room, across a landing, down a staircase and along a hall into the road,' he said.

There were marks on the dead woman's body which showed that some small quantity of moist blood was still oozing from the body. In the hallway of No. 17 Hume Street traces of blood had been found on the linoleum running from the back of the hallway down to the front door. Similar traces were also found on the stairway and on a carpet on the landing. Just outside the door to the accused's flat bloodstains were found underneath a semi-circular mat. Linked to other evidence of 'significant sounds', it was clear that the dead woman had been dragged from the accused's flat and dumped in the street.

The state pathologist Dr Hickey said that he had received a number of hairs found on the coat and on the heel of the deceased woman. Under microscopic examination the hairs were similar to those of a fur cape belonging to Mamie Cadden. The hair on the heel of the shoe found beside the bare-footed corpse had not been crushed, as one would expect if the dead woman had walked in the shoes. He had compared the hairs with samples taken from thirty-one species of animals and said he believed they had come from either a hare or rabbit. He examined hairs from the fur cape and they were probably rabbit fur, he said.

He had also examined a red dressing-gown which belonged to the accused, but could find no trace of bloodstains on it. There were two different types of human head hairs on the dressing-gown. Hairs from different parts of the body are easily distinguishable under the microscope. Head hairs are usually circular in section, and recent haircuts show square cut ends, while hair in poor condition has split ends. Hair that has been dyed, tinted or lacquered can often give forensic scientists extra clues to identity.

Pubic and body hairs are seen to be normally oval or triangular and are naturally curly. Eyebrow hairs are akin to head hairs but normally taper at the ends, while beard and moustaches hair are triangular in section, and are most likely to show signs of recent trimming and occasionally dyeing.

The yellowish coloured hairs he found on the dressing-gown were similar to those found on Mamie Cadden's comb. On the right front side of the dressing-gown he found two dark brown coloured head hairs. They were tangled together at one end. He compared these two hairs with samples of the dead woman's hair and found no difference of any sort to suggest to him that they could not have come from the same head. They were similar in colour and structure and there was a loose open wave in the discovered hairs and those of the dead woman.

He had also swept the stairs in No. 17 Hume Street for a sample of dust and hairs. He found five dark brown human head hairs and one animal hair. The human hairs were similar to the dead woman's hair and could have come from her head, he said. The animal hair in the sample was similar to that found on the shoe of the dead woman.

He had also collected some hairs and a dust sample from coconut matting in Miss Cadden's flat, he told the court. One human head hair was similar to that of the dead woman, while he found others that were similar to samples taken from her Miss Cadden's rabbit fur cape.

Dr Hickey used coloured slides to demonstrate to the jury his findings which were shown to the court, its officers and the accused.

He had carried out tests on a 'slightly shiny streak' on a piece of lino from Miss Cadden's house. His tests suggested very slight traces of blood, although the tests were not specific enough to be conclusive. He also carried out a chemical test for traces of human protein but was unable to find any. He did however find a smudge of human blood about one and a quarter inches in length on another piece of lino and on a portion of carpet also taken from No. 17 Hume Street. A flake of dry human blood was found on the inside of one limb of the forceps which was, in the opinion of Dr Hickey, 'not more than one month old and probably less than this.'

Mr Ernest Wood SC, the senior member of the legal team representing Miss Cadden, said that he had heard all the evidence presented by the state against his client at the trial. He asked for a direction from the bench on the grounds that the charge of murder should be withdrawn because it would be unsafe to leave it to the jury as the evidence was purely circumstantial. The application was refused, and Mr Wood opened his address.

He said that there was a 'whispering gallery' in the country which had already convicted Miss Cadden without ever hearing the circumstantial evidence against her. He knew the odds were already stacked against his client, an abortionist, a foreigner at that and one in a strongly Catholic country. In fact a number of doctors had been approached by the defence team to have Nurse Cadden's arthritic condition examined but all had refused. Mr Stanley Siev, Nurse Cadden's solicitor, had also asked a number of gynaecologists in the city to advise the defence in the case, but they had all declined.

His strategy was to call on the jury's sense of fair play, and during a mammoth six and a half hour address that railed against conviction on the basis of circumstantial evidence, he laid Nurse Cadden's previous criminal record before them. He urged the jury to judge her on the facts of this case, not the rumours that surrounded her life. Outside of the court she had grown in reputation to the stature of an ogre, with stories circulating of how the bodies of a number of babies had been dug up by the Gardai from the garden of her Rathmines nursing home. All the stories were without foundation, and it was to set them to rest and show the real and somewhat lesser level of her past crime that her criminal record was laid before the jury in a bid to win them over, and in an effort to show that her character had been maligned.

'I have no doubt that some of you gentlemen,' he said, 'as you hung up your hats and coats in the jury room had already heard about Nurse Cadden and her career and the Counsel for the accused came in here to defend a prisoner already convicted in the eyes of her fellow men and women of this city. Don't think I am talking with my tongue in my cheek when I say that this trial imposes the utmost limits of physical and mental endurance on those participating.

'I have not a shadow of a doubt that there is some member of the jury whose moral sense may be outraged to the extent that it activates almost a personal dislike for the Counsel for the accused. It is Counsel for the accused who asks you for still more privation and still more sacrifice, but justice must be done though the heavens fall,' said Mr Wood.

'What is there in the evidence upon which you can safely rely? I know that before this trial started this accused woman has been convicted in half the public houses of this city and that the gossip and rumour of this whispering gallery beat against the ears of probably every one of you before you went into the jury box.'

There were only two 'lay' witnesses, Mrs Farrelly and Mr Rigney, he claimed.

'Would you hang a dog on the evidence of Mr Rigney? Would you hang a dog on the evidence of Mrs Farrelly?' he asked. The jury could not, he warned them, take one inconclusive fact to strengthen or corroborate another inconclusive fact.

Mrs Farrelly's evidence was unreliable, he said, because she was perhaps over-enthusiastic. She had told of hearing two ladies talking in Nurse Cadden's room, then she heard the noise of a lady emptying water down the communal sink. Then, most significantly, from 5 am to 6.30 am with an interval of ten minutes during which time Mr Moran went down the stairs, she had heard a noise like someone moving furniture. The obvious inference was that the accused was bumping the body of the dead woman down the stairs to drag her into the street. There were glaring inconsistencies and equally glaring improbabilities in that story, said Mr Wood.

On 18 April when she was asked by two policemen if she had heard anything suspicious, she had replied 'no'. Mr Wood said that Mrs Farrelly fixed the bumping sound in her mind preceeding and of necessity succeeding Mr Moran's departure down the stairs. If her account were correct, Mr Moran must have stubbed his toe on a dead body on the stairs and not have noticed it. The irony was not lost on all the members of the packed gallery, and drew one or two smiles. People had been turned away from the public gallery, and hostile crowds had gathered as Nurse Cadden was ushered into the court where she maintained a dignified and haughtily dismissive air throughout the proceedings.

Imagine, Mr Wood asked the jury, having gone to bed at midnight and falling asleep to be awakened during the night by a loud rumbling noise. 'What you would say about it the next morning is that some confounded person in the house was bumping around and wakened you during the night. But do you think for a moment that you would be able to say afterwards that in your confused state of sleep and waking and going to sleep again that this irritating fellow lodger had been causing bumping from 5 am to 6.30 am and that it had stopped for ten minutes while one of the lodgers went out? Or is this gradually the mind playing over events?' he asked.

Mr Rigney, the milkman, had told the court of how he saw a woman in the basement by the body in Hume Street, yet in a newspaper interview he had said he saw no body. What kind of a dog would you hang on that evidence, he asked? And can you believe a witness who has made two contradictory statements, he asked?

Mr Rigney had said that he saw the sun glinting on the woman's glasses at 6.30 in the morning. But the sun did not shine on the footpath where the body lay until 8 am in the morning. Did the jury believe that Mr Rigney had that view down the road at that distance and was able to see the woman's hairstyle, the colour of her hair, spectacles, or the sun that was not there shining upon them in that fleeting moment, for perhaps a fraction of a second as the van passed by?

In an attack on the forensic evidence presented to the court, Mr Wood said that this was a trial in which science had 'gone mad'. When dealing with the scientific evidence of people like the state pathologist Dr Hickey, the accused was at his mercy, he contended. This was not merely in respect of the evidence of what was observed and examined but in so far as it was practically impossible to check his accuracy. However, he wasn't suggesting that Dr Hickey came to court to do anything but tell the truth, but at the end of the trial they would see the folly of hanging accused people on scientific evidence because, he said, it was subject to the frailties of human error.

'My cause for complaint about the way that this trial is being conducted is that it is a trial unlike any I have ever known, a trial where your prejudice must be curbed — curbed by me, my Lord, and above all Counsel for the prosecution,' he said.

Mr Wood also reminded the jury that if anyone had ever been faced with the problem of disposing of the body of a woman who had aborted, they might say to themselves that the safest place they could dump the corpse was near Nurse Cadden. 'If someone else were the criminal, then in putting the body so near to Nurse Cadden's he had chosen the safest place in Dublin,' he said.

Only a few witnesses were called for the defence. Perhaps the strongest was a consultant pathologist. He too had taken a number of hair samples from the area. He found that loose fibres and hair collected from the footpath between Nos 10 and 19 Hume Street six months after the body was found in the street were similar to fibres and hairs taken from a sweeping brush in the house in adjoining Ely Place where Mrs O'Reilly had stayed for a few nights.

Mr Noel Hartnett summed up the defence case on 1 November. He asked who owned the fingerprint found on the umbrella discovered beside the dead woman. It didn't belong to either Mrs O'Reilly or Nurse Cadden. Similarly who owned the scarf found wrapped around the neck of the corpse? 'Was there any evidence that it was ever connected with Miss Cadden? — None. Then who owned the scarf? — Perhaps the person who killed Mrs O'Reilly and left her body in Hume Street,' he said.

Hairs found on Nurse Cadden's dressing-gown could have been picked up in the police van that it was transported in after it was taken for forensic testing. The van was used by the Gardai for transporting 'disorderly people', and the jury could not eliminate the possibility that the hairs had been picked up in the van, he claimed.

The defence was entitled to greater accuracy from the state pathologist in assessing the time of death, he said before ending his four and a half hour summation.

Mr Desmond Bell summed up for the prosecution on behalf of the Chief State Solicitor. The person who dragged the body from No. 17 to the area steps of No. 15 was the murderer. It was not the best hiding place for a body in Dublin but it was the nearest one, and it could only be a person with local knowledge who knew of the coal vaults in No. 15 that would try and hide a body in its basement. No one was going to put a body into a car and drive to Hume Street to dump it there, he said.

Mr Justice McLoughlin in his charge to the jury explained why Miss Cadden had been charged with murder. In a case where death occurred by an act of violence in the course of or furtherance of a felony involving violence — in this case procuring an abortion — malice was implied by law. It didn't even matter that the perpetrator didn't intend the death of the person or that they had consented to the felony or that the perpetrator had even tried to stop the death occurring. A charge of murder would still be proferred. He charged the jury that the evidence was such in this case that they must come to the conclusion that on or about 17 April some person caused the death of Mrs O'Reilly by using an instrument or some other means in an attempt to procure an abortion which was a felony by statute.

'The jury may convict on purely circumstantial evidence but to do this they must be satisfied that not only were the circumstances consistent with the prisoner having committed the act but also the facts were such as to be inconsistent with any other rational conclusion.'

It took the jury just one hour to convict Mamie Cadden.

Asked was there any reason why the sentence of death should not be passed upon her, Nurse Cadden said, 'You will never do it. This is not my country. I am reporting this to the president of my country. This is the third time I have been convicted in this country falsely. And I will report it, and I will see about it at a later date. Thank you. Only for my Counsel I would say something you would not like to hear.'

The judge then donned the black cap and sentenced her to be hanged on Wednesday 21 November. As Mr Justice McLoughlin came to the final words, 'may the Lord have mercy on your soul', the hot-tempered Mamie Cadden shouted up at the bench, 'I am not a Catholic. Take that.'

Mr Justice McLoughlin excused the jury for twelve years and added, 'In so far as any criticisms were made of Dr Hickey the state pathologist in the course of this trial I would like to say that I regard such criticisms as being without any foundation and unjustified,' he added.

In the overhead public gallery there were a number of loud sobs as the sentence of death was passed. Outside the court, a noisy mob shouted 'hang her' as news of the verdict filtered out.

An appeal based on a number of legal points failed. A petition for clemency was lodged by her solicitor with the government, and her sentence was commuted on 4 January 1957 to penal servitude for life.

Detective Superintendent Weymes, known in Dublin as 'the big detective' subsequently pointed to the Cadden case as a first-class example of police team-work. 'Everybody knew who did it when the body was found. But it was one thing to know it and another to prove it. It was eventually proved by matching hairs and fibres — the case was written up by the FBI journal as a masterpiece of its kind — but that was the result of a team effort by dedicated and skilled policemen of all ranks and of different skills,' he said.

In August 1958 Nurse Mamie Cadden was transferred from Mountjoy prison in Dublin to the Dundrum Central Criminal Lunatic Asylum on the opposite side of the city. On 20 April 1959 the woman who became known as the Hume Street abortionist died of natural causes.

8.

The Mountbatten Murders

THE boxy shape of a yellow Ford Cortina threw its early morning shadow on the roadside outside Dermot Mullooly's house in Lisheen, Strokestown, Co. Roscommon. Mr Mullooly owned some land in the area and worked as a car salesman in a garage in the town, Westward Motors. On Saturday 25 August 1979 the brightly-coloured car was parked outside his house. It was there the following day when he jumped into his own car to collect his wife and children who were in Leitrim. They returned home in the early hours of Monday morning, and the car was gone.

A different car was now placed near the spot where the Cortina had been parked.

Shortly before 8.45 am Mr Mullooly looked out the front window of his house and saw it was shaping up to be another scorcher of a day. A few minutes later he went to his door, and saw the yellow Cortina being driven to a halt outside his door. It looked none the worse for wear to the casual observer. But to a forensic scientist, and there were two who would pay a lot of attention to this car, there were some interesting traces that one wouldn't expect to find in a car.

In the wells of the car on either side of the drive shaft were footmats. Loose sand had been ground into these mats. There were some minute samples of lime green and dark green paint found in the area between the two front seats, on the passenger seat, on the back seat and on the driver's seat. These paint flakes were so small they were impossible to pick up with a pair of tweezers; they had to be picked up using a sellotape lift. This process involved using strips of sellotape approximately six inches in length which are pressed repeatedly onto a surface and lifted until the tape has lost its stickiness, and by implication picked up whatever was on the area 'lifted'. This was then folded lightly on itself, put into an envelope, and sent to the state forensic laboratory for testing.

110

Approximately thirty-five miles away the sun was shining down on Granard, the biggest town in north Co. Longford. Shortly after 9 am on Monday 27 August Garda James Lohan, a twenty six-year-old uniformed Garda, was sent out to stop traffic on a routine tax and insurance road check. He stood in the middle of the main road, just 250 yards from Granard Garda Station, waiting for traffic. At 9.55 am a car drove towards him, and he put up his hand to wave it to a halt.

The driver was a heavily-set man with dark curling hair who needed a shave. The Garda asked him his name, and he said Patrick Rehill of Kilnaleck, Co. Cavan. Asked was that his full address the man replied yes.

The road was fairly narrow and as cars began to pull up behind the halted red Ford Escort Garda Lohan asked him to pull over closer to the kerb. Rehill went to put the car into gear but before he could find first it rolled back and almost bumped off the car that had pulled up behind it. The Garda waved on the few cars that had formed a queue behind the stopped Escort, and went over to the driver to continue his questioning.

He asked him did he know the registration number of the car and the driver said, no, in fact he didn't, as it was his brother Anthony's car. He asked him to produce his licence and insurance certificate and Rehill said that he would within the ten days allowed by law and at Kilnaleck Garda Station.

Garda Lohan asked him to open the boot of his car. Rehill got out, leaving his passenger remaining in the front seat. He fumbled with his keys and had difficulty opening the boot lock as his hands shook. As he stood at the boot, the Garda asked him about his passenger. 'I don't know who he is, I picked him up outside Edgeworthstown thumbing a lift,' he said. The man was a complete stranger to him and he had been hitch-hiking on the road, he said. Rehill had been coming from Longford town where he had gone to buy a fuel tank for his car. He'd left for Longford at 8.30 am from Kilnaleck.

The story sounded suspicious to the uniformed Garda who knew the countryside surrounding Granard well. It was only a few miles to Longford and the garages wouldn't be open until 10 am that morning, and here was this man already returning home. He radioed his station, and a Garda Superintendent arrived at the scene in a few minutes in a patrol car driven by another local policeman, Garda Geraghty. Garda Lohan asked Rehill to come with him to the Garda station and then asked his passenger his name. Thomas McMahon from Lisanisk, Carrickmacross, Co. Monaghan, he replied.

As Rehill sat into the patrol car, Garda Lohan sat into the driver's seat of the Ford Escort and drove up the road towards the Garda station. The two men chatted, 'What kind of an eejit is your man when he didn't know the number of his car?' asked McMahon. 'Is there any need for me to go to the station at all?' he asked. 'There is,' insisted the Garda as the two cars pulled into the kerb beside the station and the five men went inside.

More than seventy miles away, as the morning heat haze rose off Mullaghmore Bay in Co. Sligo, an old man was already up and pottering about his holiday home. Lord Louis Mountbatten, an uncle to the Duke of Edinburgh, a grandson and godson of Queen Victoria, the Supreme Allied Commander in South-East Asia during World War II, Britain's last viceroy in India, polo expert and a friend and confidant to numerous members of royalty throughout the world, was preparing for a day's fishing. The standards of the Earl Mountbatten of Burma flew over the castellated walls and rooftops of Classiebawn Castle to signal that he was in residence. Every August he returned to the Sligo castle which his late wife Edwina Ashley had inherited, to holiday with friends and relatives. 'What a beautiful spot to come home to,' he once said about his Irish holiday home, the nineteenth-century Gothic castle close to Ben Bulben and the Yeats country. Lord Louis was dressed in white cords, tennis shoes and a black fisherman's jumper which was a present from the crew of the battleship HMS Kelly which he had commanded during World War II, emblazoned with the phrase 'The Fighting Fifth'. He had arrived at Classiebawn three weeks earlier and was due to return to England on the coming Friday.

The well-worn sweater reminded him of more energetic days when he commanded the 5th Destroyer flotilla, which won him the Distinguished Service Medal. His ship had been mined, torpedoed and finally sunk and the survivors fished from the sea during the Battle of Crete. But today, the sun was shining, and he was looking forward to a relaxing day at sea, his first and greatest passion. After breakfasting with his house guests, his daughter Lady Pamela, his son-in-law Lord Brabourne, his wife Lady Patricia, and their twin sons fifteen-year-old Nicholas and Timothy, the dowager eighty-three-year old Lady Doreen Brabourne, and millionaire businessman Hugh Tunney, the man better known to his family as 'Uncle Dickie' went outside to inform his Garda bodyguards that the family were going fishing.

It was just 11.30 am when Lord Brabourne sat into the driving seat of the white 2.8 litre Ford Granada. As five more members of the family piled into the car, they laughed and joked at the squeeze. Mullaghmore harbour was just one mile away on a head-land jutting into Donegal Bay, but even a casual outing had to be supervised by the Garda as part of their round-the-clock seven-days-a-week bodyguard duties.

The two-car convoy slowed as they bumped over the cattle grid at the entrance to the estate, marked by a cut stone gate lodge and twin pillars with the Mountbatten crest and the motto of the British royal family, *Honi soit qui mal y pense.*

The twenty-eight-foot-long *Shadow V* had been berthed in the picturesque harbour beside another small boat, the *Celtic,* since the previous afternoon after Lord Mountbatten had inspected his lobster pots. Paul Maxwell, a fifteen-year-old from Enniskillen, Co. Fermanagh, loved boats and had a flair for mechanics, and while he holidayed with his family in their cottage nearby he had won the job of boat boy for Lord Mountbatten.

When the party pulled up in the now blazing summer heat, everybody scrambled out and began unloading equipment from the car. His armed Garda escort helped the enthusiastic but none the less elderly Lord down the steps of the quay. Bags and clothing for the day's outing were being dumped onto the deck of the boat, and the former First Lord of the Admiralty supervised stowing the equipment.

The British boating party weren't the first out that morning. The good weather had tempted out almost every boat owner in the area, and the bay was dotted with motor boats, dinghies and a few yachts. There were numerous tourists in the area and both hotels were full as it was a bank holiday weekend in Northern Ireland.

Lord Louis proclaimed that this was a good opportunity for a family snapshot and 'volunteered' Lord Brabourne to take the picture. Joking about his rightful place, Uncle Dickie stood behind the wheel of the boat, his family around him, broad good-natured grins on their faces as the shutter clicked.

Lord Brabourne, John Ulick Knatchbull, was a great-great-great-grandson of Queen Victoria and was also a veteran of the South-East Asia theatre of war, and a captain in the Coldstream Guards. He had been volunteered because of his familiarity with cameras, having gone into the movie business after the war. His most recent successes, which omitted his title on the credits shown at the end of the films, were the 1974 *Murder on the Orient Express* and *Death on the Nile* made the previous year.

It was 11.40 am when the engine burst into life, settled into a regular chug and the retaining line was cast off. Someone had put the boat into the wrong gear, and Lord Louis shouted out, 'Stern, stern' before the mistake was rectified and the bow of the twenty-two-year-old boat pointed for the harbour exit. A villager, Melim Clancy, was standing on the harbour wall with a friend as the *Shadow V* pulled away. The boat party waved at them and their Garda escort.

The Gardai had been asked on numerous occasions to relax their security arrangements by Lord Louis, but they insisted on maintaining a round-the-clock watch with up to five Gardai assigned to any of three eight-hour shifts. Lord Louis had requested that security should be stepped down three years previously. Prior to that it had been exceptionally tight around his family in the wake of tensions after bomb blasts in Dublin. At that time the Gardai had accompanied him even on fishing trips. After he had refused to have them on his boat, in his efforts to blend into the region with minimum fuss, Gardai on security detail were ordered to keep watch on the boat from the shore through binoculars.

Mountbatten remained at the wheel, steering the boat to port as they left the harbour and headed towards his twelve lobster pots. From the clifftop road skirting the peninsula his party were clearly visible. At the stern Lord Brabourne sat in the Admiral's favourite spot, the 'shark' seat. The ladies also sat near the stern, while the three teenagers moved around the deck area.

Garda Kevin Henry, who was stationed at Castlerea, had been transferred to Cliffony Station and was assigned to protection duties for Mountbatten. He watched the party as they boarded the Shadow V, then got back into the car and drove along the roadway that runs parallel to the shoreline to a lay-by overlooking the lobster pots. All the time he kept the boat in sight.

'The boat was still moving towards the pots but it appeared to be slowing down,' he recalled. 'At exactly 11.45 am when the boat was still a short distance from the pots there was a loud and enormous explosion. There was a loud bang and a huge cloud of smoke. The boat completely disintegrated. The water was rippling and there were large waves in the area and all I could see was debris. An enormous explosion broke the boat into pieces,' he said, describing the horrific scene.

As he slammed the car into gear and drove at breakneck speed down the winding road to the tiny village a few hundred yards away, his colleague flashed out a radio alert, demanding medical assistance immediately and Garda back-up.

A retired Irish army commandant, William Mulligan, who had a house in the village was on board his own boat with a group of German friends fishing when the *Shadow V* passed them. He looked up to see the boat enveloped in a cloud of grey-brown smoke and then heard the explosion. When the smoke cleared there was no sign of the boat, just flotsam, including some planks and cushions.

'I was actually looking at the boat at the time. It had just turned along the reef and had slowed down to pick up lobster pots. I would say it had actually stopped. It was enveloped in a cloud of smoke, and then came the bang. There was a delayed reaction. We saw the smoke first and then heard the bang. When the smoke cleared there was nothing but rubbish scattered about.' Within seconds of the explosion ripping through the pleasure craft he had sent out a distress signal and was turning his boat towards the floating debris, the last place he had seen the boat, in the hope of picking up survivors. Commandant Mulligan saw the first body and helped pull it into the boat. It was the body of young Paul Maxwell.

The desperately mutilated bodies of the dead were floating alongside the wreckage and the screams of the injured rent the air, piercing the smoke.

Mr Richard Wood Martin was another enthusiastic sailor. He had been following the *Shadow V* in his own boat at a distance of about 400 yards as it sailed out of the mouth of the narrow harbour. He witnessed the massive explosion and joined the rescue attempt and within minutes had fished young Timothy Knatchbull out of the calm sea as he desperately swam towards the shore.

'One minute there was a boat, the next minute there was nothing,' said another sailor, Andrew McLenehan from Enniskillen.

'After they had waved at us we heard the explosion minutes later. We went to the edge of the cliff and there was nothing left but matchsticks,' said Melim Clancy.

Fourteen-year-old Denis Devlin from Pomeroy, Co. Tyrone was sitting on the rocks by the seashore as he holidayed with his parents. 'I recognised Lord Mountbatten's boat because everyone here knows it. It was coming towards me and stopped for a couple of minutes. Then there was a terrific explosion. The whole boat blew up in the air and came down in little pieces. There were bodies in the water and people screaming,' he said.

His mother Mrs Jenny Devlin was knitting in the family caravan on the seafront when she heard the blast. 'I looked out and saw all this debris coming down. The boat had just disintegrated. It was miraculous anyone escaped,' she said.

Lord Louis was already dead. He had suffered massive injuries in the blast and was flung unconscious into the water, unable to save himself, and had drowned. On their regular shark-fishing trips Lord Louis usually sat in his favourite seat in the stern of the boat, but that fateful Monday was different. He was at the wheel of his beloved boat, a decision that cost him his life. His 'shark seat' was subsequently recovered intact amidst the wreckage.

Other holiday-makers stunned by the blast were two doctors from the north. Dr HG Best, from the Royal Victoria in Belfast and Dr Richard Wallace of the Erne Hospital in Enniskillen were in an inflatable rubber dinghy with some friends when they heard the blast. They steered for the shore. A small crowd was already gathering. The blast had been heard throughout the village but most people were unaware of the portent of the noise. The doctors climbed back into their dinghy and set out towards the blast scene. On the way they were waved to by the occupants of another inflatable boat which had already reached the scene. That boat carried the Brabournes and the dowager. The Brabournes were transferred from the tiny dinghy to the doctors' boat, and Dr Wallace scrambled onto the first dinghy to attend the dowager. The old lady was conscious but had a fracture on her forearm and some other injuries. She was transferred by ambulance to Sligo General Hospital. Dr Wallace meanwhile arranged for his two injured passengers to be transferred to the hospital and attended Paul Maxwell whose body had also been brought ashore wrapped in a blanket. He officially pronounced the boy dead.

The Garda radio alert had sent ambulances and squad cars racing to the scene, and the grim task of ferrying the wounded survivors to Sligo Hospital got underway. An Air Corps Alouette helicopter was at the scene after scrambling from Finner army camp in Donegal within thirty minutes of the blast.

One Garda who was on his annual holidays, Norman Kee, was also boating that day. He was later to tell of how he heard the explosion and then volunteered to help with the sub aqua search and succeeded in recovering the stern section of the boat, part of the bow, the shark-fishing seat, some heavy angling equipment, the anchor, chain and three life-jackets.

Garda Henry left his colleague to organise the rescue operation, and turned the unmarked Special Branch car towards Classiebawn Castle. The noise of the bomb had been heard on the estate, but no one had paid any attention to it. The young Garda drew aside Hugh Tunney on the pretext that there had been a lightning strike

116

at his factory and he needed to speak to him. Tunney, a meat trade millionaire from Clones, Co. Monaghan, had been leasing the castle on the understanding that it was vacant for the annual Mountbatten holidays in August in keeping with their holiday traditions of the past thirty years. Tunney was a guest at the castle when Garda Henry called.

He broke the shocking news to Tunney as gently as he could and asked him to keep it from the family for the time being and not to take any phone calls or callers to the house.

Meanwhile John Maxwell had been sitting in his holiday cottage with his wife and two daughters, seventeen-year-old Donna and twelve-year-old Lisa, reading the morning newspaper. He heard the explosion and went to the shoreline. When the awful truth of what had happened struck home, he dashed towards the sea, and had to be physically restrained from swimming out to the wreckage. The senior third-level lecturer had proudly watched his son Paul prepare the *Shadow V* earlier that morning before the fishing party arrived to sail into Donegal Bay.

'I heard the explosion and jumped into my car to go to a spot where I could see clearly. When I got there I knew Paul was dead. I would not plan for the future as optimistically as I would have before. Life seems more precious, more valuable. I don't think I'll ever get over the loss fully,' he said later.

The dead and injured were ferried by ambulance to Sligo General Hospital which was immediately ringed with uniformed and armed plainclothes Gardai. Meanwhile the world tried to come to terms with the atrocity: the first assassination of a close member of the British royal family since the murder of the princes in the Tower of London in the fifteenth century.

By early that afternoon the Provisional IRA in Belfast admitted responsibility for the bombing. The admission was met with a chorus of outrage from political leaders on both sides of the border in Ireland, and from London, America, India and from many other countries throughout the world.

The IRA claimed a fifty-pound bomb had been placed on the boat and detonated by remote control. The bomb was placed and detonated to 'bring to the attention of the English people the continued occupation of our country,' said the spokesman.

The Taoiseach, Jack Lynch, was in Portugal on holidays at the time and was given a full briefing on the disaster by senior diplomats from the Department of Foreign Affairs. He made immediate arrangements to return home. In Dublin the Tanaiste, George

Colley, issued a statement on behalf of the government condemning the killings. He pledged that no effort would be spared to catch the assassins. The opposition parties united to join the government in expressing horror and shame, while the President, Dr Patrick Hillery expressed his condolences to Buckingham Palace on the death of Lord Mountbatten.

From Buckingham Palace as the royal family went into mourning a brief statement was issued on behalf of the Queen, saying she was 'deeply shocked' by the murder.

But even as details of the Mountbatten murder were relayed to Dublin from Sligo, the IRA struck again. Shortly after 4 pm that afternoon a massive landmine exploded at Warrenpoint in Co. Down killing eighteen British soldiers. It was the largest killing in a single incident by the Provisional IRA.

The two outrages brought a stern promise to root out the IRA by British Premier Mrs Margaret Thatcher: 'The government will spare no effort to ensure that those responsible for these and all other acts of terrorism are brought to justice.' She paid a warm tribute to Lord Mountbatten, describing him as one of Britain's 'greatest commanders, who made a contribution without parallel to the defeat of tyranny in the Second World War'. His life was 'a sequence of service to peoples the world over,' she said.

India marked his death by seven days' state mourning. President Reddy said that he was deeply shocked — a sentiment shared by US President Jimmy Carter who described him as a 'monumental leader' in peace and war. The tributes continued to flow in over the following days as arrangements were made for a state funeral in Westminster Abbey.

In Dublin, Justice Minister Gerry Collins made immediate arrangements to visit Mullaghmore and get an on-the-spot briefing from investigating Gardai. An agenda was already being drawn up for an emergency cabinet meeting to discuss the assassination, and Mr Collins was to report to that meeting after receiving reports from the investigators at the scene, senior members of the Gardai Security and Intelligence Branch which dealt with all aspects of subversive crime. P.J. McLaughlin, who had replaced Detective Superintendent Lawlor as head of the Technical Bureau, and who was nine years later appointed Garda Commissioner, accompanied by Deputy Commissioner Larry Wren, went with the Minister to Mullaghmore.

The British ambassador, Mr Robin Haydon, arrived by helicopter in Mullaghmore in the late afternoon as the diplomatic flurry of activity continued unabated. His first call was to Classiebawn Castle to extend his own and his government's sympathy to Lord Mount-batten's second daughter Lady Pamela Hicks, the only member of the family staying at the castle who didn't go on the fishing trip. The ambassador was then flown by Irish army helicopter to Sligo Hospital where he visited the survivors.

The state pathologist, Dr John Harbison, had also been alerted and was making his way to the Sligo morgue to carry out a post mortem. His report subsequently stated that he had carried out tests on lung and liver samples which showed evidence of inhalation of sea water. The large number of head injuries established that Lord Mountbatten was unconscious when he was thrown into the sea and was unable to save himself and he concluded that Lord Mountbatten had died from drowning.

At Mullaghmore harbour, pieces of the boat were being dragged ashore by boatmen who had rushed to the scene, and soon an underwater search was being conducted by six members of the Garda sub aqua unit. All the retrieved pieces of the *Shadow V* were brought to Cliffoney Garda Station where initial forensic tests were carried out. A total of ten car trailer loads were taken from the water and transported to the Garda station in the first twenty-four hours. The Garda divers found the engine on Wednesday in over thirty feet of water. Meanwhile the boat to which the *Shadow V* had been tied up in the harbour was dusted for fingerprints by members of the Garda Technical Bureau.

One of the biggest manhunts in the history of the state now swung into action. Throughout the north-west of the country road-blocks were set up. Uniformed and armed plainclothes detectives, backed up by troops, searched cars and checked every vehicle on the roads.

The massive manhunt was led by Chief Superintendent Tony McMahon of the Bureau's investigations section, and assisted by Detective Inspector Christy McCaffrey, Superintendent Phillip McMahon, the chief of the Sligo division, and his Deputy Inspector Joseph Noonan. The latter had visited the harbour the previous evening and had noticed nothing suspicious. The harbour was regularly patrolled as part of the ongoing security arrangements made for Mountbatten's annual visit.

On the day after the explosion Inspector Noonan confirmed that Lord Louis had been 'emphatic' on the issue of his own personal security. 'He enjoyed the atmosphere of Mullaghmore and wanted to blend in as much as possible. He felt that the security arrangements hindered rather than helped him,' he said.

In Granard, over seventy miles away, both Rehill and McMahon had been put into separate cells in the Garda station. They were unshaven and appeared to be very tired. McMahon complained about the cold and put on his green anorak. Rehill smoked continuously.

Just two hours after Rehill and McMahon were asked to come to the Garda station, Lord Louis Mountbatten and his fishing party were blown out of the water. As the two men sat in their cells, the investigation was already under way.

Gardai were meanwhile continuing their investigation into Rehill and McMahon. Detectives knew a man called Patrick Rehill but he wasn't the man they were holding in a cell. It wasn't until 9 pm that evening that the man calling himself 'Rehill' was recognised by a detective as twenty-four-year-old Francis McGirl of Aughnasheeling, Ballinamore, Co. Leitrim. McGirl was a surname to conjure with. His uncle, John Joe McGirl, was one of the best-known republicans in that part of the country.

Detectives now raised their eyebrows and took another look at the story presented by a nervous driver with a famous name in a car whose number he didn't know with a chance passenger who, it now turned out, was on the intelligence files of the 'D' men — the intelligence co-ordinators in the Garda branch based in the Depot in the Phoenix Park.

Both men had earlier been arrested in the station under Section 30 of the Offences against the State Act on suspicion that they were members of an illegal organisation. 'Wee Tom' McMahon had been on Garda subversive files for eleven years at the time of his arrest, but he had no convictions. His father James lived on a twenty-acre farm about half a mile from the border town of Carrickmacross. He is one of a family of seven who have no strong background of political involvement. One of his sisters, Vera, was a lay missionary nurse in Bangladesh at the time and had previously been one of the nurses in attendance on the late President Eamon de Valera.

McMahon had met a farmer's daughter, Rose McArdle, from Sheelagh, Co. Louth, and after a two-year courtship they married in 1975 and went on to have two boys then aged three and eighteen months. Tom's father gave them a site to build a house. McMahon built the bungalow practically single-handed, calling on all his trade skills as he worked in his spare time. He neither smoked nor drank. He had trained as a carpenter and was employed by a number of local building contractors. On one occasion he worked in Dublin and while there he distinguished himself by diving fully clothed into the Liffey near Islandbridge to rescue a child who had fallen into the river.

Garda Gerald Geraghty who had called to the checkpoint and returned to the station with 'Rehill', said that both men were unkempt and dirty. He asked 'Rehill' what he did for a living; 'I work at everything and anything,' he said. McMahon said he was a fitter.

As they arrived in the station Sergeant Vincent Fanning asked both men their names and addresses and to account for their movements over the past twenty-four hours. McMahon said he would not say anything until he saw his solicitor and gave the Sergeant the name of his legal representative. 'Rehill' said nothing. Later asked by the sergeant again to give his name, 'Rehill' replied, 'Does it make any difference?'.

Detective Garda Hughes from the Central Detective Unit in Dublin had arrived at Granard Garda Station after both men had been charged with membership of an illegal organisation. The shoes, socks, trousers, shirts and jackets were placed in large brown paper bags, sealed and sent to Dr Jim Donovan in the state laboratory. Swabs were taken of their hands and under their fingernails with a 'swabbing' kit supplied by the State Laboratory. These were effectively cloths that were used to pick up traces of dust which is discharged from the barrel and breech of the gun when a round of ammunition is discharged. In that dust, trace metals can be identified which are naked to the human eye and which vanish within a few hours or if the gunman washes his hands.

Detective Garda Hughes went into the interview room at 10 pm and began his questioning by asking 'Rehill' his correct name. He admitted his name was not Rehill but was Francis McGirl from Ballinamore, Co. Leitrim and he went on to give a statement detailing how he had spent the previous day.

McGirl said he stayed in bed until 11 am that Sunday morning. He got up, read the papers and had dinner with his family. After dinner he went with his brother Michael into the town of Ballinamore to pick up three men who were members of the same tug o' war team. They then drove to Mohill, Co. Leitrim, about ten miles away. The tug o' war event wasn't due to start until 5 pm and they were over an hour early. They met up with the other two members of the team. They came second in the competition and celebrated by going to a local pub, where McGirl said he drank three pints. They decided to return to Ballinamore, and it was about 9 pm when they pulled up outside his uncle's pub, John Joe

McGirl's. He met 'Patrick Rehill' there, and asked him for a loan of his car so he could go home and change his clothes. Rehill gave him the keys and he drove towards home but changed his mind and returned to Mohill where there was a festival. He went into the Ivy Tree pub in the tiny market town and had a drink. He got sick on the drink, he said, and went out to the car. He lay down in it intending to stay only a while but he fell asleep. When he woke again it was 7 am on Monday morning. He drove on to Longford town and planned to call to Hanlon's garage in the hope of getting a job. He changed his mind when he arrived and instead turned right at the Longford Arms for the Strokestown road and called to O'Hara's scrap dealers on the edge of the town to look for a fuel tank for his car. The yard was closed, so he turned back to the centre of the town and hung around for about an hour before deciding to return home. He passed Hanlon's as he drove out the Dublin road towards Edgeworthstown, twelve miles away, where he turned off for Granard, another twelve miles away on a straight road. It was on the edge of Edgeworthstown he picked up the hitch-hiker, whom he had never met before, he said.

In Granard he was stopped by a uniformed Garda and he gave an incorrect name and address because he wasn't insured to drive the car.

McMahon said that he had spent the Sunday night in Mullingar and was thumbing from the town to Carrickmacross. He had got as far as Edgeworthstown when he had been picked up by the red Ford Escort as he thumbed at the side of the road. He had hitch-hiked to Mullingar to meet a married woman, he said, but refused to name her or where she lived in the town.

On Tuesday 28 August flags on all Irish government buildings flew at half-mast as a mark of respect for Lord Mountbatten. The government ordered that the flags should stay at half-mast until the body had been removed to England.

At 9 am that morning the dowager Lady Brabourne died in Sligo Hospital of her wounds, despite the best efforts of local doctors and surgeons and a specialist team from Belfast who were used to dealing with bomb injuries. She was the fourth victim of the bomb attack and died due to cardiac arrest brought on by shock and the injuries she received from the bomb blast.

Mountbatten's daughter Lady Patricia was still on the critical list, while her husband John and their son Timothy were improving. The survivors were visited by relatives who were flown from Classiebawn Castle, where the family standard flew at half-mast, to the hospital by Irish army helicopter after security measures around the family were tightened.

In an interview in *The Irish Times* a representative of the Provisional IRA said that they had used fifty pounds of gelignite in the bomb which had been placed on the boat and not planted in a lobster pot. 'It caused the political effects we wanted it to cause and which were expected beforehand. We will do exactly the same again against prestige targets. The man's age doesn't matter: it's what he represented. The English people would have seen him as very popular, very courageous. Well, we've been burying people for years. Now they know how we feel. Young Maxwell shouldn't have been there. Latest intelligence before the attack said that there would be additional members of the royal family, not civilians on the boat.'

Every resource available was being poured into tracking down the bombers. Over fifty uniformed Gardai were detailed to survey residents and visitors to the Mullaghmore-Cliffoney district in a bid to pinpoint everyone's movements in the area in the hours leading up to the blast. A confidential telephone line — 071-5355 — was also installed. Detectives were pulling out the stops, and acted quickly on reports of the sighting of a yellow Ford Cortina in Boyle. It was apparently coming from the Sligo direction early that Monday morning. A witness claimed he had seen a car like it in a garage in Co. Roscommon. It didn't take detectives long to trace the car to Westward Motors, Strokestown, and subsequently to Dermot Mullooly's home.

Mr Mullooly was arrested and brought to Roscommon Garda Station where he was questioned. He was held for forty-eight hours as the questioning continued before he was released without charge. He told the Gardai that when the yellow car had been missing, another car had been put in its place, and he gave detectives a voluntary statement describing the replacement car and other details.

On Sunday 2 September the yellow car was subjected to forensic examination and the samples taken were collected by Dr Donovan before he returned to Dublin. Meanwhile a large detachment of uniformed Gardai continued to search the shoreline, while pieces of the *Shadow V* retrieved from the sea and shore were brought to Cliffoney Garda Station and were then moved to the Technical Bureau's headquarters in St John's Road, Dublin in an effort to establish the type and size of the bomb used. Pieces of debris from the boat were retrieved seven miles away from the blast site off Dunkinelly on the far side of Donegal Bay.

The head of the Bureau's ballistics department, Detective Inspector Pat Jordan, supervised the recovery of pieces of the boat and its reconstruction in Dublin. He believed the blast had gone off in the cockpit, and the device had been hidden somewhere between the cabin and the engine. Detective Sergeant Michael Niland, a thin, dark-haired man who was an expert on guns and explosives within the Bureau, contradicted the IRA claim that fifty pounds of explosives had been used to destroy the boat. He estimated that a charge of between four and five pounds had been used. The explosive used was gelignite, and because of its density a charge that size could easily have been packed into a tube of about 17 inches long by 2 ¼ inches in diameter.

In 1975 the Department of Justice had established the country's Forensic Science Laboratory and appointed Dr James Donovan as its director. Prior to its establishment most scientific work had been undertaken by outside agencies. Most other European police forces had laboratories established shortly after the turn of the century. Now only four years old, and still in its infancy, the state forensic laboratory was about to face its biggest test.

Dr Donovan travelled to Sligo when news of the attack came through to Dublin. He visited the small morgue attached to the hospital where the three victims were brought and examined the bodies before the post mortems began. He was able to tell from the way in which the skin had been stripped from the bodies that they had been in a bomb blast caused by gelignite. Later he examined Lord Mountbatten's 'Fighting Fifth' sweater in Dublin. Using internationally acceptable tests and acknowledged means of identification, he was able to detect traces of nitroglycerine. Nitroglycerine, he was to explain later, was one of the two main components of gelignite.

Dr Donovan took a number of paint samples from the wrecked boat, including paint used on its decks and the protective underwater coatings. The force of the blast had embedded paint flakes from the boat into the three dead bodies and he also took samples of these. Furthermore, he arranged for the delivery of five samples of sand from different areas in the harbour in Mullaghmore, including the slipway. These were sealed in containers. On his return to Dublin he organised delivery of similar sized samples of sand from Bundoran, Achill, Strandhill, Spiddal, Salthill, Dunmore Strand, Tullen, Streega, Bettystown-Laytown and Wicklow's Silver Strand for purposes of comparison.

Superintendent McMahon and Inspector Noonan interviewed Lord Brabourne in hospital when he came out of intensive care.

He told them of the family photo that had been taken only minutes before the bomb blast, and after an intensive search of the bomb blast area the Garda divers discovered the camera and its film. It turned out to have no significance, but was just another example of the thoroughness of the investigation. The most interesting piece of information the injured man imparted was that the boat had come to a halt and was bobbing in the water when the explosion took place. They had not lifted any lobster pots, he said.

Over 700 people were interviewed in the Mullaghmore area by Gardai conducting the search for the Earl's killers. More than one hundred people were arrested by Gardai over the next few days as they searched the homes of IRA sympathisers. 'We hope to be in a position to bring charges against some of these suspects in connection with the blowing up of Lord Mountbatten's boat,' a Garda spokesman quoted in the *Irish Independent* said.

On Wednesday the 29th, just two days after the blast, twenty-four-year-old Francis McGirl and Tom McMahon were brought before the Special Criminal Court in Dublin. The court ordered their release, and as they walked away free men they were rearrested and charged with membership of the IRA. They were remanded in custody until the following day, and then charged with the murder of Lord Mountbatten.

Mr Patrick McEntee SC who was to act as senior defence lawyer for McMahon was to challenge the arrests later, saying the men were not lawfully before the court. However the presiding judge, Mr Justice Hamilton, ruled against the submission.

'Wee Tom' McMahon first came to Garda attention in 1968 when he joined a demonstration following an eviction of a family of squatters. He carried a placard that read, 'This is what the men of 1916 died for'. It wasn't the first time he had stood up for his beliefs. School friends remembered him fighting with another boy in the school-yard before he left his primary school over the interpretation of Irish history by the authors of his school-books. He later joined Sinn Fein demonstrations in counties Monaghan and Louth and was charged with membership of the IRA in 1972 after Gardai found documents containing orders from the IRA under his bed at his home. The court acquitted him because of lack of evidence on the charge after he said his brother sometimes slept in the same bed.

While he was awaiting trial in Dublin he was remanded in custody to Mountjoy jail, and it was there he joined a six-hour riot that wrecked the prison. McMahon acted as spokesman for the group, shouting their demands from the roof of B Block that there should be no reprisals and speedier trials. Garda reinforcements and troops were called in to end the disturbance after prison officers were held hostage and outside the jail Gardai baton charged a hostile crowd. After the riot large numbers of Provisional IRA prisoners were transferred to other prisons.

McMahon was again charged with membership of the IRA in 1975, but was acquitted after he pleaded not guilty and denied on oath that he was a member. Six months prior to his arrest he was in Garda custody again and his home was searched by anti-terrorist detectives. He was released without charge after spending a number of hours in custody. In the late 1970s detectives believed he had kept a low profile as he became 'active' for the Provisional IRA.

Although two men now faced murder charges, the hunt continued.

In Dublin on Wednesday 4 September — the day of Mountbatten's funeral — the President of the High Court, Mr Justice Finlay, refused a bail application by Francis McGirl. He considered an affidavit from the accused man and heard evidence from Garda witnesses, then turned down the application on the grounds that he was satisifed as a matter of probability that if granted bail McGirl would not appear for his trial. A similar application made by McMahon was also turned down by the courts.

Earlier that week, Lady Brabourne the most seriously injured of the survivors came out of intensive care at Sligo Hospital and was taken off the danger list.

A major security operation — planned some weeks previously — swung into action on Monday 5 November as the trial of McMahon and McGirl opened in Dublin's Special Criminal Court. Gardai backed up by troops manned intersections along the route from Portlaoise prison to the city centre courthouse. The route was changed on a daily basis, in case an attempt was made to 'spring' the two prisoners, and a helicopter shadowed the blue Bedford prison van that travelled in the heavily-armed convoy to and from the top-security prison.

The market streets around the jail were sealed off by steel barriers as Gardai and troops patrolled the area. Special press passes were issued for the trial. The book of evidence contained a total of 120 statements, and the prosecution warned that it might call eighty-nine witnesses over the coming fourteen days.

The well of the Special Criminal Court, overlooked by the empty jury box, was to become a battleground as the top legal brains in the country lined out against each other. The two accused sat attentively in the raised dock facing their three judges, Judge Sean Fawsitt, District Justice John Garavan and Mr Justice Liam Hamilton who presided. They pleaded not guilty to the murder charge.

The court was told forensic evidence would link both men to the murder. Mr Edward Comyn SC, opening for the prosecution, said that evidence connecting McMahon and McGirl with the explosion was largely circumstantial and based on forensic evidence. It was the state case that both men had a hand in the Mountbatten murder although it was not contended that they were at the scene at the time. There was no question of the boat having run into an explosive substance. The explosion had taken place on board the boat in full view of a number of people. There was forensic evidence to show that the blast had been caused by gelignite and although they could not prove how the bomb was detonated he would be suggesting it was by remote control. There was evidence to link them to two cars, a yellow Cortina which had been used in connection with the explosion, and the red Ford Escort to which they transferred and were arrested driving.

Further forensic evidence showed that the footwear and the clothing of the men contained traces of paint from the *Shadow V*. Because it was 'over maintained' with several layers of paint it became much easier for Dr Donovan to make the link between traces found on the men's clothing and the boat.

Furthermore, sand found on their shoes and socks corresponded to a sample taken from the slipway at Mullaghmore harbour. Traces of gelignite were also discovered on the clothes of both men, and the case would be that they were involved in placing the gelignite on the boat, that they were on board the boat and that they had explosive substances with them.

A Mr Murray had been on board the *Shadow V* at about 5 pm on the Sunday evening, attempting to repair a boat-to-shore radio link, and it was some time after his visit and the following morning that the bomb was planted, said Mr Comyn.

Both men sat tensely throughout the first day's proceedings. McGirl's chubby-going-to-fat features relaxed as the trial continued. McMahon sat beside him in a brown pin-striped suit and open-necked shirt.

Arguably the most important witness at the trial was Dr Jim Donovan, the head of the forensic laboratory, who was to detail the painstakingly gathered physical evidence. Slight of frame, he wore glasses and had dark and thinning hair. The courtroom listened in

127

rapt attention as he detailed his exact investigations over three gruelling days in the witness box, delivering his evidence and defending his methods under intense cross-examination. Among the exhibits that were to be shown in court were the control panel, a piece of the boat with its name still clearly legible in silver lettering, a torn anorak, a ripped life-jacket, some items of bloodied clothing worn by Lord Mountbatten, paint slivers taken from the bodies of the dead, and an oar from the boat.

Mr Michael Connolly, who lived at the lodge house on the Classiebawn Castle estate, had worked for the Earl for twelve years. He was the first witness for the state, and was called to prove the first link in a chain of evidence that was held together by coats of paint applied to the Earl's boat. Before Lord Mountbatten's annual August holidays he had been asked to paint the *Shadow V.* Young Paul Maxwell had helped him, and they painted both the floor and the cabin. He had painted the outside of the boat with green paint. The floor of the boat and the cabin were painted at Rodney Lomax's boat yard where it had been maintained over the past ten years. Dark grey anti-fouling was applied below the water line. The job was completed by 31 July and the boat was launched the following day. When the painting in the yard was completed he brought the tins of paint back to the castle. These were subsequently taken by Gardai for forensic testing and he identified them to the court.

Nitroglycerine and ammonium nitrate were two components of gelignite, Dr Donovan explained in the witness box. He had found traces of nitroglycerine on McGirl's jacket, and traces of the same chemical on McMahon's trousers and jacket. His forensic tests were carried out immediately after the bomb blast and took a number of weeks to complete. He found smears of green paint on McMahon's jacket and sand was encrusted in his footwear. He had taken a number of samples of paint from the remains of Lord Mountbatten's boat. By magnifying any one of these tiny samples up to two hundred times in a comparison microscope, a cross-section of the flake could then be seen as clearly as looking at the side of a dissected cream sponge cake. The numbers of layers could be counted, and comparison flakes easily compared by counting the layers of paint, chemically matching the types of paint discovered in each sample, and observing the characteristics left by weathering on the various layers. The more layers of paint and undercoat on the control sample, clearly the easier it is to compare it to a sample taken for comparison purposes.

There were three different types of paints used on the *Shadow V*, a dark green paint of unusual constituents, said Dr Donovan, a lime green paint and a white-coloured paint. Dr Donovan said that when he examined McMahon's right boot he found flakes of paint embedded in sand on the sole. He took three samples from the sole of the boot, and found one of them consisted of dark green and lime green layers.

'I found that the dark green layer of paint from the boot was the same as the dark green layer from the various pieces of the boat. I found that the lime green layer on the flake from the boot was the same as the lime green layer from the oar, the name plate of the boat and the deck,' he testified. A flake of white paint taken from the toe of McMahon's right boot, which he analysed, was the same as white paint taken from the *Shadow V*.

Dr Donovan said that he had analysed paint flakes taken from the Ford Cortina on the Sunday after the bomb blast and those samples were the same as paint found on an oar, on the name-plate and on the deck of the *Shadow V*. A tin of Interlux yacht paint which had been used to paint the boat and which he examined was the same as the samples taken from the boat and found on McMahon's boot and jacket.

Forensic scientist Dr Sheila Willis told the court that after conducting microscopic and solvency tests on the green paint, McMahon's anorak and paint scraped from the boat, she was satisifed that they were similar, and estimated the odds against them being the same as 250,000 to 1. This belief was based on tests carried out in Britain and she disagreed with cross-examining counsel Patrick McEntee that the differences in the Irish and English paint markets would substantially alter this probability.

Mr McEntee asked how dried paint could transfer to clothing. In this incidence Dr Willis cited their experience in dealing with hit and run cases where paint from vehicles tansferred to the clothing of victims. The smears on McMahon's jacket suggested that there had been a lot of friction betwen the jacket and dry paint, or considerably less friction and almost dry paint. She suspected, she said, that the paint had not been fully dry on transference.

The answer was the basic tenet of forensic science, neatly summed up by Edmond Locard, founding father of the science, when he stated that, 'Every contact leaves a trace'.

To demonstrate this she produced a standard laboratory slide of less than two square inches which had been dipped into a tin of the Interlux enamel yacht paint. The slide had been dipped in paint in early September, but even more than eight weeks later it would still be easy to break the gloss surface. She declined to rub the slide on her blazer to show how easily that gloss surface would break. However Mr Justice Hamilton held out his hand for the slide and when it was transferred from the witness box he wiped it on the sleeve of his black robes. 'It comes off quite easily,' he informed the court.

A flake of yellow paint found in the red Escort in which both men had been stopped was the same as the paint on the yellow Cortina, she said. Tests that were carried out on the clothing of both men matched sellotape lifts of fibres taken from the Cortina. She had also analysed the green paint samples found in the Cortina, and found these had come from Lord Mountbatten's boat.

Dr Donovan said sea sand was found on the boots and shoes of both accused, and this was subjected to an examination using an X-ray technique to identify its composition. The machine, a microanalyser, took X-rays of a sample and provided an elemental profile of the sample. When examined, this was found to be identical to a sample of sand taken from the slipway at Mullaghmore harbour. Both the footwear of the accused men and their socks were encrusted with sand, and it was probable that this had recently been obtained as sand was easily lost by wear, said Dr Donovan. He had arranged for samples from other seaside resorts around the country to be delivered to the laboratory for testing and he subjected them to the same examination. Each sand sample had proved to be different.

In response to Mr McEntee he said that he could not categorically state that the sand found in Mullaghmore was specific to that area only, despite the findings from his other samples. It was not possible to prove that sea sand was specific to a certain area, he explained.

He also found sand on the front seat mats of the red Escort and yellow Cortina, but because it was embedded into them it was impossible to obtain a sample in either instance.

Mr Dermot Mullooly said that the Cortina had disappeared from outside his home some time before his return from Leitrim in the early hours of Sunday morning. A red car was parked outside his house near where the yellow car had been, he said. The Cortina was not there when he looked outside his house the following morning at 8.45 am. But when he went outside he saw it driving up and two men getting out of it. He asked them what they were doing and they said they were going to the quarry. When he went back inside to put on his shoes the men got into the red Escort and drove off.

Mr Edward Comyn SC asked that the court should treat Mr Mullooly as a hostile witness, which the court agreed to after hearing evidence from a detective sergeant who gave evidence of taking a statement from Mr Mullooly at Roscommon Garda Station which he had signed voluntarily. Mr Mullooly admitted to Mr Comyn in cross-examination that he knew Francis McGirl for about four years but said that he did not recognise him as one of the men outside his house on the morning Lord Mountbatten was killed.

'It was suggested to me by the Gardai that the two men were in my house, and had washed and shaved and had been given tea,' said Mr Mullooly. 'They told me what to say. They told me to say that I recognised McGirl outside my house. They were calling me names and they were thumping the table,' he claimed.

He said that Gardai had told him he had given McGirl permission to take the Cortina, and that if he did not agree to say this in a statement they would arrest his eighty-year-old mother and he would be thrown into jail and his children would not want to know him when he got out of jail and he was so confused he signed the statement.

Asked why he had signed the statement having read it over, he replied, 'I can say I did not recognise Francis McGirl outside my house. He was not there that morning.'

Garda James Lohan gave evidence of stopping the men in a red Escort in Granard before the blast occurred. McGirl gave him a false name, and appeared to be very nervous. He had difficulty opening the lock on the boot and his hands were shaking. Mr Seamus Egan SC, who represented McGirl, asked him was it not the case that people were often nervous when stopped by the Gardai? 'Not unless they have something to hide,' replied Garda Lohan.

In reply to further questioning Garda Lohan said that McGirl had not been prompted by Gardai before he gave his proper address.

'I suggest he was brought in and Mr Hughes immediately shouted at him, "You are not Patrick Rehill, you are an IRA murderer and you are never going to see the outside world again".'

'That did not happen,' said Garda Lohan. Detective Garda Michael O'Gara from Mullingar who was also present at the interview concurred, and said there had been no shouting or screaming at McGirl. No complaint had been made to that effect and they had had a general conversation including talking about a forth-coming wedding in the McGirl family.

Detective Garda Hughes said that McGirl had given him an account of his movements on the night of the Mountbatten murder. He had started the interview by asking McGirl his correct name, and he gave it freely. McGirl later told him that the reason he gave a false name was because he was not covered by insurance to drive the car, said Detective Garda Hughes. He then told him how he had spent the Sunday by rising late, going to a tug o' war competition and then drinking in the evening, before sleeping overnight in the red Escort in Mohill and then returning home via Longford and Granard where he was stopped by a Garda.

Hughes denied that he had called McGirl a murdering IRA man or that he had accused him of telling lies. McGirl had not asked for a solicitor and he had not said he would only get him one if he told the truth. In response to further questions from Mr Egan he denied that he had told McGirl he had been seen in Sligo and Bundoran on the day before the bomb blast or that he had told him about the death of Lord Mountbatten.

Detective Sergeant Thomas Dunne from the Technical Bureau's investigation section said he wasn't satisfied with McGirl's account of his movements. McGirl was sitting at a table in the interview room smoking a cigarette when he shouted back at Dunne, 'I put no bomb on the boat.' He jumped up, clenched his fist and said, 'Fuck you', according to Detective Sergeant Dunne. 'I cautioned him and asked if he wished to sign what he said. I wrote it down but he refused to sign.'

Dunne then asked him if anyone had spoken to him about a bomb or an explosion. 'He said, "no",' said the detective. He denied that he had shouted at McGirl or used the word 'lies'.

Detective Inspector Canavan asked McGirl later what boat he was referring to after his admission but he replied he was not answering any more questions.

As detectives carried out interviews with suspects they used a number of questioning techniques. The fullest possible briefing about the suspect was a vital precursor to any interview. Inter-viewers also relied on updated information where relevant: any information unearthed by Gardai in the field as the suspect was being questioned was valuable. That constant feeding of informa-tion was considered vital in any successful interview. In their interviews with McGirl they maintained that he had been cut off from all knowledge of events in the outside world, which made his voluntary statement about what should have been an unknown event remarkable.

Francis McGirl stood in the witness box to tell the court that the Gardai interviewing him had banged the table with their fists shouting at him, and 'roaring that I was an IRA murderer'.

'They said I put the bomb on the boat. I denied putting the bomb on the boat. I said it maybe twenty or thirty times. I was told I would see no solicitor until I made a statement that I had killed Lord Mountbatten,' he said. He had been accused of murdering two children by the detectives and when he denied their charge he was told he was a lying bastard. McGirl also told the court that he couldn't sleep while he was in custody, as police officers came to see him every few minutes and kept him awake banging the door and flushing the toilet.

When the prosecution case rested, Mr Seamus Egan made an application for acquittal for his client Francis McGirl on the grounds that no case had been established against him. He contended that there were four reasons for acquittal. There were traces of ammonium nitrate and nitroglycerine found on McGirl's clothes but there could have been a large number of people with those traces on their clothes in the country that day. Evidence of sand on his shoes and socks was inconclusive; the verbal statement McGirl had made in the Garda station could not have been made unless the Gardai had informed him about the bombing; and despite exhaustive tests no particle of paint from the *Shadow V* had been found on McGirl's clothes.

The only attempt to link him with paint flakes was through the presence of paint flakes discovered in two cars, but there was no evidence forwarded to say he was in one of those cars. 'Suspicion is not enough and suspicion is all there is in this case,' he said.

Mr Justice Hamilton read out the court's decision the following day. While the evidence against McGirl may be purely circumstantial, precedent showed that this did not detract from its evidential value. The evidence of sand on McGirl's footwear might not be conclusive in itself but it was evidence that had to be taken into account with other presented evidence. The court would be entitled to find that McGirl was at Mullaghmore as the sand found on his footwear was the same as that at the slipway in the harbour. It would also be entitled to conclude that he had been at Mullaghmore a short while before his arrest as there had been evidence that sand was 'lost' quickly. The court could infer that McGirl had driven from Mullaghmore with McMahon as both men had the same sand on their footwear.

Traces of nitroglycerine and ammonium nitrate were found on McGirl's clothing and, taken with his statement to Detective Sergeant Dunne in Granard Garda Station that he had 'put no bomb on the boat', the court was entitled to conclude that he was aware of the bomb and had handled it, even if he had not put it on the boat himself. McGirl, he said, was not entitled to an acquittal at this stage.

The defence for Tom McMahon then opened its case and called its first witness, a German analytical chemist, Dr Dieter Gross. He worked at the Federal Institute for the testing of materials and had carried out tests relevant to the case in Berlin. He had written a number of articles in scientific journals, and had just completed a book about paint analysis which was due to be published shortly.

He examined the paint samples in the Irish State Laboratory and then returned to Berlin where he continued his investigations. He claimed that his equipment in West Germany was more sensitive than that used in the State Laboratory and said that there were some differences in his conclusions and those of Dr Donovan. Dr Gross said that the traces of gelignite found on McMahon's trousers were different to those found on McMahon's jacket. He had examined the white paint samples from the *Shadow V* and compared them to those found on McMahon's footwear, and he had 'severe doubts' they were the same, he told the court. He also disagreeed that it had been scientifically proved that paint samples taken from the clothing of the dead Earl and his boat were the same as those paint flake samples taken from the two cars, or those samples taken from McMahon's clothing or shoes.

Felix McArdle,an upholsterer from Courtbane, Hackballscross, Co. Louth, said that he knew Tom McMahon since he had married his sister three years ago. He employed McMahon and a part of his duties was to paint furniture frames. He had purchased about eight tins of Galoxide green paint from Tom's brother Jimmy and he had been using some of this paint in his work. Felix McArdle said he had the tins of paint for the past year.

Mrs Bernadette McMahon, Tom's mother, said that she had got the tin of paint from her son-in-law and handed it to her son's solicitor.

Summing up the defence case on behalf of McGirl, Mr Seamus Egan said that no traces of explosives had ever been found on his client's hands or under his fingernails. The court should accept that he had clearly never been on the boat. With regard to the oral statement, he said that any reasonable jury would find the prosecution case 'quite incredible'.

There could be no guilt by association, he said, and any conviction of his client would have to depend on the forensic evidence based on sand analysis which he claimed was tenuous. None of the other evidence could warrant the assumption that McGirl was in Mullaghmore. The case against his client was one of suspicion, and even if McGirl was in Mullaghmore that in itself was not enough to warrant conviction. He could have gone there to collect somebody else, he said.

Mr McEntee for the defence raised the possibility of a third person, someone not before the court, who could have planted the bomb and travelled in the car, and infected both it and his client's clothes with paint flecks. Similarly Dr Donovan or a member of the Gardai could have infected the Ford Cortina with paint flecks during their forensic examination, he claimed.

It was open to the court that some time before the bomb blast Tom McMahon could have had something to do with explosives and Lord Mountbatten's boat. But if the court did reach that conclusion it was not open to it to find that a case for murder had been made. McMahon was not to know that the intention of the person to whom he had made the bomb available was to kill the Earl. The third person could have intended to blow up the boat when the coast was clear and the pier deserted.

He discounted the sand evidence, citing testimony on behalf of the defence that there was no significant difference between sand samples from Mullaghmore and other beaches.

If the traces found on McMahon's clothing were components of gelignite, there was state evidence that such traces could remain for up to twelve months and quarrying and road cratering near where McMahon lived could account for such traces, he claimed. There was no evidence to link the traces found on his clothes to a 'pre-explosion situation', he contended. All he could say about the paint flecks was that they were of a common paint, that McMahon's brother-in-law ran a furniture business where he was employed to paint furniture, that there were other specks of paint on McMahon's footwear and that these had not been examined and neither had his place of work.

The following day, McMahon was found guilty of placing the bomb on the boat and was sentenced to penal servitude for life. McGirl was acquitted. McMahon smiled as the judgment and verdict were given. In the gallery a number of republican sympathisers gave McMahon a clenched fist salute as he was led from the dock by prison warders. He waved to his wife Rose who also sat in

135

the public gallery. He turned to McGirl and shook hands with him as he was found not guilty of the murder of Lord Mountbatten. It was shortly after midday when McGirl walked free from the court towards a pub in the market quays to celebrate his release. He was surrounded by supporters including his uncle John Joe McGirl, an abstentionist Sinn Fein Dail deputy in the 1950s. He made no comment to newsmen as he left the Green Street courthouse.

It had taken Mr Justice Hamilton twenty minutes to deliver the judgment. The evidence against each man was considered separately. In both cases it was purely circumstantial but that was no derogation of the evidence, he said. The state had claimed that McMahon was at Mullaghmore and on the *Shadow V*. The court had paid particular attention to the forensic tests carried out in this case and the methods used to reach conclusions. As a result the court was not satisfied that the sand on McMahon's footwear established his presence at Mullaghmore beyond reasonable doubt. The evidence given about paint flakes was coercive and established beyond a reasonable doubt that he had been on the *Shadow V*. The court was also satisfied that McMahon had been in contact with explosives. Both his presence on the boat and his contact with explosives were consistent with his guilt. It clearly established, said Mr Justice Hamilton, that either alone or with others he placed explosives on the boat and intended to kill or cause serious injury to anyone on or in the vicinity of the boat.

In McGirl's case it was imperative that the state should have established his presence in Mullaghmore, said Mr Justice Hamilton. However, in view of the doubt already expressed by the court about the sand evidence, it was not satisfied that the prosecution had discharged the onus that the law placed on it. The other evidence against him was consistent with his guilt, but equally consistent with an innocent explanation. If the court were to convict McGirl it would be doing so on the real suspicion that surrounded the case and his association with McMahon. The law did not allow the court to convict on those grounds and consequently there was a doubt about his guilt and the court found him not guilty.

McGirl was allowed personal bail of £100 and surety of £1,000 and a date was fixed two months forward for the hearing of an outstanding charge of membership of the IRA.

On 21 January Francis McGirl was acquitted of a charge of membership of the IRA after swearing on oath that he was not a member.

The following day Thomas McMahon told the same court under oath that he was the father of two children, that he had built his own house on a county council loan of £3,000 and that he had worked with his brother in Enniskeen, Co. Louth.

Mr Hugh O'Flahery SC, prosecuting, put it to him that he had 'no real employment for years and that you have been supported and paid by the IRA'.

'That is not true,' said McMahon.

'I put it to you that you were a member of the IRA on 27 August last,' said Mr O'Flaherty.

'No,' said McMahon. The charge of membership of the IRA was dismissed by the court and McMahon was returned by prison van to Portlaoise jail to continue his sentence.

9

Through the Bedroom Window

IN May 1946 twenty-six-year-old Alice Gerrard gave birth to a
healthy baby boy, her first child. She arrived home from hospital
with the child to her mother Mrs Mary Scott, a sixty-seven-year-old
widow. They lived together in her mother's semi-detached cottage
in the townland of Donaghmore, approximately one mile outside
Navan, Co. Meath.

Alice had married Leo Gerrard, one of six brothers from
Drogheda, Co. Louth, five years previously. She had been working
as a domestic servant in Drogheda when she met him. Times were
hard and work was scarce and there were still plenty of post-war
shortages. Leo had been working in England for a number of years
and came home very infrequently on the Holyhead boat, sending
money before him and arriving laden down with some of the
extras that weren't available after the Emergency.

Leo wasn't in Ireland for the birth. He was working in Gloucester
and made immediate arrangements to come home when the news
reached him. It was Whitsun when he travelled directly to Meath
from the boat and called to Scott's three-bedroomed house where
his wife was living. He was not the father of the child. He hadn't
been in the country at the time of the conception.

There was a terrible scene in the small cottage. Neighbours could
hear the shouting: he was going to have nothing more to do with
that bitch; it wasn't his child; he was shut of her, and wasn't going to
pay for the maintenance of someone else's child, or his wife.

Leo separated from his wife, and returned to his own family.

Behind him he left wagging tongues and the memory of a bitter
quarrel.

Later that year, on the night of Saturday 5 October, Alice went
to bed at about 11.20 pm. Her bedroom was at the back of the
house. The child, Patrick J., shared her bed and was already asleep.
The bed was against a wall and she lay on the outside to prevent

the infant falling out. She was asleep in a few minutes, and didn't hear her mother coming in about thirty minutes later. Mrs Scott came into the room to return a lamp which her daughter had brought out to the kitchen for her as she wrote a letter. She left the lamp burning on the washstand by the window which was opened about two inches.

Mrs Scott went back to her own bedroom at the front of the house, walking through the kitchen which connected to all three bedrooms, the only other rooms in the house. She went to bed and she too fell asleep within a few minutes. Some time later that night Mary Scott woke to hear her grandson crying. She lay in bed for about ten minutes as the child bawled and screamed. She called to Alice to tend to her child, but there was no answer.

'The baby stopped crying and I then heard a sound as if someone was walking in stockinged feet. I was not sure where the sound came from. I then heard four or five steps and the baby started crying again. I went to my daughter's room calling "Alice" as I went,' said her mother.

The room was dark and she groped at the bed for the child. Her hands brushed her daughter's head, and she felt blood. Startled, she rushed to the kitchen to get a match to light the lamp. 'When I took the lamp over to see my daughter I saw that she was lying on her right side and her face was covered with blood. The infant was still in the bed and crying. I took the infant out of the bed and found that his legs seemed to be caught as his mother had partly fallen on him,' she said.

Mrs Scott picked up the crying child and rushed from the room to her front door where she stood screaming into the night air until the neighbours came running to see what had happened.

The first neighbour to comfort Mrs Gerrard was Mary Rath who lived in the adjoining cottage. She had been out for the evening, had returned home at 12.30 and was in bed before 1am. The night was silent except for one car she had heard passing as she returned home. She was asleep for about thirty minutes when she heard Mary Scott calling out. She dressed and went into Scott's kitchen.

'Alice is dead. Go into the room to see her,' said Mrs Scott as she stood in the middle of the floor comforting the whimpering baby.

'I lit a candle and went into Alice's bedroom. I lifted up her head and it was all blood. The blood was coming from her mouth and nose. She was lying on her right side facing the wall. Her body was covered by the bed clothes,' said Mary Rath. 'I felt her hip and foot which were cold and she appeared to be dead.'

Convinced that Alice was indeed dead she went to raise more neighbours and called John Meleady, the Stapletons, and James Skelly who went for the curate, Fr John Herbert, who lived in the town.

John Meleady too remembered a car 'hushing' by their houses as he went to bed that evening.

Meanwhile Mary Rath was tidying up the dead woman's room. She dusted the table by the window where the lamp had stood, and the window sill. She left the cloth she had used to dust the room lying on top of a box on the table.

John Stapleton lived on the opposite side of the road to Mrs Scott. His cousin had been visiting him that evening from about 7 pm, and left at about 1.15 am. He went out to the gate to see him off. It was a dry bright night but there was no moon. He was back in bed at 2.05 am. He heard a car and after it had passed his house he thought he heard it stop. He fell asleep, and then heard someone hammering at the door. It was Mary Rath, and when she told them what had happened his wife went with her to Scott's. He then got dressed, went to Scott's himself and saw Alice Gerrard lying dead in her bed. The following morning at 8.30 am he called to Navan Garda Station and reported the death of Mrs Gerrard to Sergeant Francis Carr who was on duty and who instructed Garda Timothy Cremin to go to the scene.

It was 10.30 that morning when the Garda visited the single-storey house. He walked past the overgrown bushes that served to mark the boundary of the garden and walked up to the tongued and grooved wooden front door. It stood facing the pathway fronting a small porch. Two sixteen-paned windows flanked the porchway.

The body was still lying on its right side, and the right arm was under the body, with just the hand and wrist visible. There was blood on her right hand, but none on the left. It was covered with blankets. He lifted the dead woman's head to see if there were any marks or cuts on it, but as there were not any he placed it back on the bloodstained pillow.

There was also blood on the bedclothes and a small amount on the floor underneath the bedhead. The room looked tidy and the top of the window was open about four inches; the bottom half was covered by a net curtain. The Garda then asked Mrs Scott what had happened. Perhaps she had heard some strange noises or anything suspicious the previous evening? She told him how she had found the body but she did not mention anything about the footsteps she had heard.

The Garda returned to his station and told the sergeant what he had found. The sergeant telephoned the local coroner who asked him to contact the dispensary doctor and request him to conduct an examination of the body. Shortly after midday Dr Richard Whyte arrived at Mrs Scott's house. He went into the bedroom and examined Alice's neck and head without pulling down the bedclothes, and told Gardai that death was due to natural causes. Sergeant Carr contacted the family and said that the body could now be laid out.

It was approximately 5 pm that evening when Mary Rath and two neighbouring women armed with cloths and bowls of hot water undressed the body to wash it as part of the preparation for that evening's wake. But when the body was laid bare the women saw a large wound between the right breast and right shoulder. Mary Rath said that they would have to call the Gardai, who arrived shortly after 6 pm with Dr Whyte. He examined the body again and said that the woman had died from what appeared to be a gunshot wound and that the wound could not have been self-inflicted. Later he was to say that he had formed a certain opinion about the woman's death on the first cursory examination. He had thought it possible that she had died from TB, as he had seen similar large haemorrhages in other TB cases. He said that he wasn't satisfied with the cause of death and had intended contacting the coroner Mr Lynch. He had telephoned Mr Lynch's home in Kells three times that day, but had been told by the telephone operator that, like the past six weeks, he couldn't be expected home until after 8 pm.

That evening Patrick Gilsenan was serving behind the bar in his pub in nearby Flower Hill. Two men came into the bar together, John O'Hara who was known as 'The Yank' O'Hara and Joseph McManus. They had both worked together as general labourers and maintained their friendship, often meeting each other at the weekends in Navan. They stayed drinking together, talking quietly for almost two hours. The men in the bar were listening to the radio and when it was switched off after the national news, their talk turned to the biggest local news, the death of Alice Gerrard.

'When is the funeral?' The Yank O'Hara asked the men lined up drinking at the bar. 'There won't be one,' said Gilsenan behind the bar. 'How's that?' The Yank asked, but Gilsenan had turned to serve a customer and no one answered him.

Superintendent A.L. O'Neill who had gone to the house when the wound had been discovered, ordered that the room should be sealed off, and delegated his men to question neighbours.

Mrs Scott had heard no gunshots during the night or dogs barking or any other odd noises, she told them. Other neighbours concurred. There couldn't have been any strangers around the house as the night had been silent and no one had heard any of the neighbourhood dogs barking.

The body was subsequently removed to the morgue in Navan and a post mortem carried out by the state pathologist, Dr John 'Jock' McGrath. He had visited Mrs Scott's house and had examined the body there first. The bedclothes around the head were covered with blood and the mattress similarly was soaked through with blood which had dripped on to the floor. The room had the appearance, he said, of being partly cleaned.

He confirmed that the woman had been killed with a shotgun blast, and he found the wads of a single cartridge. He estimated that the woman would have died within a couple of minutes of being shot, and said that the wound would have been visible if it had been uncovered.

His attention to detail was renowned. He had in one instance secured a conviction after taking a cast of a man's finger which had a missing flap of skin. The positive impression was taken from the case, and it proved to match exactly a flap of skin found at the scene of the crime. Fingerprint experts in the Technical Bureau were able to prove the match not only because of the fine detail which showed the lines of the loops and arches clearly, but also the capillary ridges on the print. The skin flap is preserved in formaldehyde in the Technical Bureau to this day as a lecture exhibit.

Garda James Kavanagh from Navan had carried out a preliminary examination of the room, and found a small hole in the bottom left-hand pane of glass in the bedroom window. There was a corresponding hole in the lace curtain that covered the bottom half of the window, and the edges of the hole were blackened. That evening Detective Superintendent Dan Stapleton of the Bureau's ballistics section was called to the house. He was broad shouldered, with a beaked nose and a receding hair line that went back to the crown of his head. He had spent the past ten years as the Gardai's top ballistics officer and had gained international fame by the time he retired in 1951 for co-inventing a method of firing blanks in the Lewis gun. He also discovered that broken glass has a unique fracture pattern and his evidence convicted many hit-and-run drivers whose broken headlights were matched to glass found at the scene of the accident.

His first interest in guns came as a child when he cleaned guns stored at his father's home in Co. Kilkenny by RIC men returning from the local shooting range. Dan Stapleton had won three All Ireland medals dated 1904, 1905 and 1906 as a Kilkenny hurler. He went on to join the IRA and became one of their armourers. In 1922 he joined the Army and worked in their armoury, and by 1934 as a commandant he became ballistics advisor to the Gardai working from the barracks in Inchicore. Special legislation had to be passed in the Dail to allow him switch to the Gardai on a full-time basis and to enter automatically at the rank of detective superintendent — making him the first and only officer corps member of the Gardai — in 1936.

He ordered that the whole window including its frame should be removed and brought to the ballistics section of the Technical Bureau. He also took the curtain from the window after the room had been photographed by Detective Garda William Whelan, one of the Bureau's four photographers. The window was then boarded up. Detective Superintendent George Lawlor, who had spearheaded every murder inquiry in Ireland over the previous twelve years, was also called to the scene. The stocky, quiet-voiced man, who was once described as looking and talking like a college headmaster, began by examining the woman's bedroom.

Detective Garda Charles McGovern and his chief examined the ground around the cottage for footprints. They discovered a portion of a heel print on the ground outside the dead woman's bedroom window. The print was clear, as the ground was sodden from rain which had fallen over the previous few days. There was also a footprint made by a nailed boot in a passageway near the gable end of the house. However the heel print was without significant characteristics to make it useful for identification, and the bootprint too turned out to have no connection with the crime.

Alice Gerrard was well known in the district. She had had a child by a man who was not her husband and had a number of men friends, at least one of whom boasted of how she would open her bedroom window to let him into her bed at nights. Her husband had left her as a result of the child and had stopped sending her money from England. At the inquest on the Monday, Mrs Scott said that she did not know if her daughter was or was not on good terms with her husband. The inquest was adjourned indefinitely after Superintendent O'Neill explained that their investigations were continuing.

Gardai under Chief Superintendent Gilroy, the divisional chief in Drogheda, began to trace back Alice Gerrard's movements and associations before her death. Her mother told them that she had been in the house all day, except for a brief trip into Navan. She was home at about 2.30 pm that Saturday afternoon and both Alice and her baby were still in the house. Mrs Scott said she went out a second time, for a message, at about 7 pm and returned by 8 pm.

Alice had been friendly with John 'The Yank' O'Hara. He had been a frequent visitor to the house before the baby was born, but he hadn't been around since its birth. O'Hara was a married man. He had held down a number of jobs and had met Alice when they both worked in Flood's shop in Navan. He had first worked in Rogers Brothers the building contractors in Flower Hill outside Navan, before moving to Dublin to take up work in Musgrave's. He moved back to Navan and was employed on James Flood's farm at Proudstown. Alice had been employed there regularly for up to about twelve months before her death.

O'Hara left Flood's long before Alice Gerrard's child was born but he used to visit her while she was in hospital and bring her cigarettes. They had had a very close relationship, he admitted. Bridie Scott, who worked in a hotel in Navan, often went to dances with her older sister Alice and John O'Hara. He was employed in Rogers' at the time, and sometimes brought them into the yard where there were living quarters — a kitchen and two caravans — set aside for the firm's employees. He often had bottles of stout bought in for their visit to the yard and they always went into the caravan where O'Hara slept, to drink them. Bridie had never met any of the Rogers whenever they visited; only on one occasion did they bump into anyone, and that was another employee.

In the days following Alice's death, O'Hara, once a close personal friend of the dead woman, did not call to the house to sympathise with the family. Bridie had no recollection of meeting him at the funeral service or in the cemetery.

Meanwhile efforts were being made to trace Leo Gerrard, the dead woman's estranged husband, who had last been seen leaving the cottage in a rage.

Inspector John Crotty, Detective Sergeant Michael Comyns and Detective Garda Thomas Kavanagh all from Drogheda, were given the task of drawing up a list of possible suspects. A local Garda, George Delap from Navan, was also drafted onto the team because of his intimate local knowledge.

With the confirmation that the woman had been killed with a shotgun, the number of suspects was narrowed considerably. The Gardai had strong suspicions that the gun held by Larry Rogers in his builder's yard may have been used in the incident. The gun was a twelve bore double-barrelled shotgun which he kept in the yard and he was noted for not taking great care of it.

Thomas Friary from Trim, Co. Meath was another recent employee of the Rogers. He lived in one of the caravans and told Gardai the gun was normally lying around the caravans or the kitchen which was used by all the workmen.

Thomas Brennan from Nobber was also an employee. He recalled that the gun was kept in the caravans and on 7 October, the day after the killing, he remembered seeing the gun in the kitchen for the first time in two months. He had been refused permission to borrow the gun by Larry Rogers, but he subsequently took it and used his own cartridges to go shooting around his home. The gun wasn't missed.

Gardai had already marked down O'Hara as a suspect. Another man who lived at the yard called McManus would also have had similar easy access to the gun. Joseph McManus, a forty-year-old married man, was known to have been having an affair with the dead woman. Originally from Gortoral, Co. Fermanagh, he was separated from his wife and two children who were living in Co. Cavan. The McManus family had first come to Meath in 1945 when they had lodged with a Mrs Annie Kelly in Navan. They stayed until August of that year, and later the family split up. She had remained friendly with McManus after he had left her lodgings, and he often left his laundry with her.

Inspector Crotty accompanied by Detective Sergeant Delap went to Rogers' yard to collect the shotgun. The yardman, Thomas Brennan, gave it to them. Detective Sergeant Comyns broke the gun and looked down the barrels. They were slightly fouled. He held it carefully and asked the owner, Larry Rogers, to examine it. He too looked down the barrels and agreed they had been fouled. But he claimed that the gun was clean when he last saw it on the previous Saturday. The gun was then carefully wrapped and sent to Detective Superintendent Stapleton for examination.

The two Gardai asked Rogers where McManus was. He didn't know, he said, he hadn't turned in for work that day.

McManus had left the yard early in the morning, had borrowed a bike, and hadn't told anyone where he was going. He cycled to Drogheda, arriving shortly after 10 am. He went into Egan's pub, which was known as locally as McCourts, at 10.30 am. He had parked the bike in the yard and then ordered a bottle of stout at the bar. He stayed drinking until the pub closed for lunch at 1.30 that afternoon. The manager, Peter Smith, estimated that he had drunk nine or ten bottles of stout. McManus left the bar at lunch time and returned at 3 pm when it opened again. He stayed drinking alone until 6.30 pm, consuming about eight more bottles of stout. He looked like a man on a 'bit of a batter' said Peter Smith.

Detective Garda Kavanagh and Garda Delap meanwhile went to interview John O'Hara. He gave them a statement which told them where he had been on the Saturday night. Gardai were to check the statement which proved his innonence and removed suspicion from him. John Flood was his alibi for the time of the murder. He had dropped O'Hara home on the bar of his bicycle.

Meanwhile in Dublin, Detective Sergeant Edward Mooney in the fingerprints section examined the shotgun. He found three marks on the left side of the stock, but these were useless for identification purposes. Using a large magnifying glass he also noticed some minute particles of glass both inside the barrels and along the rib between the barrels on the outside. The Gardai inferred that Alice Gerrard was shot from outside the window by a shotgun.

The Gardai now had the suspect weapon, but there was no cartridge case in it when it was seized. A search of the cottage yard failed to turn up the missing cartridge case. Detective Superintendent Lawlor was now aware that McManus was missing. He regarded him as the prime suspect and therefore extended the search for the cartridge case to the surrounding countryside.

There were two routes from Flower Hill to the cottage where Alice Gerrard had met her death. One was by way of the Slane road, the other by Proudstown. Every house on both routes was visited by Gardai and the occupants were asked if they had seen McManus anytime after 1.10 am that early Sunday morning when he had last been seen in the town centre, having spent the evening drinking.

A number of people living on the Slane route had been going home in the early hours and had not seen McManus or anyone answering to his description. That left the Proudstown route. Teams of between twelve and eighteen Gardai spent ten days searching the route on their hands and knees. Every day Detective Superintendent Lawlor and Chief Superintendent Gilroy visisted the search party to check its progress. The team discovered four cartridge cases. All four were sent to Detective Superintendent Stapleton.

He was immediately able to eliminate three, as he compared them to two test cartridges fired from the suspect shotgun. But the fourth compared exactly to the test cartridge fired from the right barrel of the shotgun. Interestingly the cardboard wadding in the cartridge case also contained minute particles of glass.

These particles intrigued Stapleton. He had already proved to his satisfaction that the shotgun had been shoved through the glass pane before the trigger was pulled to discharge a shot. In the Technical Bureau he had set up a number of windows which contained similar glass to the cottage window which he had transported from Navan to the ballistics department.

When a shotgun was shoved through the window, it broke a small hole and the glass around the hole broke into a 'radial' fracture pattern.

In a pane of glass where the shot had been fired through it, there was a slightly larger hole, and the remaining glass had fractured into a 'morocco leather' pattern. Both patterns were distinctive, one a sharp spidery shape, the other rounder.

On the frame of the window taken from Alice Gerrard's bedroom, there were two semi-circular indentations of the gun barrels faintly imprinted into the glass putty. The glass had been broken by the end of the gun, as the scratch marks on the barrels proved. But why then was there glass in the barrels as far back as the cartridge case?

By Tuesday morning the Gardai had received a reply to their telegraph to Leo Gerrard telling him of the news of his wife's death. His reply from London put him in the clear. As the reply came through, detectives checked the whereabouts of his brothers in Co. Louth on the night of the murder. They too were all subsequently cleared of any suspicion. Gardai also discovered that the motor car heard 'hushing' past Alice Gerrard's house on the night of her death belonged to John Charles Farrell from Flower Hill. He had been driving a group of people to Gibbstown for a fare. He returned and had garaged the car at 12.45 am. He had met Oliver Flood and John 'The Yank' O'Hara on the road home, he told detectives.

Two of the dead woman's brothers, Nicholas and Bernard Scott, were also informed by telegram of their sister's death. But it was only when they arrived in Dun Laoghaire on the mail boat from Holyhead and bought the morning's papers that they realised she had been murdered. They were the chief mourners at the funeral along with their sister Bridie who had been given time off from the Central Hotel in Navan. A third brother, who was in the Royal Navy, could not be contacted.

The grief-stricken Mrs Scott was unable to attend the funeral Mass in St Mary's church in Navan and burial afterwards in Donoghmore. She took care of her five-month-old grandson as most of the parish attended the funeral.

Two people were missed by the family, John 'The Yank' O'Hara and Joseph McManus. The latter was still on a drinking spree in the area, although he had returned the borrowed bike without an apology or a word, late in the evening of the previous night. Around mid-day on Tuesday he had called to Mrs Evelyn French in Mabestown and asked her for work as a general labourer. She thanked him and said that she had already contracted a man from the west of Ireland.

McManus turned up again that Tuesday evening. Larry Ward was in the kitchen at Rogers' yard when he came in. McManus explained his absence saying he was away trying to get some money that he thought was owed to him. He didn't say anything else about the money, but announced he was going to Gilsenan's for cigarettes. As he walked towards the pub in Flower Hill he was met by a neighbour coming in the opposite direction. 'Isn't it terrible about Alice Gerrard being shot?' asked Michael McKeown.

'Lord have mercy on her,' he replied.

They stopped in the middle of the road and chatted for a minute as McKeown found a light for McManus's cigarette. McManus said he had been in Dublin trying to raise some money for his wife, and said nothing about going on the batter for two days. On his return to the yard he and Larry Ward drank tea. McManus told Ward that he had been told by Larry Rogers that the dead woman had been stabbed with a knife.

While McManus had been away a search party led by Inspector Crotty examined the outbuildings and the two caravans kept in Rogers' yard. Using a large magnifying glass he searched McManus's bed which was in the larger caravan. He found two tiny particles of glass on the patchwork quilt cover. There were four more tiny particles scattered on a wooden bench beside the bed. He noted the position of all six particles of glass and then put them into two separate clean white envelopes. These were sealed and sent to Detective Superintendent Stapleton. Inspector Crotty continued his search of the caravan but found no other traces of glass. He carried out the same meticulous search of the other caravan but again found nothing suspicious.

It was after 11 pm on Tuesday night that Sergeant Carr, who was near Rogers' yard met McManus as he returned to go to bed. He said that he had been in Dublin with a solicitor in Dame Street about money he was supposed to be getting back from his brother in Fermanagh and that he had spent the previous night in a truck parked outside Rogers' yard. McManus was annoyed and told

Sergeant Carr, 'I did not murder anybody. I did nothing wrong except to spend the few bob I had.'

Since the previous day an alert had been put out for McManus because Detective Superintendent Lawlor needed to interview him. Sergeant Carr sent word to the Garda station and Lawlor returned with two Gardai who were on duty. It took almost three hours to get a full statement from McManus. It was their first interview with him and it proved a difficult task to get a coherent time-tabling of his movements from the Saturday night. He constantly moved around the room, nervous at the attention he was receiving from the police.

'I was in Drogheda yesterday. If you will come with me in a car I will show you where I was. I am not a murderer anyway,' McManus told Detective Superintendent Lawlor. He said that he had been at Christy O'Brien's pub drinking and playing rings. Then he left at closing time and spent about twenty minutes speaking to a man named Jim Dolan. He then went back to his caravan to bed. It was some time between midnight and 12.30am when he got into the caravan, he estimated. He had no business in Drogheda on Monday, but took the notion into his head and he went there.

McManus signed the statement. Chief Superintendent Gilroy, who had also been present, said that at first McManus seemed very agitated as he was questioned, but gradually relaxed and cracked a joke towards the end of the interview. He said later that McManus had a 'very jiggy temperament'.

Gardai maintained a discreet watch on both McManus and O'Hara in the coming days as detectives checked the stories both men had given them.

Mrs Annie Kelly remained on 'ordinary friendly terms' with McManus after his family had moved lodgings from her house. She also knew Alice Gerrard. McManus had told Annie of his friendship with Alice and said he used to go to the house to play cards. When he left by the front door he would walk around the side of the house to her bedroom at the back, and she would let him in by the window. Earlier that month Annie had met McManus on the road to Navan and he said he wanted to talk to her. He asked her to go back to her house with him but she refused. He said he'd wait for her at home, but she wouldn't agree to this either.

She met him again on the Friday after the murder of Alice Gerrard. Later, she flatly rejected the suggestion that she had sought him out to gossip about the murder. When she called to him he asked her to draw his ration of butter, as he wouldn't go himself because the Gardai were after him.

'Over what?' she asked him.

'Over Alice Gerrard,' he replied.

He was edgy and nervous, and she was suprised to see him in this state, and she asked him if he killed Alice Gerrard. 'It is not now the rotten faggot should have been done but long ago,' he said and then added oddly, 'Hitler did not come near enough.'

He was drinking heavily again the following day and returned to his caravan at about 10pm. About twenty minutes later he was seen by Garda P.J. McEvilly coming out of Rogers' yard. He walked down the hill at a determined pace, and then halfway across Watergate Street bridge he glanced to his left, stopped, pulled his body up onto the side of the bridge and jumped into the river Blackwater.

Garda Dan Fitzpatrck was off duty and was standing on the corner of Blackcastle Avenue when he heard a shout that a man was in the river. He ran to the bridge, threw off his greatcoat and jumped. He swam out to McManus and tried to get a grip on his hand, missed him and when he recovered he saw that McManus was swimming with the current. He tried to get back to the wharf, but the current was too strong and he was swept along with it. He eventually managed to grab the branch of a tree and hung on until someone threw him a rope.

McManus was found a few minutes later further downstream, also clinging to a tree as the water swirled around him. Gardai pulled him from the teeming river and he struggled, shouting, 'I did not mean to drown myself.' McManus was given a couple of blankets in the Garda station and he stripped off and lay down on a stack of mattresses. The dispensary doctor, Richard Whyte, was called and examined him. McManus had drink taken and he was suffering from shock. He trembled violently and boasted loudly that he was a good swimmer. 'I shouted for help and there was not a man to come to my help. I could swim the Liffey. If it was twice as deep I would have come out of it. I could have been away with the band if I wanted to. I never did anything to anyone,' he said as he sat huddled in the Garda station. 'Didn't I tell you I would do away with myself? Listen, I did not drown myself. I was nearly gone. I am lost. Didn't I shout for help? There is a few bob in my old trousers.'

Meanwhile the tests on the samples of glass found in the gun and those discovered in McManus's caravan had all been made by Detective Superintendent Stapleton. They were all the same and were identical to the glass in Alice Gerrard's window.

After days of tests he was to be able to explain the reason why the glass particles had ended up in the barrels of the shotgun. When a shell is fired from a gun, it rushes from the barrel mouth leaving a small vacuum in its wake. As air rushes back into this vacuum it pulls in any tiny lightweight particles in the vicinity of the end of the barrel. There was every possibility that similar tiny glass fragments would have 'blown back' onto the clothes of the man who had fired the fatal shot through the broken window. The state chemist was called in by the Gardai to determine scientifically and prove beyond a shadow of a doubt that the glass found in the gun and the cartridge case were the same as that used in Mrs Gerrard's window.

The properties of the glass used in the window panes were silicates of sodium and calcium, the state chemist said in his report. The silica are added together in the form of sand and quartz, and to this is added carbonate or sulphate of sodium and limestone. These are then fused together in an earthenware pot in a furnace. The properties of the glass depend on the proportions in which they were mixed together and the purity of the constituents. There are two ways to identify this glass, either by its density or its index of refraction. Its density could vary from 2.23 to 2.54 times the weight of an equal volume of water. This was measured by placing the sample glass in a mixture of bromoform and benzene. The test sample would move around in the liquid. When the mix is changed by adding more of either of the two chemicals, its density changes, and this process is continued until the glass sample remains static in the liquid, indicating it had exactly the same density as that liquid. Secondly if a glass sample is placed in a liquid having the same index of refraction as itself, it appears to vanish when they are examined under the microscope. The liquid mixture for this test is made up of clove and cedar oils.

In the Navan case the index of refraction of glass taken from the pane and that found in the gun were the same, 1.5213, and the density of both samples of glass from the gun and the pane were the same, 2.510. Placed in a flame they all coloured it yellow and a colour test showed it contained sodium. 'From these results it was concluded that they were all sodium silicate crown glasses, similar in composition,' the report stated.

McManus was kept in Garda custody that night and on the following Monday he was charged with the murder of Alice Gerrard.

McManus was twice judged unfit to plead. Dr John Dunne RMS, from Grangegorman Mental Hospital in Dublin said he examined

McManus on 28 November. He believed him to be a manic depressive. He examined him again on 4 January and said he still considered him insane and unfit to plead. He subsequently examined him before his trial started on 14 January and he found him sane and fit to plead. While he awaited trial in Mountjoy jail McManus claimed 'little men' came into his cell. Dr Dunne said that he had formed the opinion that at any time McManus was not absolutely normal, but he told the trial judge that he would know the difference between right and wrong.

McManus pleaded not guilty on the first day of his trial which lasted for over two weeks. Fifty-five witnesses gave evidence for the prosecution and most of those were brought by bus each day from the Navan area to the court in Dublin city centre. There was only one witness for the defence.

On the Monday after the murder Inspector Crotty had taken a very full description of McManus from his employer. The description was accurate except that there was no account of what type of footwear McManus was wearing. The only footwear he possessed was a pair of boots and these were still in his caravan. Larry Rogers discovered that his own pair of black patent leather dancing shoes were missing. He had last seen them in the caravan under McManus's bed on the Friday before the killing.

When McManus returned it was found he was not wearing the black patent shoes, but a pair of brown shoes which were owned by Tommy Rogers, Larry's brother. They had been taken without Tommy's permission. Because the black patent shoes were missing, it was surmised that McManus could have worn them to commit the crime and then discarded them. Inspector Crotty advised the team searching the fields for cartridge cases to be on the lookout for a pair of black patent shoes. A Miss Bridget Gibney found them in her field on 10 October. The field was in a direct line between the caravan where McManus slept and Alice Gerrard's house, which was a walk of approximately thirty minutes. John Flood testified that McManus regularly walked that route across the fields when he employed him.

Prosecuting on behalf of the state, Mr R.J. McLoughlin SC said that the accused had been drinking in pubs in Navan. When the pubs closed he stayed in the town and had a cup of coffee in Flood's soda fountain cafe. He was last seen at about one o'clock by Anthony Smith who saw him walking in the direction of his caravan. He knew where the shotgun was and he also knew how to use it from his days in the Local Defence Force in Swanlinbar, Co.

Cavan. He knew that he could take the gun, use it and replace it without being caught, said Mr McLoughlin. He knew the dead woman and used to visit her until August 1946. He knew how to make his way secretly and quietly to Alice Gerrard's home. 'This crime as you will realise must have been premeditated,' he said.

The evidence was there to show that Rogers' gun had been used to carry out the murder. Glass found on his bed and beside it linked him to the gun. He lied about his whereabouts on the day after the murder and his behaviour was consistent with his being the person who brought the gun to Mrs Gerrard's home and with his being the person who committed the crime with which he was charged. The liaison with Alice Gerrard would provide the motive for the murder. This was the substance of the prosecution case.

Tommy Rogers told the court that he had received a number of letters from McManus's wife complaining to him about monics her husband owed her. He had told McManus that he had to do something about these complaints or else he'd have to find work elsewhere. McManus had been a regular visitor to Alice Gerrard's home. He knew her sister Bridget and two of her brothers. However he did not go to the funeral and ignored them when he met them after her death.

John 'The Yank' O'Hara, once a suspect, was now a leading prosecution witness. He had first known McManus when he worked at Flood's. After he left there he told McManus about his relations with Alice Gerrard which dated back to before the time all three worked together in Flood's. McManus told him that he used to visit her on Sunday nights. Those visits through the bedroom window continued after the child was born, O'Hara said McManus told him. He had also told him that Alice Gerrard had asked him to go away with her to England. He told her he had a wife and two children of his own and asked her how he could do that.

O'Hara had seen McManus in Navan town on the Saturday night Alice Gerrard had been shot. He had seen him dance a jig in the street and also saw him in Flood's soda fountain. The following day he called to Rogers' yard and spoke to McManus as he washed himself in the kitchen. McManus told him he had not sent his wife any money that week or for the past few weeks and he was afraid his failure to support her would be reported to the authorities. He was very annoyed and said he didn't know where or how he was going to get the money to send to her. He had been thinking of leaving the job and just 'going away where he would never be seen or heard tell of any more'. He had a ten shilling note and some small change and said there would be no point in sending that to his wife. He turned down O'Hara's invitation to go to Navan saying he was 'desolated with the dirt', and instead the two men went to Gilsenan's pub and had a few drinks.

Mr Vivion de Valera SC, defending McManus, said there was a complete absence of proof as to where McManus was before he retired to his caravan on the night of the crime. Was there any evidence to show that McManus had continued his liaison with Alice Gerrard? McManus had stayed in the area after the crime and there were no fingerprints or evidence to link him to the shotgun, he said. McManus was not the only person with access to the gun on that night and he asked was there anything to bring that gun closer to him than it was brought to anybody else.

In his summing up for the jury Mr Justice Overend asked them if the person who was going to commit a crime of this kind would consider doing it silently, and if so would he wear hobnailed boots or light leather shoes. Patent leather shoes seen under McManus's bed on the Friday night before the killing were next discovered in Gibney's field on 10 October. He also asked the jury to ask themselves why the shoes were found on substantially the same line as the cartridge case. He said that because of the way the shooting had happened he did not know if it was the killer's intention to shoot both the mother and the child.

The jury took four hours to reach a guilty verdict with a recommendation of mercy. When the verdict was announced the judge said he entirely agreed with it, and said the jury had given great consideration to the case and done their duty as good citizens. He then asked McManus if he had anything to say before he passed sentence on him, to which he replied, 'I want to thank your lordship and also to congratulate Mr Teevan and Mr de Valera on the grand defence they put up for me.'

Judge Overend then sentenced him to be hanged on 13 February. The case was appealed, but after a two-day hearing the case was dismissed by the Court of Criminal Appeal and McManus was ordered to be hanged. The sentence was carried out in Mountjoy jail on Monday, 31 March 1947.

10.

Murder in the Park

GARDA Michael Reynolds was rostered for night shifts at Clontarf Garda station in Dublin. He had been there for three years having spent his first two years as a Garda in Kilmainham on the south side of the city. The enthusiastic thirty-year-old came from Ballinasloe, Co. Galway. He was a broadchested man with a round, honest face and ready smile.

Michael had two brothers and two sisters, one of whom, Kathleen, was a Bangharda in Dublin's Pearse Street Garda Station. On 11 September 1975 Michael finished night duty at 6 am, went to his home in Ardmore Drive, Artane and slept for a few hours before having a late breakfast. It was pay day and he had to go to Raheny Garda Station to pick up his wages. He planned to go shopping in the city that afternoon with his wife Vera and their two-year-old daughter Emer.

On the other side of the city two men were in the car park at the front of the Hospitals Sweepstakes headquarters in Ballsbridge. A number of cars were parked there but they were only interested in a four-door car, and picked on a green 1970 Ford Cortina, registration number XZU 844. It was a company car, and had been parked there at 1.45 pm. It wouldn't be missed until its owner, Ross Connolly, finished his working day at 5 pm and left the offices to drive home. One of the men broke the lock of the driver's door, opened it and sat into the driving seat. He leaned across, lifted the locking button of the passenger door and his accomplice sat in. It took only a few moments to start the car. Both men acted casually so as to attract no attention, then drove through the silver gateway and onto the busy Merrion Road.

It was just 4 pm when the green Cortina drove up outside the Killester branch of the Bank of Ireland. Killester is on the north side, lying between Clontarf where Michael Reynolds worked and Artane where he lived.

The bank was a two-storey building, with private houses, a shop and a freezermarket to one side and a laneway on the other. The public area was confined to the ground floor. The manager's office was to the left of the entry door, the two tellers' cash boxes to the right. A large semi-circular counter ran around the room linking the tellers to the manager's office. Behind the counter almost directly opposite the front door was the large safe.

The stolen car parked outside the bank facing towards the city with its four wheels on the wide path. Three people jumped out and rushed into the bank. The driver remained behind the wheel of the car with two doors still swinging open in the rain and the engine running.

Once inside the bank, the three fanned out, shouted and produced guns and two bags made of a silky brown material. 'This is a raid,' shouted one of the men as he pointed a gun at the staff. 'Move back from the counter.' He stood at a pillar inside the door where he commanded a clear view of the bank floor. He levelled his revolver at the tellers, swivelling it from employee to employee as he watched them.

'Don't panic and nobody will get hurt,' he shouted. He had a green woollen mask pulled down to his nose. There were eyeholes cut in the mask. He had a long drooping dark moustache, and was wearing what looked like an old army combat jacket. He stood at about five feet five inches and was in his mid twenties.

There was one woman in the gang. She was thin and had long straight ash blonde hair which was so striking that one witness guessed it was a wig. The female robber carried a revolver in her left hand. She also wore a mask and a similar combat jacket with a green jumper and a pair of slacks and black shoes. She walked with a masculine stride and was aggressive. She climbed over the counter and shoved past Deirdre Stevenson, the teller in the number one cash box, knocking over a weighing scales and a blotter in her haste to grab bundles of money. She stuffed the bank notes into the bag she carried.

The manager, John Dawson, was in his office interviewing a local woman who was the only customer in the bank when the door was kicked in. 'A man stood there holding a gun in his right hand. He said "Put your hands up and no pressing alarms"', Mr Dawson recalled. The customer said she heard the wicket door opening in the counter and then the door 'just burst in'. The man's accent was difficult to distinguish: it was neither from the North nor a Dublin accent. He too was masked and was probably in his early twenties. He had long brown hair and wore a grey sports jacket. The raiders who had climbed the counter went into the open safe room, but there was no cash in it.

In the bank Patricia Horan thought she was going to faint and a colleague led her to a desk where she sat with her head in her arms. One of the male raiders who had watched her misinterpreted her actions, and called out 'Don't cry, no one will get hurt.' The three raiders had scooped up over £7,000 and some foreign currency. 'No alarms and thanks,' shouted one of the men as he turned towards the door.

It was after 3 pm when Mick Reynolds, comfortable in his casual clothes, was ready to go to town. He pulled the front door of their semi-detached house behind him as his wife sat into their beige Vauxhall Viva with their daughter. They called into Raheny Garda Station on their way and Mick picked up his pay. They set out for their first stop on the shopping trip, Dorset Street in the north city centre.

It was just after 4 pm when the Reynolds were coming abreast of the Killester shopping centre. A cassette was playing in the tape deck. The couple were unaware of the drama unfolding just hundreds of yards away from them.

The raider with the Mexican style moustache backed out of the bank, his gun covering staff as the other two ran for the car. One of the staff immediately hit the alarm button in the banking hall. In his office the manager did the same. The girl raider stumbled as she ran to the roadside rear door, and all three piled in as the driver raced the engine.

A number of people had seen the car parked on the pavement and were suspicious. One woman looked twice at the driver who sat hunched over the wheel. 'He looked like James Bellamy of "Upstairs Downstairs",' she told interviewing detectives later. Another woman thought the driver was edgy and agitated.

The bank was alarm wired to Raheny Garda Station and the Chubb monitoring headquarters. Chubb's duty officer Fintan Deegan in South Leinster Street alerted the Gardai. The Gardai received two other 999 calls about the raid within minutes of each other.

Outside the getaway car lurched onto the road as the third door slammed shut. The driver hit the accelerator and the green car surged in front of Mick Reynolds's car as it drove towards town. Reynolds had to swerve to avoid him. Reynolds hit his horn, but the getaway car was accelerating fast.

'I bet that's a stolen car,' Mick said half turning to his wife as he gave chase.

'I told him to be careful they might have guns, but he just laughed and said there was nothing to worry about,' said Vera. He had previously been a patrol car driver.

At 4.02 pm the first 999 call was logged with the Garda control room in Dublin Castle. Five Garda cars were raised on their car radios, the local crime patrol cars Juliets one and two, and cars from the neighbouring Coolock, Whitehall and Ballymun stations. As they sped to the scene with sirens blaring the radio dispatcher was reading them out a description of the car and its plate number. A fourteen-year-old boy who was passing saw the raiders leave, and a potato delivery man delivering a few doors away saw the near collision and also wrote down the registration number.

A third car also joined the chase. It was driven by Oliver Byrne, a wholesaler from Raheny who had seen the gang run from the bank. Garda Reynolds blew the horn on his car continually. Inside the getaway car there was panic. The three raiders shouted and screamed at the driver, urging him to go faster. There were no traffic lights on the route — suggesting it had been preplanned. They turned into Dunseverick Road, left onto Castle Grove, left again onto Castle Avenue, right onto Vernon Avenue, and then left at Sybil Hill Road.

In the third car, Oliver Byrne was losing ground. He eventually lost them, but as he was from the area he guessed they would come out at Castle Grove. He waited at a junction and was proved correct. He gunned the engine and vowed to stick to their tail, doing almost 60 mph through the suburban streets.

Beside St Paul's College the Cortina turned into St Anne's Park followed by Garda Reynolds. They drove along the main avenue accelerating all the time.

Mr Byrne stopped his car outside the Park, then turned back to the bank to alert the Gardai. He had to knock to get in and told detectives who had already arrived at the scene what had happened. They ran to their car and radioed for support.

A thirteen-year-old girl, Lucia McMahon, was in the park when she saw the Cortina racing up the avenue, a cul de sac, and take a corner on two wheels. The car's speed increased until it reached the end of the avenue when the driver jammed on the brakes and the car slid to a halt under a grove of trees. The four jumped out and Vera Reynolds could see the driver. He had long black hair with a black moustache and wore a medium-length coat. She guessed he was in his twenties.

Mick Reynolds had his own door opened before the car had even stopped. Three of the occupants of the getaway car ran along a pedestrian walk. Mick Reynolds chased the fourth, the driver who tried to escape across the grass. Vera Reynolds stayed in the car minding the child. All five were out of sight within seconds.

'My husband went after them and I waited in the car with Emer. I was waiting only a few minutes when I thought I heard a shot, but I wasn't sure. I thought it might have come from the cassette which was playing in the car.'

Two local children, Brian Collins and Coleman Burke, saw three people running. One man was outpacing the other two runners, the second man kept pulling along the third person who had long blonde hair and a 'girlish face' and could have been a woman said the two boys. Lucia McMahon saw all four fugitives running. One carried a suitcase. Moments later she heard the same sound Vera Reynolds had heard.

The woman raider was running with a bag of money clutched in her left hand and a revolver in her right hand. The safety catch was off. She had the second gun in the pocket of her jacket. As they ran from the car she saw a man running from the trees in their direction to cut them off. He looked fit, and she was already beginning to tire. As they ran along the bank of the small river Nanikin which flowed through the Park, Garda Reynolds made a diving tackle on the male raider and they fell to the ground struggling. The woman screamed 'Let go my fellow,' and shot Garda Reynolds. A bullet from the Colt .45 smashed into the off-duty Garda. As he lay on the ground the man and woman ran off, leaving him lying on the bank of the stream.

He was found by Raymond Baragy who was in the park with a friend when he saw the chase. He saw a man jump from the yellowish car and chase one of the four people running from the Cortina. After the driver and the man chasing him had disappeared he heard a shot. He went over to the Vauxhall Viva and asked Mrs Reynolds what was happening and then followed Garda Mick Reynolds. He found him lying on the far bank of the stream with his legs in the water. There was nobody in sight.

Detective Garda Jim O'Malley of the drugs squad, Liam Byrne and Noel Clarke were the first members of the force at the scene of the shooting. They had been patrolling in the Fairview area when they heard the Garda radio control centre's bank alert. They had been directed to the Park, and were to radio for an ambulance.

Gerard Bell and Brian McGeehan of the Dublin Fire Brigade were in the ambulance that answered the radio alert. They were escorted to the spot where Garda Reynolds lay. He was still alive but bleeding profusely from a wound in the head. His pulse was feeble.

Gardai, plain clothesed and uniformed, were arriving in the area by the minute.

Mrs Reynolds stood by the car for twenty long anxious minutes, waiting for her husband to come back. 'A plain clothes Garda came along and I asked him if my husband Mick was alright. He said he didn't know my husband but there was a man lying in a pool of blood in the ditch. I knew it was Mick.'

Inspector John Duff from Raheny Garda Station had gone to the Killester bank immediately after the robbery. While there he learned that a man had been injured in a shooting incident which was connected to the bank raid. He immediately went to St Anne's Park. As he arrived at the entrance gates he met the ambulance as it sped towards St James's Hospital in the city centre.

The tree-lined avenue on which the chase had taken place was over one and a half miles in length. To the right of Inspector Duff as he drove along the avenue was the famous Rose Garden, to his left the pitch and putt course, and in the distance he could see the old clock tower. In addition to those officially despatched to the scene, members of the force from throughout the city were arriving, anxious to do anything to help. The shooting of a Garda was something they all took personally. By evening time it was estimated that over a hundred Gardai were involved in the manhunt, at the scene and in the immediate vicinity.

Even as the ambulance was leaving the Park, the getaway car had received its first cursory examination. It showed that the gang which had carried out the raid were wearing disguises. A false beard and a false moustache were found in the back seat along with a woman's handbag and a number of other items.

Teams of search parties began to comb the 260-acre Park which included forty-five soccer pitches, eighteen tennis courts, a pitch and putt course and car parks as well as shrubberies and grassy open spaces. They were to be backed up later in the evening by troops and an Air Corps helicopter.

Tracker dogs were brought to the scene in the hope of picking up a scent. The Technical Bureau also arrived and within the hour were organising the first search parties.

Four fingerprint experts and one photographer were despatched to the Bank of Ireland in Killester. One mapper, one photographer, two ballistics men and one fingerprint expert were sent to St Anne's Park.

Under Detective Chief Superintendent John Joy the park was surrounded and a search of the ground commenced. A van with a loudspeaker toured the park urging everyone to leave immediately. As people filed out of the park gates they were checked by Gardai. Roadblocks were set up around the city as motorists were checked. The descriptions of four people were broadcast on RTE and the following morning's papers carried the descriptions and an appeal for information.

A total of forty-five detectives were pulled from other duties and assigned to the dual crime. The senior detectives investigating the incidents under Chief Superintendent Joy were Detective Inspectors Hubert Reynolds, Paddy Culligan, Myles Hawkshaw and John Courtney. An incident room was established in Raheny Garda Station.

At Jervis Street Hospital a desperate battle was being waged to save the life of Garda Reynolds. He was unconscious when admitted to the casualty department within half an hour of the shooting. An immediate operation was undertaken but was unsuccessful. Garda Michael Reynolds died at 6.10 pm that evening. Vera Reynolds heard the awful news at home. She hadn't gone to the hospital as she had been told her husband would be alright.

He was the second Garda to be shot dead in the 1970s, and the twenty-first shot dead in the line of duty since the foundation of the force. The last fatal shooting of a Garda prior to the Killester incident had also been a bank robbery. On 3 April 1970 Garda Richard Fallon of Lorcan Drive, Santry, a forty-four-year-old father of five, was shot as he tried to stop four armed men who had held up the Royal Bank of Ireland at Arran Quay in Dublin.

The female bank robber had run through the park and evaded the Garda dragnet. There were sixteen official public entrances and exits to the park, but many more unofficial ones. As she crossed the road to stand at a bus stop a squad car passed her by. She stood nervously at the bus stop, then boarded a number 29A bus, and returned home. Her husband was one of the raiders too, and he arrived home before her.

She listened to news bulletins with growing horror. 'I heard on Radio Eireann that a Garda had been shot. First they said he was critical. Later they said he was dead. I was dazed for a time. I will never forget that man 'til the day I die — just crumpled up.'

Among the people who went to the park that day was Jack Marrinan, the general secretary of the Garda Representative Association.

'Essentially we are an unarmed force and I think that the public outrage which will follow the killing of this officer will be a protection for our members in the future,' he said. He paid tribute to the dead man and condemned the shooting. 'The whole force is shaken by it. Our entire resources will have to be mustered and put into operation to ensure that this is the last of these abominable crimes.'

The debate about arming the Gardai has surfaced at regular intervals — mostly prompted by a particularly violent incident — since the unarmed force was first established in 1922. The Commissioner, Edmund Garvey, had just started in his new post nine days earlier. By coincidence he had given an interview to *The Irish Times* after his appointment, and it was printed two days after the shooting. In it the new Commissioner spoke of the upsurge in armed robberies and the decrease in the murder rate. 'When you come to talk about armed robberies you must remember two things; there are very few people who are not afraid of the gun, and secondly even though we are law abiding in Ireland we are not very security conscious.'

A hard-working, religious man and a member of the force since 1939 when he was twenty-four years of age, he spoke of the respect unarmed Gardai had been earning since the force was founded and voiced his view that Gardai should remain unarmed. After the shooting of Garda Reynolds he said, 'He was one of the finest men we had. He showed great courage in anything he did and nothing would deter him from his duty. In following the killers he showed a complete disregard for his own safety.'

The post mortem was carried out that evening by Dr Niall Gallagher, the consultant pathologist in Jervis Street Hospital. There were no flesh burns or powder marks made by the gunshot. The entry wound was slightly irregular and had penetrated the head at the frontal bone of the skull on the left hand side of the forehead. It had caused multiple fractures of the skull. Death, concluded the post mortem report, was due to laceration of the brain associated with fracture of the skull due to a gunshot wound.

The bullet was retrieved for forensic examination. Forensic studies have shown that the lack of black soot and tatooing marks made by tiny fragments of unburnt powder driven into the skin around such a wound suggest that the bullet was fired at a range of over two feet. A gunshot wound and the marks around it can help identify the range and type of weapon used, but in cases where a handgun is used the range of markings are only illustrative of distances of less than two feet from the mouth of the gun.

The getaway car was sealed and taken by tow wagon to the Technical Bureau. Within minutes of the Hospital Sweeps reporting one of their cars missing, Gardai interviewed its driver, Ross Connolly. After the car had been forensically examined for hair, fingerprints and other evidence, he identified his family's belongings from items found in the car.

Among the items that the raiders had left behind were a lady's dark blue handbag, a biro, a fifty pence piece, some paper with handwriting on it, a false moustache and beard, a blue coat button and a lady's hairbrush.

The search of the park continued through the weekend. The Gardai's meticulous search of the murder scene turned up many items. Two knives, two gloves and other bits and pieces were found to have no evidential value but were put through the same stringent examination procedure before being eliminated from the inquiry.

The following morning, Friday the 12th, the cabinet met. Top of the agenda was the shooting of the unarmed Garda. After the meeting Justice Minister Patrick Cooney announced the government's offer of a £20,000 reward for information leading to the arrest and conviction of the killers. It was the largest ever reward offered by the state.

The cabinet had not discussed the question of arming the Gardai, which he said was a move the members of the force themselves were against. The best deterrent to criminals is the certainty of apprehension and punishment. 'Those who have introduced this cult of the gun into Irish society have a lot to answer for,' said Mr Cooney. Proportionate amounts of the sum would be paid for information of value to the Gardai in the hunt, he explained, before calling to visit Mrs Reynolds in her home.

The printing section of the Technical Bureau churned out 'Reward' posters which were distributed to Garda stations throughout the country. The posters listed four Dublin phone numbers the public could contact, or alternatively any local Garda station. Members of the Garda sub aqua unit joined the search teams in the park to trawl through the waters of the two ponds and the river for the murder weapon and possible clues. Mechanical diggers were called in to help clear dense undergrowth in the area where the body was found.

In Killester, Gardai took statements from members of the banking staff. Other teams of Gardai were carrying out questionnaire interviews of people in the area. A watch had been put on all sea and airports in case the gang tried to leave the country. Senior

163

investigators believed the killers were lying low in the country, but no chances were being taken that they would evade the dragnet.

The Provisional IRA issued a statement saying it wished it to be known that no members of their organisation were involved in the bank raid or shooting. The Provos' decision to issue the statement was a sign of the intensity of the Garda investigation, as touts were contacted and suspected members of the organisation throughout the country questioned. The Provisionals have always been quick to deny any involvement in such serious crimes where massive Garda operations in their aftermath bring unwanted attention on their members and make life uncomfortable.

On the day after the shooting questions were being asked about Garda Reynolds's actions. Was he on duty and was he empowered to act? A spokesman for the force said that a Garda is always on duty. Even when not rostered he still maintains his power of arrest. It was a point that was to be discussed subsequently as the question arose as to whether the shooting constituted a capital crime or not.

That evening the removal of the body of the murdered Garda took place to Saint Paul's Church, Mount Argus, Harold's Cross. The state, government and its institutions turned out in a massive demonstration of solidarity with the Garda Siochana at both the removal and the funeral. The Taoiseach, Mr Liam Cosgrave, and the Minister for Posts and Telegraphs, Dr Conor Cruise O'Brien, attended the short service and afterwards spoke to Mrs Reynolds. Two Garda land-rovers were piled high with wreaths and floral tributes from Garda stations all over the country and the Garda Representative Association. Wreaths were also sent by the Bank of Ireland.

The following morning at 10 am the funeral mass was held. The Garda choir sang and six colleagues from Clontarf Garda Station acted as pall bearers. Three station wagons carried wreaths from Ireland and from police forces throughout the world. The coffin was draped in the tricolour. A small bunch of pink roses lay on top of the coffin. The attached card simply read 'To Daddy from Emer'.

Along the route through Dublin city, through Lucan, Kinnegad and to Ballinasloe, Co. Galway thousands paid their respects at the sides of the road. In Ballinasloe, the Commissioner marched behind the coffin in front of a large contingent of Gardai. Several thousand people attended the burial. The Garda band led the funeral procession playing the 'Dead March', 'Wrap the Green Flag Around Me' and 'Nearer my God to Thee'.

The principal celebrant, Fr Clarence Daly, the acting Garda chaplain described Garda Reynolds as a courageous man. 'It was this dedication to duty that dictated his actions on Thursday afternoon. He was a dedicated man, a brave man, a fearless man,' he said.

The Gardai's questionnaires and taking of statements were producing results. Reliable descriptions of the gang members were being fitted together gradually. More information was coming in by phone, sometimes from anonymous callers, sometimes people prompted by the offer of a reward, others prompted simply by their civic spirit.

Within a few hours of the shooting Garda telephonists had logged over a hundred calls. Days later, after the reward offer, Detective Chief Superintendent Joy estimated that the number of calls taken in connection with the shooting had exceeded a thousand. 'It is too soon yet to say whether any of the messages will be of value but we are carefully checking out all tip-offs,' he said.

Those tip-offs varied greatly in both detail and relevance. Some came from people in the Killester area or in the park at the time of the shooting. A number came from members of the underworld with snippets of information and a request for money. Others were from householders suspicious of their neighbours. One of the unexpected but welcome effects of the flood of information from the public was that detectives were able to solve a number of outstanding cases with information that turned out to be irrelevant to the Reynolds investigation but was otherwise useful.

Gardai decided to issue details of the people they were searching for in a bid to trace them beyond the killing zone. They knew the gang had worn disguises, so the descriptions they issued to the public concentrated on unalterable details rather than have the public hunting for bearded and mustachioed bandits when clearly their quarry were clean shaven.

At about 4.20 pm on the day of the killing two men had been seen together in St Anne's Park, near the junction of Watermill Road and James Larkin Road. They split up and one of them ran along by the football pitches towards Raheny village. He was described as twenty-one to twenty-three years of age, five feet seven inches or five feet eight inches in height with black, shoulder-length, fluffy hair, sallow complexion, medium build. He wore glasses with black square rims and was wearing a black jacket probably made of leather. He was carrying a briefcase.

The second man went across the park in the direction of the boundary wall at the junction of Watermill road and James Larkin

Road. He was described as in his early twenties, five feet ten inches to five feet eleven inches with fair hair, pale complexion and slim build. He was wearing a light blue polo neck sweater and blue jeans.

At approximately the same time a man was seen walking along the causeway joining James Larkin Road to the Bull Island near its boundary with St Anne's golf links. He was walking on the grass although it was raining heavily at the time. He was described as in his early twenties, about five feet eight inches or five feet nine inches of proportionate build wearing a blue pullover and dark pants. He had short sidelocks and his hair was saturated with rain. His hair was a darkish colour.

Four days after the incident the photofit pictures of three of the four gang members were circulated in the media and to all Garda stations. Gardai also appealed for three witnesses who were seen outside the bank to come forward as they wanted to interview them: a woman with a ponytail wearing a black pvc raincoat; a woman pushing a pram and the man who accompanied her.

The search of the park turned up a number of pieces of evidence. A pair of sun-glasses, a balaclava and a wig, a black leather glove, two false moustaches, a blue macintosh and — most importantly — a spent cartridge case were all found near the abandoned getaway car. The bullet case was found within the first hour of the search getting underway at the scene of the shooting.

It was an exhaustive inquiry. Senior investigating officers briefed the Commissioner on a daily basis telling him that it was slow work and that there was little likelihood of any immediate development.

For instance one of the labour-intensive aspects of the investigation was an effort to trace the false wigs and moustaches and to identify the owners of the clothing and the woman's handbag. That meant detectives checking out theatrical shops and joke and novelty shops with the same wearying questions. Do you sell items like these, when did you sell them, who did you sell them to, what did they look like, do you know their names, do you know where they live now, do you know any other shops that sell false wigs or moustaches?

The same small teams of men were also trying to track down the other items found in the getaway car.

Recently rented houses were also being checked out on the theory that the gang could have holed up together.

Detectives also drew up a list of suspects based on their own intelligence files and criminal records. Some of the suspects had been involved in previous armed robberies, others were suspected of involvement, others still had been seen consorting with previously armed criminals, and some had connections with the IRA and consequently had access to guns.

Mrs Christina Doyle, an elderly attendant in the ladies public toilets on Marine Road, Dun Laghaoire, was at work four days after the shooting. As she entered one of the cubicles to clean it she noticed a large brown paper laundry bag. Suspicious but pressed for time she put it into her locker deciding to examine it later. It was the first break in the case. It wasn't until after 10 pm that night that she examined the contents of the bag. It was from Terenure laundry on the south side of the city and contained two chocolate-coloured pillow cases of a silky type material, a false moustache, a grey woollen balaclava helmet, two sections of a green woollen material, a gaberdine jacket and some Bank of Ireland paper cash bags. A single one pound note fell from one of the pillow slips when it was opened.

The huge publicity and the massive public outcry following the shooting alerted her to the possible importance of her find, and she put it back into her locker and contacted the local Gardai. They collected it and passed it onto the Technical Bureau for examination.

The toilets were beside a bus stop and close to the Sealink terminal and the railway line. The discovery of the bag at the far side of the city suggested a number of things — that the gang lived or had business in Dun Laoghaire, that they knew the area, or that they could have travelled there by public transport. The same railway line also ran close to St Anne's Park on the North side. There was the further possibility that they had fled the country, dumping the bag in the toilet before boarding the ship to Wales — although this was considered unlikely as the bag could have been more easily disposed of at sea simply by dropping it overboard.

On the list of possible suspects was a husband and wife team. The man, Noel Murray, was twenty-five years of age, Marie his wife a year older. They were on the list of suspects drawn up on the basis of past form and likely access to weapons.

Noel was born in Celbridge, Co. Kildare, and was the youngest of a family of seven. He was apprenticed to CIE as a metal fabricator, and was with them for six years before working in Tallaght with a firm of fabricators. He was on the run for the past year with a warrant out for his arrest on charges of possession of explosives and firearms, and robbery. He met his wife at an Official Sinn Fein meeting and they had married in 1973. They had no children. He had a slight build, with bony features and fashionable long hair.

His wife Marie was born in Castlepollard, Co. Westmeath. She was adopted as a child, but when both parents died, she was taken into care by a family in Co. Clare. She seemed set to become a daughter to be proud of: she was intelligent, achieved five honours in her Leaving Certificate, and got a steady job in the civil service. She worked in the Department of the Gaeltacht for nine years until she left in 1973 when she married. She was remembered as a round-faced chubby girl with poor eyesight. Eight months after their marriage she was charged with receiving £500 taken in an armed robbery. She pleaded guilty to the charge of receiving, and was sentenced to two years imprisonment suspended on her keeping the peace for two years. Her husband was wanted in connection with that robbery.

Information was given to the murder hunt that the Murrays had been living in the Ranelagh area of the city, the southside flatland. Detectives swamped the area, checking with business premises and other people who might have known their whereabouts. Dozens of premises were checked out by the teams of detectives and gradually the net spread wider throughout Dublin 6 and Dublin 4 and then nearer to the city centre until a man identified Marie Murray from a picture a detective showed him. But that wasn't the name she was using, he said.

It was another week before the government's reward prompted the information that the Gardai needed. The new name Marie Murray was using was Ann Finlay. Their information also gave them an address near Dun Laoghaire, information that tied in with the discovery of the dumped bag of robbery equipment. However the address proved to be incorrect, and it took more vital time before No. 15 Grangemore Estate, Raheny was pinpointed.

It transpired that although Marie Murray lived on the north-side she continued to take the train across town to shop in the Dun Laoghaire area where she had previously lived.

Three detective inspectors led by Myles Hawkshaw of the Special Detective Unit based in Dublin Castle — which normally deals with subversive crime — led the raid on the Murray's home. It was timed for 7.30 am in the morning. Back-up came from one detective sergeant and six detective Gardai. There was no response to their demand to open up and so they forced the door. A quick search showed that no one was home, so they hid themselves in the house to await the return of the occupants.

The house was a rented, two-storey semi-detached off the main estate road in a cul-de-sac. In November 1974 the owner Sean

Kiernan was emigrating to Canada, and decided to set the house. He advertised in the *Evening Press* and a woman called Ann Finlay answered his advert, saying she was willing to pay the £60 a month rental, which was to be paid into his bank account. She said her husband was working in England and she was living in a flat in Monkstown. Two days before the Garda raid Kiernan had returned to the house to say he was home, and would be taking possession on the 17th of the month and gave them notice to quit. Fair enough, said Marie, they had put a deposit down on a house they were going to buy.

Detective Garda Brian Kelly from the Criminal Detective Unit was in the upstairs bedroom looking out to the front of the house when he saw the Murrays arriving at approximately 8 am. They had been walking their Alsatian dog. Noel walked up to the front door, turned the key in the lock and went into the house followed by his wife Marie. They were met by Gardai armed with revolvers and machine guns.

Noel Murray was searched by Inspector Hawkshaw who took a gun and a matchbox containing a number of bullets from one of Murray's pockets. A second gun was found in another pocket. Marie Murray was searched by a Bangharda who found a screwdriver, a pair of pincers and a purse in the pockets of her anorak.

Hawkshaw cautioned Noel Murray and asked him if he had any other guns or weapons in the house. Murray led them upstairs and pointed out where he had hidden a gun under the mattress of the double bed in the back bedroom. He was not the owner of the gun but he had put it there, he said. He had no firearms certificate for either gun, he added. Murray also brought him to a hot press and showed him an ashtray, which held some detonators. He had rented the house in the name of John Finlay and told the landlord he was a writer.

The raid was well timed. In eight days' time they would have gone, and the trail would have gone cold. The couple were taken to different Garda stations in the city for questioning. Detective Inspector William Byrne of the Technical Bureau had supervised a search of the Bank of Ireland in Killester and now organised a search of the Murray home.

Drawers were emptied, furniture moved and the attic checked in a search that went on until the late afternoon. One of the most dangerous discoveries made in the house were two copper pipe bombs and six fuses. These were made by stuffing a pipe with explosive and beating both ends flat to make a package, and then inserting a fuse and letting it protrude from one end. He also found a large blue suitcase which contained two bags, one of paper and one of plastic. They were stuffed with bundles of money. He estimated there were thousands of pounds in the case in Irish currency notes. There was also some foreign currency.

Detective Sergeant John Garavan had twelve years' experience of fingerprints behind him in the Technical Bureau. He had attended courses at both Scotland Yard and the St Andrew's police headquarters in Glasgow. He had tested the Killester bank for fingerprints but had been unsuccessful. Now he watched as Detective Inspector Byrne opened the suitcase and took out the cash bags. They contained bundles of banknotes which were bound together with rubber bands which had slips of paper shoved under them with figures written on each of the slips. He was subsequently able to develop fingerprints on four of the slips and one palm mark on the brown paper bag. There were no marks on the plastic bag.

He tested the four pieces of paper which were used to bind the notes for fingerprints and found that, after enlarging them photographically, the prints on three of them had been made by Noel Murray's left thumb. There were twelve points of similarity between the scraps of paper and the fingerprint form on which Noel Murray's prints had been taken when he was held in custody. He also found Marie Murray's right thumb print on another piece of the paper and he was satisfied that a palm mark taken from the paper bag which had been in the suitcase had been made by Marie Murray's left hand.

On 10 October Detective Sergeant Garavan brought the cash with Detective Sergeant Diggin to the Bank of Ireland in Killester where two officials counted out the money into bundles. It totalled £7,576 and $28. Detective Sergeant Diggin had also searched the Murrays' house on 8 October and found six sticks of Frangex, a brown explosive from the dynamite family, in the bottom drawer of the kitchen fridge. Lt Col James McDevitt from McKee Barracks in Dublin was subsequently given the explosives after a sample had been preserved for forensic examination. He detonated it that day at Kilbridge military firing range and was able to write a report saying the explosives were in good condition.

Detective Sergeant Diggin was also present when the Colt .45 was retrieved from the bedroom. During the search he also found a book on theatrical make-up, which told how appearances could be changed, and two American dollar bills. In the drawers of a room divider he found a spent cartridge case and a live round of ammunition, a spool of blue grey thread and a red hairbrush.

A bank official in Killester, Patricia Horan, the cashier who felt weak during the robbery and had to be helped to a chair, identified figures written in biro on the banknotes as her writing. The hairbrush was later traced to a local shop in Donaghmede where the shop assistant remembered Marie Murray also purchasing hair colourants.

The forensic evidence was slowly mounting up.

On the day of the raid, bags of items taken from the Murray home were being delivered in relays to the forensic laboratory. Dr Jim Donovan, its director, also visited the scene that day for a first-hand examination. Among the exhibits delivered by Detective Sergeant Diggin were a sample of the Frangex found in the fridge, a lady's plaid coat found in the attic, other pieces of clothing, a green combat jacket, a hairbrush, a reel of thread, a false beard, moustache and sidelocks, two hair nets and a bottle of mastic gum.

Dr Donovan also received the bullet taken from the body of Garda Reynolds, a .45 cartridge case found at the scene of the shooting and a .45 bullet found at the Grangemore Estate. The bullets had the same colouring, shape, weight, diameter and metal content. The bullet taken from the head of the dead man and the one found in the house were both composed mainly of silver and copper. There was only a slight difference in weight but this was probably because the bullet used in the killing had lost some metal when it struck bone. He concluded that the indications were not only that they were similar but came from the same factory batch. The cartridge cover found at the scene had strikingly similar characteristics to bullets found at Grangemore Estate and he said he believed it too was from the same batch.

Dr Donovan spent days examining the articles brought to him in the laboratory before clearly establishing a link between the four sites; the park, the getaway car used in the robbery, the toilet in Dun Laoghaire and the Murrays' home. Adhesive found on the false moustache found in the toilet was the same as that used with the moustaches and beards found in St Anne's Park. The same adhesive was also used on the beard found in the getaway car, and similarly on false sidelocks and a false beard found in the Murray home in Grangemore Estate.

Stains made by this adhesive were also found on the sleeve and in the right-hand pocket of the jacket which was found in the toilet. Similar adhesive stains were also found on the sun-glasses, the mirrors of the powder compact, the car, and a black glove found in St Anne's Park.

The beard taken from the car matched one of the moustaches taken from the park in colour and composition. The fibres used to make the false beards, moustaches and sidelocks were all so unusual that they could not be expected to occur coincidentally, concluded Dr Donovan.

A tiny bottle containing some of the adhesive was found in the handbag in the getaway car and a bottle of the same fluid adhesive was also found in the Murrays' house. Chemical tests identified the adhesive as one sold under the name 'Mastix spirit gum'. It was not commonly available, and had limited uses as it was a very light adhesive. Dr Donovan explained that the difficulty in using it might explain the staining on a number of items, including the glove.

The green cloth material found in the toilet was the same as that used in the balaclava found in St Anne's Park. Each item had the same composition, with the same dye and the same stitch in the knitted material. In addition, some stray acrylic fibres found on each piece suggested a common origin. The cloth probably originally came from a garment such as a scarf.

The pale mauve thread used to sew a tear in the brown jacket found in the toilet was the same thread as used to sew together the top of the balaclava helmet, he wrote in his final report.

The pair of sun-glasses found in the car were similar to the pair found near the body of Garda Reynolds.

Man-made fibres found in the car on the hairbrush with the black handle were the same thickness and colour and composition of the fibres used to make the wig found in the park. Human hair found on the hairbrush was the same colour and thickness as hair found on the hairbrush in the house as well as the hair on the collar of the plaid coat found in the attic.

The large blue button found in the car matched the buttons on the lady's blue plaid coat found in the attic in Grangemore Estate. The top button of the coat was missing. The button was the same in all respects as the buttons remaining on the coat. The thread ends were jagged, suggesting it had been torn from the coat. The buttons were similar in colour, the number of thread holes, their design, and their size and composition. The buttons were also unusual and distinctive.

A long red nylon fibre entangled in the bristles of the brush found in the car was the same as the fibre found entangled in the bristle of a red hairbrush found in the house, and may have come from a red nightdress found in the house. A number of pine-needles were found among the grit from the car and were similar to those found in the pocket of the green combat jacket in the house. These were sent to UCD for microscopic testing by natural history scientists there.

The left-hand black glove found in St Anne's Park was part of a pair with the right-hand glove found in the Murrays' house. There were a number of similarities: the black material was the same composition and design and had white lining; the white cotton thread used to sew the seams was the same in each glove; the fastening stud on each glove was red and had the legend 'Newey — England' stamped on the inner surface. In addition the degree of wear and tear on both gloves was the same, they were of the same size, and most convincingly of all each glove was stained with the light adhesive found on the false beard, moustaches and sidelocks.

The thread in the green balaclava found in the park had the same colour, composition, thickness and dye as the reel of pale mauve thread found in the Murrays' home. The thread was also similar to that used to sew the jacket found in the toilet and the balaclavas. Dr Donovan's forensic evidence had linked the four locations together through the disguises, the adapted balaclava-type masks and other evidence.

The .45 Colt pistol was subjected to rigorous testing by Detective Sergeant Timothy Jones of the ballistics section of the Technical Bureau. He carried out tests using the ammunition found in the Murrays' home in the Grangemore Estate, and estimated that powder burning of the skin could take place only at a range of over thirty inches. The bullets found in Grangemore were of a slightly smaller calibre than those normally fired from such a gun, and had a smaller propellant charge. Consequently there would be less marking of the bullet in the barrel and the gun would be less accurate. He had carried out tests on the gun, and found it accurate to twenty-five yards, but at fifty yards it pulled about eight inches to the right.

The gun had two safety catches. One was on the left-hand side of the gun, the other on the butt. Both were in perfect working order. His tests showed that it was impossible for the gun to go off accidentally. The pressure a gunman would have to use to pull back the trigger was seven pounds. The normal pressure on similar weapons was five and a half to six pounds. This meant that the gun was in fact safer than similar marques.

It was not possible to say whether the bullet taken from Garda Reynolds had been fired by the pistol. However, the marks found on the spent cartridge case near the body were consistent with having been ejected from the gun. The gun had an erratic trajectory of spent cartridges.

Noel Murray was brought to Harcourt Terrace Garda Station where he was again cautioned by Inspector Hawkshaw who asked him if he was the owner of the gun. Murray replied that he wasn't and that he had been keeping it for another person.

Detective Inspector Edward Ryan said that at Harcourt Terrace Garda Station he had told Noel Murray that he believed he could help their investigation into the bank robbery and the shooting of a Garda. 'I can't help you, I can't help you,' Murray said. He asked Murray what had he been doing on 11 September, and Murray had said he had brought his Alsatian pup for a walk and had then watched television and read. 'I knew this day would come sooner or later. Is it possible for me to speak to my wife? I don't know what to do. If I could speak to my wife first I would know what to do.'

Inspector Ryan explained that as soon as it was possible she would be brought to the station. At about 3.30 pm he left Murray, taking his clothes from him for examination by the Technical Bureau. Murray was given a new set of clothes.

Marie Murray had been taken to Ballymun Garda Station for questioning. But she refused to answer, saying she would talk only to Detective Inspector John Finlay. He was an experienced detective stationed in Donnybrook, and had had previous dealings with Marie from the time she and her husband lived in Ranelagh. She cried when he came into the interviewing office and then composed herself. He said that he wanted to know about the murder of Garda Reynolds. 'I will tell you a lot about it, but not everything,' she told him.

He asked her who had carried out the robbery. 'Noel and I and two others,' she said before breaking into tears. It was to take some time before Marie Murray spoke about the murder. 'I will tell you everything but the circumstances make it impossible to tell you that,' she said when asked who had fired the gun. Detective Inspector Finlay decided to jog her memory and her conscience with a return visit to the park, the scene of the murder.

Bangharda Noeleen Firth who had searched her that morning gave her the loan of a coat and head scarf. Detective Inspectors Finlay and Reynolds and Bangharda Firth accompanied Marie Murray. It was 10.30 am. They drove from the station in the unmarked car to the Murrays' rented house at Grangemore Estate, and she then directed them from there to the Bank in Killester and then to St Anne's Park. Marie gazed out of the window for much of the journey.

They got out of the car in St Anne's Park and asked Marie to show them the scene. She refused, saying 'I am not going to walk into that park.'

Inspector Finlay asked Marie if she was aware that a car had been chasing them. 'I was aware of it because there was a lot of excited talk and shouting in the car,' she replied.

They returned to Coolock Garda Station, where Inspector Finlay interviewed her alone. Bangharda Firth asked Marie Murray did she want something to eat. 'Just a cup of tea,' she said, explaining that she hadn't been able to eat for the past month. 'I'm glad it's all over. It shouldn't have happened.'

It was just after 1 pm. Detective Inspector Finlay asked her to make a statement and she agreed. He spent the next four hours writing down the statement. When it was finished he read it out to her. She initialled some alterations, but said she wouldn't sign the statement for the time being. At the end of the statement in her own writing she wrote, 'I have read over this statement with Detective Inspector Finlay. The only correction I wish to make is that in the Bank of Ireland there were two teller's boxes and only I, and I only, entered one of them and the big safe. The statement is correct otherwise. I do not intend to sign the statement now, but maybe later.'

She told Detective Inspector Reynolds she wouldn't sign the statement because 'Noel would be mad with me if I signed it. I would prefer not to. He told me to never sign a statement,' she said.

Detective Inspector Reynolds asked her to identify a number of items. The first was a wig which she had last seen worn by Noel 'on 11 September'. She identified false moustaches worn by the men during the bank raid, a zip jacket worn by her husband, and pillow cases and balaclavas which were similar to the ones they had used in the raid.

The handbag found on the back seat of the car was hers, as well as a leather purse and a blue button which had probably come from the coat she was wearing during the raid. She also identified the items she had left in the toilet in Dun Laoghaire, a blue suitcase which had been used to store the bank haul, and bundles of money it contained.

The statement said that both she and her husband had been unemployed since early 1974. A few days before 11 September they had met two men, and the four of them planned to rob the Bank of Ireland in Killester. The men were to provide the car, they would provide the guns.

They arranged to meet in St Anne's Park on the afternoon of the 11th. She left home between 2 and 3 pm that day with her husband. As they waited in the park for their accomplices they walked around some new tree plantations. One of the men met them near the trees, and they went with him to join the third man in the stolen car which had been brought to the park.

'Noel, one of the men and myself entered the bank by the front door. The other man and myself scrambled over the counter. I had a woollen mask and a long-haired blonde wig. I had one of the two guns I have already mentioned and a soft bag rolled up. I wore slacks and a green pullover. I scooped up all the currency notes in the tellers' boxes. I also entered the open safe room, but I got nothing there.

'Noel stayed outside the counter all the time. Nobody gave us any opposition at the bank. The three of us ran from the bank to the car where the other man was waiting behind the steering wheel. We drove off and arrived at the entrance to St Anne's Park. We jumped out of the car. I had most of the money from the bank, the guns — the small one in my pocket and the big gun in my hand. Someone said, "get away quick" and I can remember running from the car. Noel was a bit in front of me and I was not able to keep up with him.

'I next saw a man who looked very fit running from the trees on our right. He tackled Noel fiercely. The man had a hold of Noel. The man's back was to me. I was panicking and screamed "let go my fellow". All I could think of was that Noel was caught and I moved in to take Noel from him. I am not clear what happened. I think I made a swipe at the man with my right hand. This was the hand in which I had the big gun. It was a Colt .45. Obviously I had not put the safety catch on. As I made the swipe my gun went off. There was a shot and the man crumbled up. I could not believe what happened. The man was there one minute and next he was down. After that I don't know. I have been saying that ever since. I never intended this to happen. I never intended to hurt anyone.

'It did not register with me that he had actually been shot. You cannot believe you have done something like that. Everyone scattered and I ran alone, feeling unreal.'

Marie Murray was brought from Coolock Garda Station across the city to Harcourt Terrace at approximately 6 pm. As she waited to see her husband she talked to a number of Gardai, and said to one Bangharda, 'I only intended to hit him. He crumpled up. It was terrible.'

Mrs Murray said that the incident had left her in a daze for days, she hadn't been able to get it out of her mind and she could neither eat nor sleep. At this time she named the driver of the getaway car, but said he had nothing to do with the shooting.

Mrs Murray was brought into a room where she met her husband and they talked for about half an hour together. There was no one else in the room with them. Through the window they could see two Gardai walking up and down the laneway outside.

The ballistic and post mortem evidence was that there was no powder burning or 'tattooing' on the body as would have been the case if the shot was fired close to Garda Reynolds. Because of the absence of such marking it was clear the gun shot had been fired at a distance of over thirty inches — although Marie Murray said she made a 'swipe' at him. The ballistic evidence also showed that the gun could not have gone off mistakenly and that it needed stronger pressure on the trigger than other similar guns.

At 6.50 pm Detective Inspector Ryan spoke to Noel Murray again. Murray told him that what Marie had already told the Gardai was true, and that he would make a statement but wanted his solicitor present to help him phrase it. His lawyer, Brian Doolan BL, met Murray in private and raised no objection to two Gardai patrolling the laneway outside the consultation room.

Inspector Ryan returned at approximately 8.30 pm. He cautioned Murray, who said: 'I have been advised not to make a written statement. He [Mr Brian Doolan] says making a statement will not help Marie in any way. She has told you the truth about everything that happened in the Park.' Before he could make a reply to this, Murray added, 'This doesn't mean I won't make a statement, but I must have time to think.'

Murray was then shown about fifty different items taken from the house in Raheny and found at the scene of the shooting. Murray only identified a matchbox which contained three detonators. At about 10 pm that evening Mr Doolan returned with Mr Carroll, a solicitor, and held private consultation with Murray. They made out a statement and had it photocopied. It read that, after consultation with his legal advisors, Noel Murray did not wish to make verbal or written statements in connection with the murder of Garda Michael Reynolds or other offences, and was signed 'N.A. Murray'. Despite an exhaustive search, the document could not be found subsequently in Raheny Garda Station.

That evening Bansergeant Sarah McGuinness who was attached to Store Street Station said she had seen Mrs Murray a number of times that day. At 10.30 pm she talked to her. She was calm and relaxed. 'She said she got a surprise that morning when she was arrested but she was relieved now. She knew it had to come sometime. She mentioned the bank raid and said "You know what happened after that, I did it, you know that,"' said Bansergeant McGuinness.

The Sergeant later told a court that she did not take a note of the conversation at the time. 'I asked her if she knew he was a Guard. She said that she did not, that she heard it on the news. She said he caught one of them; she only intended to hit him. He crumpled up. It was terrible. She said there was panic and confusion.'

It was some hours later that Detective Inspector Ryan was told that Murray wanted to make a statement. It was about 2.30am, and he wrote out the statement as dictated by Murray, who then initialled it. Murray was composed, he recalled. Murray also volunteered to identify some of the items found in the park and his home which had been shown to him earlier but which he had refused to identify.

'The stuff the other detective showed me tonight — if he shows it to me again I'll tell him about it.'

Detective Inspector Ryan left the room to get the exhibits, but was back within two minutes to tell Murray they had been taken back to Raheny Garda Station. Murray said, 'It doesn't matter. The wigs and the moustaches were the ones used in the raid. The brown pillow cases were the ones used by my wife and the other man to take the money.' The jacket he had been shown earlier was the one he used in the raid, he said. 'Believe me we never intended to hurt anyone, never mind kill a person. I am completely against violence of any kind. I feel sorry for that man's wife and child,' he added.

Noel and Marie Murray were charged with the capital murder of Garda Michael Reynolds. They were also charged with armed robbery, three separate charges of possession of firearms and possession of explosives. They both pleaded not guilty to the charges.

The trial in the Special Criminal Court spanned seven weeks and a considerable amount of that time was taken up with complex legal argument. For much of the time the defendants heard the case from the holding cells beneath the well of the court through loudspeakers, as they were ordered out of the dock for abusing the court.

Their Counsel also raised the question even before their arraignment as to whether they were fit to plead, and later as to whether one of the three trial judges who had previously convicted Marie Murray of receiving stolen money could sit on the bench, and in another attempt to get a new trial alleged that a trial judge was unfit to sit on the bench.

In the course of the trial Noel Murray made an unsworn statement in which he made serious allegations of ill-treatment and threats by the Gardai. When asked by the court if he would give evidence under oath about those allegations, Noel Murray refused.

Mr Justice Pringle, the President of the court, said that the allegations were not substantiated by any evidence. It was significant that Noel Murray had been given facilities for two private consultations at Harcourt Terrace Garda Station, the first for forty minutes from 7.35 pm and the second for forty-five minutes at 10 pm. If Mr Murray was to be believed he had been kicked, punched, beaten and subjected to other forms of abuse before either consultation had taken place. Yet neither his solicitor nor his Counsel had made any complaint to the Garda authorities. After he was moved from Harcourt Terrace to the Bridewell he had another legal consultation, and again no complaint about abuse was made. 'The court is quite satisfied that none of the cases of ill-treatment or threats alleged by the accused in fact took place.'

After the prosecution case had ended Noel Murray told the court that the case against him was that the money found in their home was the proceeds of the bank raid. He wouldn't speak on oath, however, but said, 'This money was from collections made for the anarchist movement, the Black X. I intend to claim it. I want it back.' Marie Murray said that all the evidence against them was circumstantial and could be explained away in many ordinary ways.

On Wednesday 9 June the three judges of the Special Criminal Court retired after a one-hour review of the case. Seven hours later they emerged, and Mr Justice Pringle read out their verdict of guilty. The penalty for capital murder, he said, was to be hanged in the prison they were taken from, and buried in the grounds of that prison.

In addition, sentences of twelve years on a charge of armed robbery and six years each on the possession charges were also imposed.

They were refused leave to appeal against the sentence, but were advised that they had the right to appeal against the refusal to the Court of Criminal Appeal. The date for execution was set for 9 July 1976.

The couple appealed to the Court of Criminal Appeal, and the hearing was set for the end of July. On 30 July it dismissed the appeal which was based on the argument of lack of knowledge that the man who had been shot was a Garda. A new execution date was set, this time for 17 August 1976. However the court accepted that because this was an exceptional point of law they were prepared to certify for a final appeal to the five judges of the Supreme Court.

That appeal was fixed for 1 November. Because capital murder was a new offence — dating back to 1964 when the death penalty was abolished for murder except in certain cases — state of mind was of prime importance. The charge of capital murder was quashed for both husband and wife. Noel Murray's penalty was converted into life imprisonment for non-capital murder and the court ordered a retrial for Marie Murray. She was re-tried on the charge of non-capital murder, was found guilty and was sentenced to life imprisonment.

On 16 July 1976 the Garda Commissioner paid tribute to Garda Michael Reynolds. Mrs Vera Reynolds received posthumously on behalf of her husband the highest honour awarded to Gardai for outstanding bravery, the Scott gold medal.

11.

Genetic Fingerprinting

SANDY-HAIRED Carol Carpenter had just completed her Intermediate Certificate in the summer of 1988 at her school in
Blackpitts and was waiting for her results. The fifteen-year-old was
one of a family of eight children living in a Dublin local authority
house in Donomore Avenue on the outskirts of Tallaght.

On Friday 26 August, Carol had taken out the family lawn-
mower and hired herself and machine to neighbours to cut their
grass. She had a number of regular customers and it was a good
source of pocket money. Later that morning Carol had been seen
in good spirits laughing with neighbours as they gave a car a push-
start outside her home down the sloping road which was lined
with terraces of two-storey houses. At about 4.30 pm she left her
home and called to the mobile shop in Donomore Green, a few
minutes walk from her house, where she bought a canned drink.
Then she returned home at about 6 pm and had her tea. It was
about 8 pm when she left the house again saying she was going on
a message and wouldn't be long. Approximately one hour later
she visited a neighbour, Carol Hughes, who lived just a few doors
down the road, to sell her a set of tools for her husband. She
stayed for about twenty minutes and then left for home. It was still
a bright summer's evening as she walked up the road wearing her
distinctive denim jacket which was bedecked with badges and
teenage scribbling. It was one of the last times she was seen alive.

The following morning, Saturday, shortly after 3 am, the phone
rang in the ultra-modern blue-paintwork and grey-bricked Garda station in Tallaght. Twenty-two-year-old Ann Carpenter was on the line
and she wanted to report her sister missing. She hadn't been seen for
hours. It wasn't like her at all. They'd searched everywhere, she said.

She described Carol as a little over five feet tall, with short hair
and a small scar on her chin. She wore a denim jacket, black
trousers and had a white shirt and black suede shoes.

Carol had never run away from home and there was no reason for her family to think she had done so now. They were worried sick. They called to neighbours' houses and asked if she had gone to the disco that night. Ann had just arrived home with her father when they decided it was time to ring the Gardai. Something must have happened to her; they could only hope for the best and avoid thinking the worst.

Gardai estimate that over one thousand people are reported missing in Ireland every year. In 1987, the previous year, 1,300 people were reported missing. The majority turned up within forty-eight hours — most of them reacting to domestic disputes of one kind or another. By the end of the year only twenty of those people were unaccounted for: some were thought to have left the country; others were known victims of depression and it was likely they had drowned themselves and that their bodies had not yet been found.

Sunday 28 August 1988 was another hot summer's day. The park in Killinarden estate, Tallaght wasn't as busy as usual despite the summer holidays. Plenty of kids were running around, but it wasn't as full as you'd usually expect on a normal hot Sunday afternoon.

The forty-acre park had opened only three years earlier. Thousands of trees planted in the park had still not matured, and only bushes gave body to the planned shrubbery areas. The park was situated less than half a mile from the centre of Tallaght, the suburb that had grown into a sprawling town.

The park was surrounded by houses in the Killinarden local authority estate and was regularly used not just for recreation purposes but as a short cut from one side of the estate to the other. At the top of Donomore Avenue there was a pedestrian entrance to the park. From the entrance you could look down for miles towards the city centre. This was the foothills of the Dublin mountains, the furthest point out on the south west of the city.

At about 4 pm some local boys were playing 'chasing'. Thomas Tolan aged fourteen and his twelve-year-old brother David were looking for their elder brother, fifteen-year-old Jimmy. They were due back at their home nearby shortly as their youngest brother Ciaran was due to be christened in the nearby Church of the Sacred Heart. The two boys were near the vast shrubbery that grows in the centre of the park area, on the opposite side of the playing pitches.

They shouted and called for Jimmy. It was time to be going home, they had to go to the church. As there was no response they thought he might be on the other side of a shrubbery. They shoved through the bushes on the edge of the shrubbery and saw what they thought was a doll. It was big, and lying on its side. But it wasn't a doll. It was a body. 'Hey, mister, mister,' they shouted at a man who was playing nearby with four children, 'Mister, there's a body here.'

Twenty-nine-year-old Kevin Berry wasn't inclined to believe them, but there was something insistent in their voices, and he went to look for himself. He saw a body lying on its side. There were bits of sticks and twigs thrown over the lower half of the body and the top was bloody. It was impossible to tell whether it was male or female. He alerted the Gardai.

In the next twenty-five minutes the Gardai had arrived, the scene was sealed off and a doctor was on his way. An hour later the doctor, Perceval Patton, had pronounced the body, that of a girl, as dead.

The lazy Sunday afternoon atmosphere had been electrified. News of the horrific find ran through the community like wildfire. Even as Gardai began to seal off the area by stretching the distinctive yellow tape with 'Garda — Crime Scene' stamped on it around the shrubbery, an estimated 300 to 400 local people were arriving in the park.

Despite Garda appeals to the crowd to stay back from the crime area they kept pushing forward. They wanted to see what was happening. The Gardai insisted, however, appealing to them to stay back and the mood of the already tense crowd turned to anger and frustration. That feeling was expressed by a small section of the crowd who chased after a marked Garda patrol car, throwing objects at it when it left the scene. In another incident they smashed the windows and car radio and kicked in a door of another marked patrol car.

'I had only four Gardai with me and we were sealing off the area. A very large group of about 300 to 400 mainly young people kept on insisting they wanted to get into the area. I appealed to them repeatedly to keep back and they vented their frustration by smashing a marked Garda car, damaging the door and smashing the windows and the radio,' said a shocked Superintendent William McMunn. Asked by newspaper reporters about the possibility of the killer striking again, the superintendent urged prudence. 'As a precaution we appeal to parents to keep their children at home — particularly at night,' he said.

At his home, Peter Carpenter was comforting his family. There had been no word about Carol, although he had searched the area for her with family and friends. There was no confirmation as to the identity of the body. The Carpenters didn't even know if it was male or female; it was too soon to know. They could only hope it wasn't Carol. 'I have not seen the body yet. We are hoping it's not Carol,' he told reporters who called to the family home.

Arrangements were made to have the body moved to the City Morgue. It was 10 pm that night when the body arrived in a hearse with a Garda escort at the City Morgue in Store Street.

As people in Killinarden discussed the murder, one woman spoke of how her daughter had been attacked by a man in the park on the Friday night — the same night Carol had gone missing. Sixteen-year-old Rita Ryan from Donomore Park was passing the youth club in Killinarden when a man approached her. He had one hand in his pocket, and Rita thought he was looking for a light for a cigarette. She thought that because she was on the way to the shop herself to buy cigarettes for a friend. Instead, without warning or any provocation, he punched her in the face. She was knocked unconcious and fell to the ground. When she came to, she estimated about four or five minutes later, her attacker was gone. She stumbled towards the nearby disco in the community centre and told the bouncers on the entrance doors what had happened. They put her into a van and immediately drove around the area looking for the attacker.

By now Carol Carpenter was missing — but no one was aware of that fact yet.

Rita Ryan said her attacker might have had a few drinks on him. She guessed he was probably about thirty years of age. As they toured the Killinarden estate and turned onto the main Blessington-to-Dublin road, memories of other attacks on children in the area were uppermost in their minds. The park wasn't always considered safe. There were rowdy kids and occasional joyriders. A girl had been shot in the park a year earlier. Despite an extensive tour of the area they didn't see anyone whose description vaguely tallied with the still-shocked teenager. They brought her to the Garda station. She spoke to the Gardai and they brought her home. Later that evening her mother brought her to hospital. Rita's nose was fractured and an eye was starting to close as it puffed up.

In the cold and comfortless surroundings of the City Morgue with its line of ceramic examination trays, the body was formally identified as that of Carol Carpenter. It was a numbing blow to her family. The people of Tallaght united with the family in their grief for the young girl who had suffered such a sad and tragic death.

The post mortem carried out by the state pathologist Dr John Harbison showed that the girl had been dead for not more than forty-eight hours. She had been battered, and stabbed six times in the chest. But the cause of death was asphyxia due to strangulation.

Detectives investigating the case hoped they had an early lead in the case. There was only one shoe on the body. In addition she had been seen leaving her own home and her neighbour's wearing her denim jacket but that had not been found in the park either. Gardai using slash hooks and shovels cleared the area around the body, as a minute search got underway. They found a haversack harness, a shoelace and a plastic sack near the body. These suggested that the body had been dumped in the bushes, but that the killing had taken place somewhere else.

House-to-house inquiries in the estate began that Sunday afternoon as detectives traced her last hours and the people she had met in that time. The last person she had met was her killer. As the Gardai talked to people in the area, they realised she had spent most of the Friday evening on her own road. She was seen alive at approximately 9.30 pm. They therefore had to account for those forty-three hours before her body was found.

It was only as Gardai made house-to-house inquiries that an important piece of physical evidence came to light. A woman on Donomore Avenue had seen a black suede shoe in her back garden on the Saturday afternoon, but paid no attention to it. When the Gardai called she told them about the shoe and gave it to them. She had paid no attention to the shoe on the Saturday, but with the death of young Carol and the presence of the Gardai on her doorstep it suddenly might be extremely relevant. The two Gardai who called to her door that evening took possession of it.

The shoe was identified by her family as belonging to Carol. It was covered in black suede material and had an easily identifiable white motif on one side. She had been wearing it on the night she went missing. Detectives surmised that it could have fallen off her as she was brought to the park and that her killer had got rid of it by throwing it over the woman's fence into her back yard. If so, that brought back the time of death closer to the time when she had gone missing, and cut down the number of missing hours considerably.

The Gardai set up a special confidential telephone line in Tallaght and urged people to call them if they could help the investigation in any way.

'Death is always sad. But in this circumstance it is an especially harrowing experience and a barbaric measure of the times we live in,' parish priest Fr Paddy Sheehan told hundreds of people who crowded into the Church of the Sacred Heart at Killinarden for the removal on Tuesday evening. The little prefab church was filled to overflowing and outside dozens listened to the service and the choir of Knockmore national school singing. The following day the senior Auxiliary Bishop of Dublin, Most Reverend Dr Joseph Carroll, presided at the funeral mass. A guard of honour was formed by the dead girl's schoolmates as the cortege left the church for Bohernabreena cemetery. At the graveside the Carpenter family stood numb with grief.

That evening Gardai said they were satisfied that the man responsible for the killing had local connections.

On Thursday 1 September a twenty-year-old youth, a neighbour of the Carpenters, was charged with murdering Carol in Donomore Avenue. Joseph Mark Dowling was alleged to have killed Carol Carpenter in a house on the avenue where, ironically, her brother had been living and which he had been asked to keep an eye on while he babysat the children of friends gone to England.

Detectives investigating the case had had their suspicions raised early in the investigation by the unemployed Dowling. He had been questioned within a short time of the discovery of the body in what was a brief but intensive investigation.

Dowling was brought to Rathfarnham Court on the following afternoon after he had been charged. Superintendent William McMunn arrested him. 'In reply to the charge the accused shook his head,' he said.

Dowling was wearing a pair of blue jeans, white running shoes and black leather jacket. As he entered and left the tiny, narrow courthouse his head was covered with a jacket. He did not speak during the four-minute hearing, and shook visibly. He was granted free legal aid and was remanded in custody. Dowling broke down in the courthouse, tears streaming from his face. He was comforted by his mother and his younger brother. After a number of subsequent court appearances, he was remanded to the Circuit Criminal Court on 1 May. As the trial opened, Dowling pleaded guilty to the murder charge.

The prosecuting counsel, Feargus Flood SC, said that they were entering a *nolle prosequi* on the second charge which alleged that Dowling had raped the victim. The trial was expected to last a week, but was over in less than three minutes. Mr Justice Richard

Johnson imposed the mandatory sentence of life imprisonment. Dowling was taken to Mountjoy jail.

If the case had come to trial, a legal first would have been established in the attempt, successful or otherwise, to introduce as evidence a revolutionary new technique of identification. The process had only been discovered four years earlier and was being marketed commercially by Cellmark Diagnostics, the Oxfordshire-based section of ICI, as 'the most positive scientific method now available for identifying individuals'.

By 1984 a thirty-four-year-old English genetic scientist, Dr Alec Jeffreys, was working on a study to determine how genes evolve and was also studying gene coding for proteins which carry oxygen to the muscles.

DNA, or Deoxyribo Nucleic Acid, is the very basic genetic material contained in all living cells in the human body. It is the material from which chromosomes are made which carry the genetic code and determine our characteristics, such as the colour of our eyes and hair. It is the ingredient which makes us individual. DNA was discovered in the early 1950s. The DNA molecule has a long chain-like structure which is made up of two spirals. These are held together, like rungs in a ladder, by chemical bases. It is the different order of these bases which gives a person his or her own characteristics. The only exceptions to this are genetically identical twins. These specific twins are formed from the division of one fertilised egg in the mother's womb. As a result they have exactly the same DNA structure and are therefore identical.

While stretches of this DNA ladder are common to all people, there are areas of this code which are individual. Dr Jeffreys, who worked in Leicester University, discovered that this sequence of genetic information repeated itself within the DNA molecule, and it is the length of this repeated sequence, the number of repeats and their location within the molecule, which makes that person unique. He was able to identify these individual marker bases using a complex series of chemical, radioactive and X-ray techniques.

The final result on an X-ray film is something similar to a supermarket bar code. The new identification system, derived from any sized sample of biological material, has a number of popular names: genetic fingerprinting, DNA profiling or biological blue-printing. In November 1984 Dr Jeffreys spoke twice to scientific communities about nature's own identity code which is indelibly stamped on each human being. His patent application lists him as inventor, and vests the patent rights in the Lister Institute of

187

Preventative Medicine. ICI were selected as the sole licensee for the discovery.

In March 1985 Dr Jeffreys published his discovery, saying: 'You would have to look for one part in a million million million million million before you would find one pair with the same genetic fingerprint, and with a world population of only five billion it can be categorically said that a genetic fingerprint is individually specific and does not belong to anyone on the face of this planet who ever has been or ever will be.'

The enormity of this claim was soon tested. On 21 November 1983 a fifteen-year-old girl was sexually assaulted and strangled with her own scarf on her way home just a few miles from Leicester. Two and a half years later, on 31 July 1986, another fifteen-year-old girl was sexually assaulted and murdered just six miles from Leicester.

Aware of the new technique which had never been tried before, Leicester police asked Dr Jeffreys to test the suspect genetically. Dr Jeffreys proved that he wasn't the killer after he had carried out a genetic test on the man's blood. However after he had tested stains on the clothing of one of the girls and a vaginal swab from the other, he could tell them that the killer had been the same man in both cases.

Leicester police announced that they would hold a voluntary 'blooding' for 5,000 men living in the area. That meant that a blood sample was taken voluntarily from every man in the area, and each genetic fingerprint tested for a match against the killer's.

But the killer duped another man into taking the test for him. The impersonator bragged about his feat of hoodwinking the scientists, and when a co-worker heard the story in a pub she contacted the police. They arrested both the impersonator and the killer. The impersonator was given an eighteen-month suspended sentence. The killer, Colin Pitchfork, was sentenced to two terms of life imprisonment to run concurrently. It was the first use of genetic fingerprinting to solve a crime in the world, and curiously it happened on the doorstep of the man who invented it.

Cellmark Diagnostics markets genetic fingerprinting as a technique that can be applied to a number of situations: a bloodstain at the scene of a crime; a semen sample or stain in a rape case; fingernail scrapings or intact hair pulled from an assailant in an assault case; or body tissue in a hit-and-run case.

The odds of a number of the bar code bands matching are millions to one. The odds of four bands matching are rated 250 to one, of six bands matching 4,000 to 1, of ten bands matching one million to 1, of fourteen bands matching 268 million to 1, of eighteen bands matching 68,000 million to 1, and of twenty bands matching one billion to 1. In their promotional brochure, Cellmark Diagnostics say: 'Essentially where any form of DNA containing biological material is found at the scene of a crime, the DNA profile from it may provide a conclusive link to the person or persons who committed that crime. Clearly a major use of this new technology in criminal investigations is the positive identification or elimination of suspects.'

Because DNA is found in every living cell of our bodies there is no shortage of materials from which samples can be taken. Foetal tissue and post mortems can both provide material for such forensic testing. However the most common material sent to the Cellmark Laboratories are samples of blood, semen, hair roots and saliva.

In June 1988 a twenty-one-year-old man was jailed for life in a Belfast court. He was the first person caught and convicted in Northern Ireland using the technique of genetic fingerprinting. Kenneth Henry Callaghan pleaded guilty to the murder of his neighbour Carol Gouldie, a receptionist with a motor company, at her home in Colvil Street, East Belfast. Callaghan had battered the woman to death when she discovered him in her living room when she returned from work. She had been found badly beaten and dead, slumped over a couch. Her hands were tied behind her back with a pair of tights and she was hooded. Crown Counsel, Ronald Appleton QC, said that a blood sample taken from Callaghan compared with a swab taken from Ms Gouldie proved he was the killer. The DNA test carried out at the Home Office Research Centre in Alderson showed there was only one in a ten million chance that Callaghan was not the attacker.

Just eight months after Colin Pitchfork had been convicted and two months after Callaghan's conviction, Dublin detectives decided to back up their evidence in the Dowling case with the DNA fingerprint technique.

Superintendent McMunn had been keeping abreast of the development of genetic fingerprinting and its implications for crime detectors for some time. He discussed the new technique with members of the Technical Bureau. In the Carpenter case they believed the test would conclusively link Dowling to the dead girl. He had already been inextricably linked to the house on Donomore Avenue where the killing took place. However although Carol's jacket was discovered in the house, investigating Gardai needed conclusive proof. The owners had cleaned the house before they left it in Dowling's charge. Now there were blood-stains in a number of places, and tests showed the bloodstains didn't belong to Dowling. The odds were they belonged to the murder victim but the odds weren't good enough, Superintendent McMunn felt. A sample of blood was taken from Dowling with his consent while he was in Garda custody.

It was sent along with a sample of the murder victim's to the Cellmark Laboratories in England. A third sample of blood, taken from the spattered fridge in the kitchen was also sent.

According to the laboratory the genetic testing showed that the blood sample taken from the top of the fridge matched the Carpenter sample, pointing to Dowling's guilt.

It was the first time that DNA profiling had been used in any criminal case by the Gardai. It was subsequently used in a number of rape cases — in some cases to clear suspects.

At the time of writing, one of the State Laboratory's forensic scientists, Dr Maureen Smyth, has already undergone training in DNA profiling. This involved a number of months in the Medical Genetics School in Trinity College, and subsequently a course at the British Home Office's research centre. Further staff were also in the process of being recruited for genetic profiling duties in the state forensic laboratory, and a bill was before the houses of the Oireachtas to allow Gardai take forensic samples from suspects.

As fingerprints had revolutionised crime detection techniques at the turn of the century, DNA profiling is set to change current detection techniques radically.

Although DNA profiling represents a huge advance in the science of detection, it further underlines the principle of scientific crime detection formulated by Edmond Locard at the beginning of the twentieth century: 'Every contact leaves a trace.'